D0962356

BAGEHOT

ALSO BY JAMES GRANT

Bernard Baruch: The Adventures of a Wall Street Legend

Money of the Mind

Minding Mr. Market

The Trouble with Prosperity

John Adams: Party of One

Mr. Market Miscalculates

Mr. Speaker! The Life and Times of Thomas B. Reed

The Forgotten Depression

No portrait of Walter Bagehot is known to exist except for the famous profile that a photographer snapped in Bagehot's middle years. The image you see here is the product of the remote collaboration between the former New York City Police Department forensic artist, Stephen Mancusi, and the illustrator and book designer, Katherine Messenger. Together, the two have imagined the face in full that no one has seen since Bagehot's death in 1877.

BAGEHOT

The Life and Times of the Greatest Victorian

James Grant

W. W. NORTON & COMPANY
Independent Publishers Since 1923
NEW YORK • LONDON

Photographs © National Portrait Gallery, London, unless noted otherwise. Cartoon of "The Old Lady of Threadneedle Street" and photograph of Richard Holt Hutton are in the public domain. Material relating to Stuckey's Bank, including directors' minutes, financials, and the data used to create the "Victorian Money Machine" chart, from the Royal Bank of Scotland Archives. Endpapers: *London from the Monument*, William Wyllie c. 1870 (private collection).

Excerpts from *Till Time's Last Sand* © David Kynaston, 2017, *Till Time's Last Sand: A History of the Bank of England 1694-2013*, Bloomsbury Publishing Plc.

For information about permission to reproduce selections from this book, write to Permissions, W. W. Norton & Company, Inc., 500 Fifth Avenue, New York, NY 10110

For information about special discounts for bulk purchases, please contact W. W. Norton Special Sales at specialsales@wwnorton.com or 800-233-4830

Manufacturing by Sheridan
Book design by Ellen Cipriano
Production manager: Beth Steidle

Library of Congress Cataloging-in-Publication Data

Names: Grant, James, 1946- author.
Title: Bagehot : the life and times of the greatest Victorian / James Grant.
Description: First edition. | New York : W.W. Norton & Company, [2019] |
Includes bibliographical references and index.
Identifiers: LCCN 2019004287 | ISBN 9780393609196 (hardcover)
Subjects: LCSH: Bagehot, Walter, 1826-1877. | Bankers—Great
Britain—Biography. | Essayists—Great Britain—Biography. |
Journalists—Great Britain—Biography. | Economist (London, England :
1843)—History. | Great Britain—Politics and government—1837-1901. |
Great Britain—Economic conditions—19th century.
Classification: LCC HB103.B2 G73 2019 | DDC 330.092 [B]—dc23
LC record available at https://lccn.loc.gov/2019004287
W. W. Norton & Company, Inc., 500 Fifth Avenue, New York, N.Y. 10110
www.wwnorton.com

W. W. Norton & Company Ltd., 15 Carlisle Street, London W1D 3BS

1 2 3 4 5 6 7 8 9 0

for Edward Chancellor,
who insisted

We are looking for a man who was in and of his age, and who could have been of no other: a man with sympathy to share, and genius to judge, its sentiments and movements: a man not too illustrious or too consummate to be companionable, but one, nevertheless, whose ideas took root and are still bearing; whose influence, passing from one fit mind to another, could transmit, and can still impart, the most precious element in Victorian civilization, its robust and masculine sanity. Such a man there was: and I award the place to Walter Bagehot.

—G. M. Young, "The Greatest Victorian,"
Spectator, June 18, 1937

CONTENTS

AUTHOR'S NOTE

"The immense fluctuations in our commerce, caused by protection, were aggravated by immense fluctuations in our credit, and the combined result was unspeakably disastrous."

—Walter Bagehot on the commercial and monetary conditions prevailing in England around the time of his birth[1]

IN 1832, JEREMIAH HARMAN, a long-serving director of the Bank of England, testified before a parliamentary committee on how the Bank rose to meet the occasion of the Panic of 1825. It was a desperate time, and the Bank lent money in unprecedented ways. "We lent it by every possible means, and in modes that we never had adopted before," Harman explained;

> we took in stock as security, we purchased exchequer bills, we made advances on exchequer bills, we not only discounted outright, but we made advances on deposit of bills of exchange to an immense amount; in short by every possible means consistent with the safety of the Bank; and we were not upon some occasions over nice; seeing the dreadful state in which the public were, we rendered every assistance in our power.[2]

Bagehot (pronounced Badge-it), who wrote the still-canonical pre-scription for stopping a run on the banks, *Lombard Street*, never recom-mended a policy so extreme. Faced with a crisis, he famously asserted, a central bank should lend freely at a high rate of interest against good banking collateral. He said much more than that, but those words—customarily abbreviated to omit the part about the high interest rate—are invoked to this day. No sooner do the banks bring down a crisis on themselves, or stock prices take a tumble, than the call goes out for the Federal Reserve to infuse the market with emergency credit. In his memoir of the Great Recession, *The Courage to Act*, Ben S. Bernanke, chairman of the Federal Reserve from 2006 to 2014, cited Bagehot more frequently than any living economist.

Bagehot was a banker, a man of letters, and a financial journal-ist; most famously, he edited the *Economist*. But he was no economist himself—that is, he made no original contribution to the body of eco-nomic theory.

It is a comment on the nature of economics as much as it is on the genius of Bagehot that his dicta on central banking continue to hold sway almost a century and a half after he propounded them. In the physical sciences, progress is cumulative; we stand on the shoulders of giants. In economics, the most ostensibly rigorous of the social sci-ences, progress—and error, too—are cyclical; we keep stepping on the same rakes.

There is a misconception that Bagehot originated the idea of a lender of last resort. It's obvious he could not have done so; Jeremiah Harman and his fellow directors were doing more than Bagehot would later recommend two months before the author of *Lombard Street* was even born. He did, however, popularize and legitimize the proposition, controversial at the time but now taken as revealed truth, that a central bank owed a public duty to private persons dealing with large sums of money. Unfortunately, he seriously underestimated the extent to which this supposed obligation would induce people to take risks they would not otherwise accept in the absence of expected government help.

Perhaps Bagehot himself would agree. He believed—at least, at age thirty-nine, when a monetarily astute friend took the trouble to make a careful inventory of his views—that money was gold and silver and that alone. All forms of currency, including the notes of the Bank of England, were credit instruments, no different than personal checks, from which it followed that the government had no business intervening in the business of banking. Bagehot came to modify his ideas about financial regulation—but, unacknowledged by the many who approvingly quote him on the imperative of central bank crisis management, he never changed his publicly expressed view about the gold standard or the abomination of fiat currency.

Bagehot was not the only virtuoso writer on money and banking in nineteenth-century England: Karl Marx, London correspondent for the *New York Tribune*, was an accomplished financial reporter (bear markets brought out the best in him). George Goschen's brilliant matched set of essays, "Two Percent" and "Seven Percent," can be read for sheer pleasure—no small feat considering the subject matter is interest rates.

Yet Bagehot—eclectic, fearless, aphoristic, prolific—stands apart. The twentieth-century American journalist A. J. Liebling said of himself that he wrote faster than anyone who wrote better, and better than anyone who wrote faster. Bagehot made no such claim—it would have been un-English. But with a glance at periodical journalism in the 1850s, 1860s, and 1870s, the boast would have been defensible.

An adviser to statesmen, notably the Liberal parliamentarian and long-serving prime minister William E. Gladstone, he himself failed to win election to Parliament in three attempts. Nor did he make a fortune in the City of London. His writing is what secured his reputation, and it certainly won my admiration. Forty years ago, I discovered bound copies of the *Economist* from the Bagehot era on deposit at the

New York Public Library. Bagehot's articles, like everyone else's in that newspaper, were unsigned, but his style was unmistakable. His output astounded me—5,000 words a week at least, and each word placed just where it should be. Was such a thing possible?

Nevertheless, the reader will find that my Bagehot comes in for a certain amount of criticism. I spent three years in his biographical company, and have had my fill of his hauteur, his studied forgetfulness about forecasting errors, however understandable, and his embrace of the dubious notion, so corrosive to financial prudence, that the central bank has a special obligation to the citizens who present themselves as borrowers and lenders, investors and speculators. No other class of person enjoys access to the government's money machinery. On the credit side of the ledger—I draw up the assets and liabilities with a libertarian's biases—Bagehot opposed the demand of aggrieved English bondholders that the British Foreign Office intervene on their behalf with the governments of defaulting states. As a financial journalist, the editor of the *Economist* possessed another, apolitical virtue: his paper was evidently incorruptible.

Bagehot himself, like many in the age before antibiotics, was susceptible to bronchial disease—yet during the period of his worst illness, he produced his most celebrated work. In sickness or health, he wrote as few have ever written, before or since.

PROLOGUE: "WITH DEVOURING FURY"

The Panic of 1825 almost pushed Britain to the pre-banking dark age—to "within eight and forty hours of barter."

The remote cause of the upheaval was the great war with France. In 1797, four years after the start of hostilities, there was a run on Britain's banks, including the Bank of England. The depositors demanded gold in exchange for paper pounds, which was their right, but King George III, Prime Minister William Pitt, and Pitt's senior ministers judged it impossible. An Order in Council on the morning of Sunday, February 26, 1797, relieved the Bank of England of its obligation to pay gold coin in exchange for paper currency.

The suspension was a stopgap; a subsequent act of Parliament ordered gold payments to resume within six months. But the war dragged on for another eighteen years, and the paper pound remained the functional coin of the realm for nearly another quarter century.

The Panic was a consequence of this monetary experiment, and of the attempts at financial reform that followed the crisis.

•   •   •

THE TWENTY-FIRST-CENTURY READER, accustomed not only to paper money but also to digital scrip—accustomed, too, to the institution of deposit insurance, and the idea that some banks are too big to be allowed to fail—will require some acclimation to this financial world. Following the paper-pound interregnum, money was gold; small change was silver. This was the monetary foundation, over which rose credit, the promise to pay money. The English house of credit, haphazardly designed, was prone to structural problems, and from time to time it nearly collapsed. The interplay between money and credit was the source of the recurrent cycles of boom and bust that bedeviled the nineteenth century—and continue to plague and mystify the twenty-first.

There was no standard, uniform, nationally circulating paper currency at the time; many private banks, essentially unregulated, issued their own. In law, the bearer might present these notes to the issuing bank in exchange for a like amount of gold. In any case, such notes were not legal tender. Neither were the notes of the Bank of England. Gold was the only money that a creditor was bound to accept in payment of a debt.

The institutions of nineteenth-century banking bear only small resemblance to their millennial descendants. The Bank of England was the hegemon: in contemporary American terms of reference, a cross between JPMorgan Chase and the Federal Reserve. It was the government's bank but it belonged to its stockholders, conducting a private banking business while discharging a limited number of public duties. Up until the 1797 restriction of gold payments, and following the 1821 resumption of gold payments, the Bank's one and only formal public obligation was to keep the gold value of the pound on an even keel—to make sure it did not significantly vary from the statutory, or Mint, price.

The Bank was a monopoly, no better loved than a twenty-first-century cable TV provider. In London, no private institution was allowed to issue currency; that right was the Bank's alone. And no

English private bank, in or out of London, could organize itself with more than six shareholders. Only the Old Lady of Threadneedle Street—the Bank was an Old Lady even then, so depicted in 1797 in a famous cartoon by James Gillray*—was allowed to achieve a tolerable scale of operations.

The shareholders of any bank bore considerable risks. The law regarded them as general partners, responsible for the solvency of the institution in which they owned a fractional interest; if their bank should fail, the owners were personally liable for its debts, "down to their last shilling and acre." The depositor's only security against loss was the prudence of his bankers and the assessable wealth of the bank's shareholders.

Wealth was measured in pounds, shillings, and pence. Twenty shillings, or 240 pence, made a pound; 240 silver pence, properly struck, weighed a pound. By the 1820s, Britain was formally on the gold standard, no longer the century-old mixed, bimetallic standard of gold and silver. A pound was defined in law as 123¼ grains of 22-carat gold. Three pounds, seventeen shillings and ten and one-half pence, expressed £3 17s 10½ d, was exchangeable for an ounce of gold.

At the outbreak of war with France in 1793, £1 coins, called sovereigns, furnished the principal portion of the British money supply. Twenty to thirty million pounds' worth was in circulation or under lock and key. The rest of the circulation was filled out by roughly £12 million in Bank of England notes and another £12 million in the notes of more than two hundred small private banks—including Stuckey's.[1] Vincent Stuckey, eponymous president of the small family bank, boasted that his customers, given the choice, would pick Stuckey's notes over the Bank of England's (which were easily counterfeited) or even over gold

---

* In the drawing, a suitor, William Pitt the Younger, the prime minister of Great Britain, is wooing a woman of a certain age who has seated herself on a money chest. She—which is to say, the Bank of England—is properly suspicious of his advances. To wage his war with France, gold is what Pitt needs and doesn't have.

coins (which were sometimes short of standard weight).[2] Even under the gold standard, many preferred portable paper to bulky metal.

Still, the 1797 suspension of gold payments was a shock to the monetary system; to some it seemed a catastrophe. In 1798, the first full year of the suspension, British consumer prices actually declined, and it seemed as if the Bank were managing its issuance in accordance with the doctrines and signposts of the gold standard. But it later came to light, amid stiff inflation, that the Bank was not steering by the gold standard—neither by the relation of the quoted price of gold to the official Mint price, nor by the value of the pound against foreign currencies. By 1809, the gold value of the pound commanded not its customary 123¼ grains but only 113 grains. A parliamentary commission called the Bullion Committee resolved in 1810 "That the only certain and adequate security to be provided, against an Excess of a Paper Currency, and for maintaining the relative Value of the Circulating Medium of the Realm, is the legal Convertibility, upon demand, of all Paper Currency into lawful Coin of the Realm." Parliament voted down that contention by a margin of two to one.

After Waterloo came peace and—again—the monetary question: Should Britain return to gold? If so, when and at which gold value should the pound be set? Should it be the old familiar one or some new measure, adjusted for the myriad changes that war-induced finance had brought about?

Years of easy money had facilitated many necessary and pleasant things: victory over Napoleon, high wages, high and rising crop prices. The English usury law capped interest rates at 5 percent, a respectable rate in times of stable prices, a cheap and bewitching one in times of hot inflation. Seizing that rate, squires had borrowed to expand their profitable farming operations, high wartime crop prices having furnished the profit. The government had borrowed to fund the war, running up a national debt of more than £800 million (compared to £247 million in 1793). Debtors wanted a cheaper pound, creditors a dearer one. Radicals—such as Thomas Atkinson, a Birmingham banker and crusader for monetary notions that only entered the public policy mainstream in the mid-twentieth century—made cause with the debtors, proposing the adoption of cheap silver, or much cheaper paper, in lieu of gold.

The Atkinson radicals made no headway. Resumption of gold payments at some undetermined rate of exchange had been on the political agenda since the moment of the 1797 restriction. Resumption would re-anchor the value of sterling. It would, its proponents promised, restore banking discipline and furnish a check on public spending.

It would also return the monetary antennae to working order. The option to convert paper into gold, and gold into paper, was the sensory device of the monetary system, and the Old Lady was determined to give that device free play: "The Bank," said one director, "are very desirous not to exercise any power, but to leave the Public to use the power which they possess, of returning Bank paper for bullion."[3]

A high and rising demand for coin would have told the Bank's directors, if they'd been listening, that paper money was in oversupply. To set matters right, the Bank had to reduce its note issuance and raise its interest rate, in order to assure the note-holding public that its claims on gold were promptly payable.

The gold standard was no mere domestic contrivance. In theory and practice, it integrated the economies of all who played by the gold standard rules. The first of these conventions was that gold should move freely across national boundaries. If, for instance, the metal bought more in France than it did in England, watchful people would collect gold sovereigns—those common £1 coins—melt them into ingots and ship them across the Channel. Losing gold, the banks—especially the Bank of England, whose job it was to defend convertibility—would curtail lending. As credit tightened, commercial activity would stall. To raise cash, merchants would sell whatever they could. Prices and wages would fall. They would not fall indefinitely, because the very decline in

domestic prices and wages would make England a more desirable destination for foreign capital. The pound, its purchasing power restored,
would appreciate against the currencies of Britain's trading partners.
Gold would retrace its steps back to Britain. Such movements of gold
and credit, with minimal direction by governments and central banks,
served to balance the accounts of one gold-standard nation with another
and to stabilize prices across national boundaries. The adjustments
were irksome but salutary.

Still, monetary virtue, like many another kind, was more popular
in the abstract than in the living moment, and not a few bankers were
attached to the paper pound. The gold standard clipped their wings.

IN PARLIAMENTARY HEARINGS AFTER the dust of the 1825 panic had
settled, an inquisitor asked a former governor of the Bank of England
about the nature of the business in which he and his brother directors
were engaged. Is not "the essence of banking," came the question, that a
man "issues promises which it is universally known by the takers of those
promises that he cannot fulfill?" The witness, John B. Richards, hedged,
but the short and correct answer would have been, "Sometimes, yes."[4]

Accidents occurred in banking, just as they did on the newfangled
railroads. The bankers, like the engineers wrestling with steam power,
were only just beginning to understand the risks and power of the forces
they were attempting to harness. In banking, though, accidents came in
clusters. Bank runs, unlike train wrecks, were contagious.[5]

Cascading mishaps are in part owing to the nature of banking. Even
the most liquid institution would be hard-pressed to return every shilling to every depositor if all came running at once. But the particular
nature of English banking was another source of distress. The banking
business in the early nineteenth century was stunted by the law that no
more than six partners could share ownership of a single institution. Nor
were the half dozen invariably informed, attentive, or proficient. Vin-

cent Stuckey disparaged the quality of his country competition: "they lent their property on very inadequate security," he testified, "and we have seen the unfortunate result in many instances."

Stuckey's criticism of the banking profession might have almost passed for praise six years later. *The Times*, assigning blame for the 1825 panic even while it raged, charged that "In large Provincial towns, certainly, the word Bank makes a showy figure, and is placed over a respectable structure; but we have known cases in which the word Dairy, or Cheese-Room, would be a much more suitable description of the tenements from which so great a proportion of the circulating medium of England issues, than that of a Bank."[6]

But the Bank of England itself was no model of managerial competence. The merchants, insurance underwriters, industrialists, ship owners, and mining executives who oversaw the direction of the Bank—no commercial bankers were allowed—lacked neither intelligence nor business experience, and over the course of a twenty- or thirty-year tenure they did develop banking experience. However, as to the day-to-day business of lending and deposit-taking, not to mention the more rarefied work of crisis management, they had to learn on the job.[7] When the House of Commons registered its lack of confidence in the Bank in 1819, it was not "from any doubt of its wealth, or integrity, but from a conviction of its total ignorance of the principles of political economy."[8]

WHEN THE SHOOTING STOPS, governments reduce the pace of their spending and borrowing. Shipyards and munitions makers lay off workers, who compete for peacetime employment with demobilized soldiers and sailors. War-inflated prices and wages start falling—or, to say the same thing, the value of money starts rising.

In England, many regretted the transformation. The country had had twenty years to adapt to the paper pound. Debtors in particular had welcomed it, as the money they owed had become easier to obtain than the money they had borrowed. Farmers, industrialists, wage-earners, and merchants had all come to terms with the new inflated state of things. At the end of the war, England resembled a middle-aged man who finds he can no longer fit into an old pair of trousers. He must either lose weight or see his tailor.

Should Parliament validate the wartime inflation by redefining the pound as a lighter weight of gold? Or reaffirm the inviolability of the pound by sticking to the old standard of £3 17s 10½ d? Something had to give: either the value of money or the wartime level of prices and wages.

Sir Robert Peel, a rich factory owner and father of a rising Tory politician—also Sir Robert Peel—pushed hard for the adjustment to fall on the pound, not prices. The Bank of England took the same side.

Opposing them were the young Sir Robert, chairman of the House of Commons committee investigating the monetary question, and David Ricardo, Parliament's trusted voice on economic questions. The economist expected no difficulty in resuming gold convertibility at the old rate: a decline of 3 percent in prices and wages should do the trick. It would not come close to doing the trick, countered Hundson Gurney, MP for Norwich and a non-economist but a member of the Royal Society and heir to a Quaker banking fortune. Prices would have to fall by as much as 20 percent, Gurney predicted.

Young Sir Robert got his way—in 1819, Parliament voted to return to gold at the prewar rate, with the transition occurring in stages, starting in 1821—but the critics proved the wise ones. Britain's gross domestic product, as historians piece it together, reached a postwar peak of £462 million in 1818 and proceeded to plunge. At the bottom of the business cycle in 1822, it registered £399 million. The hard times left deep scars. On August 16, 1819, at St. Peter's Field, Manchester, tens of thousands gathered to protest against a system of parliamentary representation that left hungry and jobless Britons politically mute. When the people refused to disperse, a pair of local cavalry units, green and excitable, charged them with sabers drawn. Fifteen civilians were killed, including a mother of seven, a two-year-old boy, and a veteran of the Battle of Waterloo. Five hundred more were hurt. "Peterloo," the citizens of Manchester bitterly called the massacre.

Low grain prices, a transatlantic depression, high unemployment, and tight money sent up a clamor for relief. Heeding the call, the Bank of England, with encouraging prods by the government, took steps to make credit cheaper and more abundant.

On June 20, 1822, came a laconically worded announcement of the first adjustment to the discount, or lending, rate of the Bank of England to take place in more than a century. "Resolved," read the text in its entirety: "That Bills and Notes approved in the usual manner, and not having more than 95 days to run, be discounted at the rate of 4 per cent. on and after the 21st of June 1822." The rate had not wavered from 5 percent since 1719.

Changes almost as historically momentous followed. In May 1823, the Bank announced its intention to lend against mortgage collateral. In September it widened the class of assets against which it was prepared to lend to include government securities and shares of the Bank of England itself. A stockholder-owned business, the Bank needed profits, and its mainstay line of commercial lending was not supplying them.[*]

To RESTORE BRITISH MONETARY affairs to prewar trim meant a wider circulation of gold coins and a smaller issuance of currency; the country

---

* Mortgage lending, in particular, represented a radical turn in policy. The asset of choice for any well-tempered bank was the short-dated commercial IOU. Cash changed hands at the end of its brief life more or less automatically. There was no such assured liquidity in a mortgage, which took years to mature. And when a mortgage did fall due, there could be no guarantee that the property that secured its value could find a buyer. If a central bank prizes liquidity, it should confine its investments to self-liquidating assets and gold, no matter the temptation to earn a higher yield. This doctrine the Bank laid aside. L. S. Presnell, *Country Banking in the Industrial Revolution* (Oxford: Clarendon Press, 1956), 477–79.

banks' £1 and £5 notes, especially, were on the chopping block. But the push to boost lending—and thus, it was hoped, spread prosperity—caused the government to backtrack. In 1822, Parliament enacted legislation to allow the banks to continue to emit small-denomination notes through 1833.[9] These reflationary policies bore fruit, as prices, wages, and national output recovered from the depression lows of 1822. Princess Lieven, wife of the Russian ambassador to Britain, sensed that something new and cheerful was in the wind. "I have lived in this country for eleven years," she wrote to Prince Metternich in Vienna in August 1823, "and for the first time I hear no grumbling."

Falling bond yields contributed to the high spirits. The British Treasury had borrowed at high rates of interest during the war, and now refinanced at lower rates. In 1823 it exchanged a 5 percent issue for one paying 4 percent, and, in 1824, a 4 percent issue for one paying 3½ percent. In response to falling interest rates, securities prices rallied. Savers abandoned safe, sane—and now low-yielding—gilt-edged securities for the high-yielding alternatives.

Alternatives abounded in South America. As the armies of Simón Bolívar pushed Spain and Portugal out of the New World, British capital, encouraged by the foreign secretary, Lord Canning, came rushing in. In 1822, the brand-new republics of Chile, Colombia, and Peru raised £3.4 million in London at rates of interest more than double the yield available on sovereign British debt. Brazil, Buenos Aires (then a sovereign borrower), Mexico, and Guatemala followed in 1824 and 1825.[10] Also in 1822, a Scots adventurer named Gregor MacGregor succeeded in borrowing £200,000 at 6 percent on behalf of a supposed Principality of Poyais, situated in what today is Belize. The country was a fraud and MacGregor was a fabulist.

Whatever else the Bank's and the government's policies achieved, they quelled the long-running monetary controversy. The gold pound was back, and people rushed to invest it. The Liverpool and Manchester Railway, organized in 1823 as the first British steam-powered line to provide intercity passenger service, found seed capital. So did a less promising £1 million scheme to plant mulberry trees in order to propagate silkworm culture.[11] The teenaged Benjamin Disraeli quit his legal training to write purple marketing copy for South American mining promotions. Foreign governments and domestic joint-stock companies raised £42.9 million in the London capital markets in 1824 and 1825—not much less than the combined market value of all listed equities on the London exchange in December 1825.[12] "There never was a period in the history of this country," declared the Lord Chancellor, reading the King's Speech at the opening of Parliament in February 1825, "when all the great interests of the nation were at the same time in so thriving a condition, or when a feeling of content and satisfaction was more widely diffused through all classes of the British people."[13]

Arthur Wellesley, 1st Duke of Wellington, dissented from the royal view. He warned the diarist Harriet Arbuthnot in March that "all the companies are bubbles invented for stockjobbing purposes & that there will be a general crash, which [would] be almost as fatal as the failure of [John] Law's schemes." Law, as the Duke's contemporaries were well aware, was the Scottish adventurer whose monetary innovations first inflated, then deflated, Regency France a century earlier.

It was a point in Wellington's favor that "the foreign exchanges" were adverse —the Bank of England was paying out more gold than it was taking in. Between October 1824 and November 1825, £7.5 million's worth of coins and bars left the Bank,[14] or 62.5 percent of the treasure that the Old Lady's vaults had held as recently as 1821. In July 1825, Vincent Stuckey found it singular and worrying that the ship on which he was crossing the English Channel was carrying almost £1 million of sovereigns earmarked for French buyers.[15] Money left England in loans to foreign governments, in payment for shares in South American mining speculations, in exchange for commodities—for there was a bull market in produce as well as in bonds and shares.[16] The loss of gold was public proof that the Bank had lent too much or that the interest rate it charged was too low, or both.

In Bristol, in June 1825, Frederick Jones presented himself at the Castle Bank, handed six £1 Castle notes to the clerk, and demanded six gold sovereigns in exchange. The clerk, refusing, offered notes of the Bank of England instead. Jones turned on his heel, left, and returned with £45 of Castle Bank paper for which he again demanded the gold equivalent. Again he was refused. Incensed, Jones took his case to Joseph Hume, his MP, who presented it to the House of Commons. The treatment of his constituent by the Bristol bank was no isolated insult, Hume contended, but a "disgraceful and growing evil"[17]—and grow it did.

By mid-July, bankers all over the country were denying accommodation to loan applicants accustomed to hearing a cheerful "yes." By the end of July, the Bank of England had restricted lending against the unimpeachable collateral of British government securities. In September, the country banks began to turn away applications for loans against the all too impeachable collateral of South American bonds. The Plymouth Bank stopped payment altogether in late November.* There was a spate of failures across the West Country.

On December 12, the crisis shook London. Pole, Thornton & Co., the London correspondent for more than forty country banks, had been stretching to earn the extra income that safe investments never pay.†

---

* The Plymouth Bank went wrong by lending against illiquid mortgages, the *Morning Chronicle* reported. "It would have been well if the Bank of England had not set the example of this mode of extending the paper circulation." *Morning Chronicle*, November 30, 1825.

† *The Times*'s post mortem read in part: "The decline of this house in credit is generally attributed to the anxiety felt by the partners at the time when the rate of interest was low, to make a profitable use of their capital, and hence they were led to employ it on securities capable of being realized only at a distant period, or of an inferior degree of credit."

Not even a £300,000 advance from the Bank of England, whose directors gathered on a Sunday morning to discuss the situation,[18] could save it.

Now crowds replaced Frederick Jones at the counter of the Castle Bank in Bristol. The notes of local banks, so readily accepted in boom times, were money no longer. Frightened people demanded cash, meaning gold, and the notes of the Bank of England. To obtain them, country bankers trooped to London to beseech their correspondents or the haggard Bank clerks, bringing gilt-edged British securities, exchequer bills, prime commercial bills, and first mortgages to offer in exchange for cash. The quality of the collateral was pristine—but there was, simply, no cash to be had.

To get gold—to bring it in from abroad and shake it from the grasp of frightened Englishmen—the Bank returned its discount rate to 5 percent. A certain "eminent capitalist," perhaps Nathan Rothschild, imported £300,000 of sovereigns, which he deposited at the Bank of England. The exchanges began to turn in favor of the pound, but not fast enough.

Would the government not lift a finger to help? It would not, said Lord Liverpool, espousing faith in the curative properties of markets.[19] The directors of the Bank of England acted to push the healing processes along, and lent against the shares of their own institution and against the bonds of the British Treasury, classes of securities they had previously held to be ineligible for discount. The volume of their discounts—that is, funds advanced against collateral—had jumped from £7.5 million on December 8 to £11.5 million on December 15 and to £15 million on December 29.[20]

The demand for sovereigns seemed insatiable; the Royal Mint, working nonstop, was unable to keep up. The Bank of England's £1 notes were as good as sovereigns, though none had been printed for many years and, for all anyone seemed to know, no adequate supply existed. It was therefore a godsend when the Bank discovered a sizable cache of previously unissued £1 notes, precious pieces of paper that the clerks duly started handing out.[21]

No formal announcement told the public that the Bank was relaxing monetary policy; it fell to the press and the financial community to sense that things had changed. "[N]ot only liberal, but profuse," *The Times* characterized the Bank's new M.O. In subsequent parliamentary testimony, Bank of England directors revealed that they had lent against merchandise—not securities but goods themselves—and the most marginal categories of commercial bill.

The Bank, a profit-making institution with some definite but indistinct obligation to help in times of crisis, was stretched thin. No government guarantees were in place to save it should it suffer a debilitating loss,[22] and its gold reserve was being fast depleted. Its staff worked through the night so they could be ready to distribute signed notes to clamoring customers the next day. The Bank had suspended gold convertibility in 1797. In the third week of December 1825, it was rumored that the Old Lady had only 60,000 sovereigns to her name.

"The evil will cure itself," Liverpool had prophesied, and so it did—with more than a little help from the Bank. The crisis subsided just before Christmas. Even at the worst of the December panic, the pound had held its own on the foreign exchanges; it was the English people, the Frederick Joneses—not the foreigners—who ran on the banks.

There had been 770 banks in England before the panic; seventy-three failed. To prevent a recurrence of the disaster, Parliament, in May 1826, enacted a law to allow joint-stock banks the freedom to expand beyond a 65-mile radius of London (provided they had no office in the capital city) and to permit them any number of partners they wished.

Stuckey's was among the first to avail itself of the new freedom to expand, counting twelve partners and fourteen branch offices by 1832. The crash had brought the number of Bristol banks down from ten to five, and before long, the premises of the now-shuttered Castle Bank housed the Bristol office of Stuckey's Banking Company. The Panic of 1825, the undoing of so many, was the making of the enterprising Vincent Stuckey. It would likewise furnish an important case study for any who would delve into the workings of the British financial system—for one, Stuckey's nephew, Walter Bagehot.

BAGEHOT

CHAPTER 1

"LARGE, WILD, FIERY, BLACK"

Walter Bagehot was born on February 3, 1826, in the West Country market town of Langport, in the county of Somerset, England. Bank House, on Cheapside, part of the main street in Langport, was the family residence as well as his birthplace. Immediately adjacent was Stuckey's Banking Company, otherwise known as S & G Stuckey & Co., which employed Walter's father. It was said in later years that the townspeople could set their clocks by Mr. Bagehot's arrival at work in the morning.

Nobody in Langport, population 1,100 or so, had far to travel to reach any local destination. Hemmed in by hills and wetlands, it was compact, beautiful, and ancient. Romans, Saxons, Danes, and Britons had lived there (at times fighting over it) for 1,600 years. The Chantry Chapel of the Blessed Virgin, locally known as the Hanging Chapel, dated from the thirteenth century. In 1645, Oliver Cromwell's New Model Army defeated the royalist forces of Charles I at the Battle of Langport. Market days and annual fairs, exciting fixtures of town life, had their origin in the charter that Elizabeth I signed in 1562. A nine-arched medieval bridge crossed the river Parrett, which ran through the center of town and was Langport's commercial lifeblood. The town was planted at the first ford from the mouth of the river; it's the point at which the Parrett meets the river Yeo to form a navigable waterway to Bridgwater and to the sea beyond.[1]

As a Langport pedestrian of 1826, you could walk the winding main street, called Bow at one end and Cheapside at the other. You could climb Herd's Hill, overlooking the town from the west, or Langport Hill, which peers down from the east, and pause to absorb the view: to the north, the tower of St. Mary's church in nearby Huish Episcopi, where members of the Bagehot family sometimes worshipped; to the west, the Burton Pynsent monument, a 140-foot-high tribute to the man who settled a fortune on William Pitt the Elder, the statesman having removed a tax that weighed on his benefactor's cider business.

You could look in on the bustling quay, where dockworkers loaded the barges that plied the Parrett to Bridgwater and back. You could walk up the slope leading to All Saints church, with its octagonal tower, its fifteenth-century stained-glass window, and its ornamental "punky dunks," as the Somerset people called them—not gargoyles, exactly, as a proper gargoyle serves an architectural function. You could not range far into the surrounding flood-prone moors before getting your feet wet. In winter, the wettest part of the year, the townspeople sometimes traversed the streets in rowboats.

In 1826, the floodwaters were financial. Walter's father, Thomas Watson Bagehot—Watson to friends and family—was thirty years old when the storm broke. More than an officer of Stuckey's Bank, he was one of its six partners. This lofty station carried with it an unlimited personal liability. As he earned his pro rata share of the profits of the bank, so was he responsible for his portion of its debts.

Fearful though the times were, the new father did not despair. Having survived the panic, Stuckey's stood to gain in prestige, therefore in depositors, and business value.[2] There was a second cause for confidence: Watson had married a Stuckey. His wife—Walter's mother—was a widow named Edith Estlin. Born Edith Stuckey, she was the sister of

Vincent Stuckey, chairman of the bank and nephew of Samuel Stuckey, the founder.

Marriage and money had bound together generations of Stuckeys and Bagehots. Before the bank opened its doors in or about 1770, the families were partners in a shipping business. At the moment, Vincent was a business partner not only of Watson Bagehot but also *his* father, Robert Codrington Bagehot, grandfather of the newborn Walter. Watson's sister, Mary, was married to John Stuckey Reynolds, whose mother was Vincent Stuckey's sister.[3] Altogether, Watson's banking career was probably as safe as any in the midst of Britain's worst financial upheaval.

Watson and Edith had married in 1824; she was thirty-eight, he twenty-eight. In Langport, the union was accounted a dynastic inevitability. The townspeople likely banked at Stuckey's if they banked at all, and not a few of them worked on Stuckey and Bagehot barges, or in the Stuckey and Bagehot salt works. As between the two clans, the keepers of local reputation accounted the Stuckeys the richer, the Bagehots the better bred. A Sir Thomas Bagehot, Master of the Buckhounds to King James I, and a number of generations of major landowners at Prestbury, near present-day Cheltenham, figured in the family history.

Edith had a quick wit, a sense of fun, good looks, and a volatile personality. She was given to acts of charity—thrusting a £5 note into the hand of a needy visitor, raising funds to build a church for the poor, dispensing smiles and friendship all around, and with none of the condescension that might have been expected from a member of a prominent local family. People loved her—and they pitied her, too, as she was known to be mad.

Widowed at the age of twenty-eight, Edith brought three sons to her marriage with Bagehot. Vincent, the eldest, was born feeble-minded. A second son died of illness and a third in a carriage accident. Walter was the second child of her second marriage. The first-born, Watson, was three when he died in 1827. A second Watson, called Watty, the son of a widowed naval officer of some family relation, arrived years later to become Walter's foster brother. Some ascribed Edith's mental illness to the many deaths she bore. It wasn't uncommon in those days; of the ten children born to Vincent and Julia Stuckey, eight died young.[4]

Edith was an adherent of the Church of England, and few sects were further removed from her conception of true religion than the stripped-down Protestant faith of Walter's Unitarian father or of her first father-in-law. John Prior Estlin, LLD, was a Unitarian divine who conducted a literary correspondence with Samuel Taylor Coleridge and Robert Southey. John Bishop Estlin, a brother of Edith's deceased husband, had earlier married Watson Bagehot's sister Margaret. *She* died in 1821, after the birth of her first child, Mary Anne. The widowed Estlin, himself a Unitarian, became a famous ophthalmic surgeon, the founder of a charitable dispensary for the treatment of eye disease in Bristol, a writer in support of Christian miracles, and an adherent of temperance, abolition, and religious tolerance. Mary Anne, taking after her father, was likewise a Unitarian, a feminist, and a radical abolitionist, who pressed England's antislavery organizations to take up the uncompromising ardor of the American radical William Lloyd Garrison.

A snapshot of life at Bank House was furnished by a visiting cousin, George H. Sawtell, in about the year 1835; Walter was nine, Vincent was twenty-nine. (Watty, a boy about Walter's age, goes unmentioned.) Recalled Sawtell:

> I was introduced to the scene of [Walter's] studies which were being conducted (in the room over the entrance door of the Bank House) after a very singular fashion and apparently with a view to induce concentration of thought. He was "doing sums" with about twenty clocks all ticking in unison and striking to the minute around him (such being Vincent Estlin's whim of the hour), while his mother read "Quentin Durward" in as high a key and as rapidly as was possible, for the benefit of poor Vincent.[5]

The head of this manic household was second in command at the bank, a junior partner in the various Stuckey and Bagehot shipping, warehousing, and merchant enterprises. It was he, Watson Bagehot, who could be counted on in directors' meetings to move that a portion of the bank's earnings be paid out as bonuses for the employees. Bagehot worked the then customary six days a week. On the seventh day he led Unitarian services in the family parlor. In the few free hours left over, he painted watercolors, carried out landscaping projects, or drove into the surrounding countryside to be alone with his thoughts. From time to time, he served as a school trustee and as the town's port supervisor. He said that he didn't mind the occasional bout of illness as good health afforded him so little rest.

A photographer captured the elder Bagehot in prime middle age. The subject is seated, his left arm slung over the back of the chair, his right leg half-crossed over the left. His face is composed, his posture upright. Evidently he is healthy—indeed, he would outlive his famous son. "Remarkably plodding," cousin Sawtell called Watson.[6] One might rather have judged him overwhelmed. He lived in two shadows, his wife's at home, his brother-in-law's at the bank.

Vincent Stuckey was Langport's grandee. He planned canals, bestowed gifts, testified before Parliament, maintained a fashionable house in London, gave balls, kept hounds, owned land, manufactured salt, and ran the bank.* A portrait depicts him in muttonchop whiskers. His face is wide, his eyebrows heavy, his torso thick. His eager eyes are those of the young man who, in 1790, approached a high-placed Somerset neighbor out of the blue to ask for an introduction to the prime

---

* Everybody knew he was rich, including the criminals. In 1827, William Kerslake broke into the Stuckey mansion and carried away a quantity of silver plate, a pocketful of small change (which some charity girls had turned over to Stuckey for safekeeping), and a mustard spoon. When Kerslake was caught, his pocket was still smeared with mustard. He was tried, convicted, and hanged, along with three other thieves, in front of Ilchester jail; 10,000 people watched.

minister, William Pitt. "Well, I do not see why I should not," replied
Lady Chatham, who happened to be Pitt's mother. Her letter in hand,
Stuckey went to London, presented himself to Pitt, got himself a clerk-
ship at the Treasury, served in positions of increasing responsibility that
brought him into personal contact with Pitt and the financial authority
William Huskisson, and, after ten years of service, returned to Langport
to marry his first cousin, Julia, the youngest daughter of the founding
banker, Samuel, in 1801.[7] Before long, Vincent was on the Stuckey payroll; by 1807 he was effectively the bank's senior partner; in 1812, upon
Samuel's death, he became the head of the institution in fact; in 1826,
he was made chairman of a merged collection of banks gathered under
the corporate banner of Stuckey's Banking Company.

Vincent didn't just go looking for money; money also seemed to go
looking for him. Sometime after his return to Langport, he found that
a certain Squire Stuckey of Branscombe, in the county of Devon, had
remembered him in his will. Vincent was no relation of the deceased
but had rather dropped by to introduce himself, one Stuckey to another.
The visitor charmed the squire, and vice versa, and the two stayed in
touch. Vincent called the unexpected bequest—a life interest in two of
the squire's estates—his "shower of prosperity." He pumped the proceeds into his bank.

All doted on little Walter. According to the loving testimony of
his paternal grandmother, the newborn was a "large, handsome fellow
who can already make the nursery ring with his strong voice, tho he
is generally quiet." Before long, it wasn't the boy's voice but his eyes
that excited comment—"large, wild, fiery, black," as they struck one
observer years later.[8]

It was clear from early on that Walter was different. At age four or
five he was starting to write. At six, he was complaining that he had
read the covers off his copy of *Daily Food for Christians*, a collection of
365 meditations. As children's literature was scarce, the eager pupil was
directed to Sir Walter Scott and Charles Dickens.[9] When he was seven,

Walter was writing poetry. His father commended him on this feat in a letter dated June 17, the day before the anniversary of the Battle of Waterloo. To mark the famous victory, Watson presented the boy with a sword and asked him to ponder: "How would you have liked living at Brussels when the cannons began to roar and the soldiers were summoned to the field?"[10]

Edith Bagehot knew some Greek, read voraciously in English, and self-published some devotional verse. The elder Bagehot was a sturdy reader and possessed an extraordinary memory—he could "quote chapter and verse, any part of the Bible you can name," Edith boasted. Both parents were determined to give their precocious son the schooling which they had not had. "Every day," the father wrote to his boy, "I feel how much I have lost in not having had such an education as I wish to give you, and you need not therefore fear that anything will be wanting on my part to secure to you its advantages."[11]

At the age of eight or nine Walter began attending classes at the Langport Grammar School under the more than capable master, William Quekett. At age twelve, he was writing extracurricular essays for his father on topics including the Battle of Marathon, St. Augustine, and Julius Caesar. The thirteen-year-old student had read the *Aeneid* (in Latin, of course), among other works of Virgil. He had conquered some mathematics and probably read some Wordsworth; master Quekett and the poet had been schoolfellows. Some hint of the high quality of Quekett's teaching is evident in the lives of his own four sons, two of whom achieved eminence in science, with John, a histologist, becoming a member of the Royal Society; another in the clergy; and a fourth achieving, if not eminence, then competence, in finance, as the secretary of Stuckey's Bank.[12]

Langport was a scrum of contending Christian faiths when Walter was going to school. More than one family was split as the Bagehots were, with adherents of the established church lined up against dissenters. Walter, attending Unitarian services with his father in the morning and Anglican services with his mother in the afternoon, favored the Church of England. The town made room for Baptists, Wesleyans, Plymouth Brothers and Sisters, and members of the Home Missionary Society. It set a place for heathens, too. "From time immemorial," contended James Moreton, a dissenting minister, "Langport was a stronghold of the powers of darkness, proverbial for ignorance of spiritual things, prejudice and wickedness."[13]

Be that as it may, the market town was putting aside some of its eighteenth-century folkways. Walter was born too late to partake in the bull-, bear-, and badger-baiting, pugilism, backsword play, sword-and-dagger contests, and dueling that had delighted earlier and rougher generations of townspeople.[14] Still, drunks spent time in the stocks, and people turned out for the festive "Hang Fair Days" in nearby Ilchester. Changed was the composition of the crowds. When the trapdoor opened under the feet of the condemned, fewer spectators of the Bagehot and Stuckey social stratum were likely to be cheering.[15]

A transportation hub, Langport had the sights and sounds to entrance a little boy. Stuckey–Bagehot barges moved goods to and from Bridgwater. At Langport, the cargo was unloaded and piled on to waiting horse-drawn carts, which could line the length of Bow and Cheapside. The London–Taunton–Barnstaple coach changed horses next to the family quarters at Bank House.[16] The mail coaches pounded up to the Langport Arms. Returning from a season in London, Vincent Stuckey would sweep into town in his carriage with postilion.[17]

Not long after Walter's birth, his town-dwelling paternal grandparents built a higher and drier house on Herd's Hill, a two-story Regency-style villa set on spreading grounds. Walter loved to play there. Whacking his sword this way and that, he annihilated his enemies (the heaps of dead resembling weeds and flowers). He moved with his parents into Herd's Hill upon his grandfather's death in 1836, Watson taking care to transplant a prized mulberry tree from the Bank House yard.

In some visible ways, young Walter was an ordinary boy. He

delighted in climbing trees and running around the observation deck of the Pynsent monument with his mother watching below, her heart in her mouth. Riding since the age of four, he thrilled to hunt; on horseback, he was accounted something of a daredevil.

In other respects, Walter was not so much a boy as a miniature middle-aged man. He complained of a weak chest, nervous strain, headaches, and the none-too-extreme heat of the Langport summers. And it was no ordinary boy who marveled that Dr. Johnson preferred "Goldsmith's history of Greece to any composition of Robertson or Hume."[18]

Walter went as far in the Langport Grammar School as Mr. Quekett could take him. In 1839, at the age of thirteen, his parents enrolled him in Bristol College, founded eight years earlier by Unitarian freethinkers. That fact commended the place to Watson Bagehot, who knew Bristol as the home of a thriving Stuckey's office. Edith Bagehot judged the city heretical,[19] though there was one mitigating factor: Dr. James Prichard, a renowned anthropologist and physician, was on the college's faculty. Prichard was married to Anne Maria Estlin, a daughter of her first father-in-law. The scholar, a kind of brother-in-law, was an Anglican.

Bristol College offered instruction in science—a rarity in secondary-school curricula of the day—as well as the classics; optional was the teaching of doctrine of the Church of England. The school's Unitarian progenitors could see that the times were changing. Popular pressure for the expansion of the electoral franchise crystallized the Great Reform Act of 1832. In and out of Parliament, there was agitation for a reapportionment of political power away from the old landed interests and in favor of the rising commercial classes, well represented in Bristol—and, indeed, at Herd's Hill in Langport.

The reformers were not mistaken in their reading of English political currents. The year 1832 brought not only landmark reform but also the famous Bristol riots, an explosion of popular fury against the English ruling classes, both political and ecclesiastical. Mobs attacked the cathedral and burned the bishop's house. In the aftermath, four alleged ringleaders were tried and condemned to death. Ten thousand citizens signed a petition for clemency, in vain.[20]

Perhaps Walter's mind was elsewhere. Besides classics, he studied Hebrew, German, and mathematics. Under the instruction of Dr. Prichard, he was exposed to the exciting new doctrine of evolution. "I dined at the Prichard's a day or too ago," the rapt pupil reported home. "The Doctor had two friends there talking about the Arrow-headed character and the monuments of Pentapolis, and the way of manufacturing cloth in the South Seas."[21]

"Work as hard as you can, but be modest," his father admonished him, "for to be so is a great charm in boys, and the more so, the cleverer they are." Try as Walter might, there was no hiding what lay behind those burning black eyes. He counted only a few of his thirty-odd classmates as his intellectual equals. He scorned the others, calling them the "mob," and they returned the compliment. "I was carried out just now to play with some of the other boys," Walter reported to Langport from what seems the early phase of his school career:

> I wanted to do my mathematics and to mug China; but they took me out, and because I would not play when I got out there, tied me up to the railings and corked me as hard as they could with a ball which made me play whether or no. They very often beg me to come out, when they have not enough to make up their game; and it is hard to spoil their game; and if I do; I get a kick every now and then; and sometimes a blow for every time I open my mouth. It is not at all a pleasant thing to be on bad terms with any of one's schoolfellows, much more with all. This has prevented me from doing as much mathematics with Mr. Bromly lately as before.[22]

It must have seemed at times as if he were going to school for his father as much as for himself. "I wish I could be with you," Mr. Bagehot wrote shortly after dropping off Walter for his first term at Bristol, "but as that cannot be, we must gladden each other's hearts by writing as often as we can, and telling each other, not only what is passing without, but within us, and keeping up a constant interchange of thought."[23]

His father sent him the highbrow quarterlies and briefed him on current affairs. In politics, it was like father, like son: both supported free trade, opposed the Corn Laws—the high tariff on imported grain, a gift to the country gentlemen at the expense of the consumer—and stood with Lord Palmerston against the landed interests. Walter was grateful to be furnished with Anti-Corn Law arguments for debates with the protectionist college master. "What makes Mr. Booth a Corn-Law advocate?" father inquired of son by post. "I hope he has an old rich Uncle with many fine acres, all of which are to be his!"[24]

Watson and Walter saw eye to eye in the matter of party politics, too: they were against it. A letter from Walter deploring the blind partisanship of the Whigs and Tories afforded his father the opening for some moral instruction. "A strong love of truth and the seeking it for its own sake, must be the ground on which all our endeavors must rest," he wrote,

> but there are too many enemies ready to displace us, so that we must be ever on our guard, and ready to defend ourselves. A love of ease, and an unwillingness to examine into the foundation of things long settled, as far as we are concerned—a fondness for our own opinion, and a dislike of allowing that we were, or are mistaken—are some among the numerous enemies to be resisted, beside the heavy and weighty troops of pounds, shillings and pence, and patronage and power.[25]

Man and boy shared another interest: Edith's flights of madness frightened and tyrannized them both. In the absence of effective medical treatment, it fell to family and friends to help, and the job fell increasingly to Walter. His personality more closely resembled his mother's than his father's. Sharing her gift for nonsense, he could sometimes jolly her back down to earth.

"Walter told us," relates his sister-in-law and biographer, Emilie Barrington,

> of a characteristic scene which took place towards the end of her life. One morning, for some unknown reason, she got it into her head during breakfast that she could not speak to Walter, and therefore remained dumb; but this silent situation before long became dull; so she wrote on a slate something she wanted him to know, and hung the slate around her neck and appeared in his study where he was writing. She was standing mute in the doorway when he looked up suddenly, and saw her and the slate, and the two burst out laughing together.[26]

It was as a peer and fellow sufferer that Mr. Bagehot wrote to Walter in 1842 to report that his mother had had one of her spells. Worse, she had had it while he was home sick, "so I have not had so much to delight me as in some of my illnesses." He had so looked forward to a few days of peace.

Walter strained to succeed for his parents as much as for himself; he would fall asleep over his books rather than disappoint them. He had been at school only a few months when he reported that he would soon discover whether he stood at the top of the junior division in only German and theology or in classics, too; he was number two in mathematics—"but," he added, "I am afraid I am building castles in the air . . . I scold myself for being so anxious."[27] Two years later—just before Christmas 1841—he was writing an essay on "the comparative advantages of the Study of Ancient and Modern Languages" not because he had to, but because he wanted "the practice in composition."[28]

Walter was away at school when Edith sat her husband down and read to him the letters that Stuckey Estlin, the son from her first marriage who was killed in a coach accident, had written to her. Then she sat down with paper and pen. "My dearest Walter," she wrote,

> I have been reading over many of my beloved Stuckey's letters to dearest Papa this week, and he and I were much struck with the similarity of the style with yours and in affection for his own Mamma—or rather in parental affection I hope you resemble each other. Oh! I have the blessed assurance that that is a feeling which survives the grave and lives purified and anew through all eternity.[29]

Not every schoolboy would be equipped to receive such a letter. Nor is it clear that Walter was.

By the age of fifteen, he was immersed in Newton's *Principia*, studying integral calculus, and reading Homer and Cicero. At sixteen, he returned to school from the Christmas holiday for his final term at Bristol to discover that he would be placed, literally, in a class of his own.

The former victim of his classmates' envy and loathing had by now grown into his skin. Cousin Sawtell recalled that "he was all himself, with his standing leaps, his daring ventures on horseback, his absorbing love of children, and his conversational freshness, chiefly, as far as I was concerned, interrogatively as to what I, three years older, learnt and saw and heard in the great city, always with the result of making me feel that I had got hold of the little end of the stick."[30]

After graduation, it was to the great city—London—that Walter repaired.

CHAPTER 2

"IN MIRTH AND REFUTATION—
IN RIDICULE AND LAUGHTER"

There would be no Oxford or Cambridge for Walter Bagehot. Britain's ancient universities required entering students to subscribe to the tenets of the established church; Watson Bagehot, the Unitarian, refused to hear of it. So, for Walter, it was off to London to study with the sons of Catholics, Jews, and Protestant dissenters.

There was nothing very ancient about University College London. Founded on February 11, 1826, the school was eight days younger than the incoming first-year student from Langport. Walter arrived on the campus at Gower Street, Bloomsbury, in October 1842.

London was new, exciting, and hideous. Stinking cesspools, rank cemeteries, fetid alleyways, and soot-filled air accosted the rural nose. The urban mud—57 parts horse dung, 30 parts abraded stone, 13 parts abraded iron, according to the City of London's medical officer—was sticky enough "to suck off your boots."[1]

Perhaps the only slightly familiar aspect of collegiate life for the sixteen-year-old alumnus of Bristol College was the hostility of the English establishment to the liberal institution in which he was enrolled. "The radical infidel college," some called it, there being no chapel and no religious instruction. Fastening on the inclusive social profile of the student body, others sneered at "the Cockney college." As money was short, the grand, neo-Grecian design of the college architect, William Wilkins, had been only partially realized. The magnificent portico, critics smirked, was "the grandest entrance in London with nothing behind it."

The founders, a pair of Scotsmen, the poet Thomas Campbell and the lawyer and parliamentarian Henry Brougham, were undaunted. They passed the hat for seed money in much the same manner as the joint-stock companies had raised funds in the boom of 1825—a method that proved another incitement to ridicule. They secured enough money to open the doors to the first students in 1828. Campbell, writing to Brougham, envisioned "a great London university," for "effectively and multifariously teaching, examining, exercising and rewarding with honors, in the liberal arts and sciences, the youth of our middling rich people."

The spirit of the times, if not the disposition of the then-sitting Tory government, smiled on the project. In 1819, across the Atlantic, Thomas Jefferson had founded the University of Virginia. Seven years later in England, Brougham, championing popular education, had established the Society for the Diffusion of Useful Knowledge. London, the biggest city in Europe, was the only capital without a university. Campbell and Brougham set out to fill the void.

University College could hardly have hoped for a brighter light than Bagehot. A preliminary examination found him qualified in Latin, Greek, natural philosophy, English, and mathematics. Homesick, the devout and brainy country boy found solace in the dense pages of books such as *A Second Defence of Dr. [Samuel] Clarke's Demonstration of the Being and Attributes of God: In Answer to the Postscript Published in the Second Edition of Mr. Law's Translation of Dr. King's Origin of Evil.*

There were no dormitories at University College; the students settled in nearby lodgings. Bagehot took a room at 39 Camden Street, the home of Dr. John Hoppus, the college's first chair of logic and philosophy of mind.[2] A fellow student also living under the Hoppus roof happened to be conducting an affair when he ought to have been in class, and a second student seemed ready to do the same. Apprised of these facts, Bagehot resolved to step in: "This certainly must be stopped, and I possess no other means of doing so, but informing Dr. Hoppus immediately." Hoppus showed the offending students the door and the tattletale became a pariah. "It is my first taste of the troubles of life," Bagehot wrote to his father. "Henceforth, I shall perhaps never be wholly free from them."

The prig soon lived down his infamy. If some of his classmates shunned Bagehot, others stood in awe of his mind or were charmed by his conversation. He made friends: William Caldwell Roscoe, grandson of William Roscoe of Liverpool, the historian of Lorenzo de' Medici and Pope Leo X; Timothy Osler, a distant relative whose family had befriended him in Bristol; and Richard Holt Hutton.

Hutton, the son of a Unitarian minister and future critic and journalist whose life and career would intertwine with Bagehot's, chafed at his friend's "superciliousness" and "arrogance." But he recognized, too, the basis of Bagehot's youthful conceit; he really was smarter than the others.[3] In later years, Hutton wrote critical essays on the arts and religion and turned the *Spectator* into a profitable and respected weekly journal. "Both wore beards and glasses," Alastair Buchan, a twentieth-century Bagehot biographer, observed of the two collegiate friends, "but Hutton's beard did not curl nor his eyeglasses flash as Bagehot's did. One of Hutton's best characteristics was that he was fully aware of this, from the day when he was struck 'by the questions put by a lad with large dark eyes and florid complexion to the late Professor De Morgan.' "

Augustus De Morgan, like Bagehot, had entered university at the age of sixteen—in De Morgan's case, Trinity College, Cambridge. And, like Bagehot, De Morgan wound up at University College because he bridled at a religious test. Arriving at Gower Street to take up the chair of mathematics at the age of twenty-one, the prodigy was the youngest of the original University College faculty and, by some accounts, the most brilliant. The chemist Sir Henry Roscoe, a few years behind Bagehot's class at University College, judged De Morgan to be "one of the profoundest and subtlest thinkers of the nineteenth century."

The deviser of eponymous laws in the fields of Boolean algebra and propositional logic, and the author of a volume entitled *Trigonometry and Double Algebra*, De Morgan sometimes looked out into a class of blank faces. "We have," reported Bagehot, "been discussing the properties of infinite series, which are very perplexing—one is harassed by getting a glimpse of theorems and then to find that they are to be taken with so many limitations, that one has still greater difficulty in seeing them at all."[4]

The mathematician brought whimsy as well as rigor to his lectures, for he was a collector of riddles and puzzles. Paradoxes, he called these intellectual curios, and paradoxers, he called their authors: "the squarers of circles . . . constructors of perpetual motion, subverters of gravitation, stagnators of the earth, builders of the universe."[5] Bagehot, though his head sometimes reeled, followed De Morgan through the labyrinths of pure and applied mathematics.*

Classical languages were an essential part of the Victorian curriculum, even at University College, which prided itself on the new teaching of science.† George Long, the professor of Latin, was a Cambridge

---

* On a page of his mathematics notebook, Bagehot jotted, "[T]his professor is intoxicated."

† In an 1838 address concerning the introduction of the natural sciences into the University College curriculum, Henry Malden, a professor of Greek, added a good word for the ancient languages: "If we prize exactness in the use of speech, even in our own language, we shall encourage our pupils to study it in languages which are in themselves more exact, and on which, as new and external objects, the mind can fix an attention, such as, without this discipline, it never can be taught to fix upon the mother tongue, which use has made all too familiar to be so contemplated, and the idioms of which have become confounded with its own modes of conception." Henry Malden, *On the Introduction of the Natural Sciences into general education: A lecture delivered at the commencement of the session of the faculty of arts, in University College, London, October 15, 1838* (London: Taylor and Walton, 1838), 5.

man and, like De Morgan, a favorite of Bagehot's. For many years the editor of the *Penny Cyclopedia*, the classicist was deeply imbued with the ideals of the founders of University College. Elected professor of ancient languages at the new University of Virginia in 1824, he had returned to England in 1828 to assume the chair of Greek at University College. He gloried in the promise of a university "offering," as he put it, "the advantages of higher education to all classes, but particularly to those who had before been excluded from it." Learned, versatile, and witty enough to bring tears to Bagehot's eyes, Long was a founder of the Royal Geographical Society, a contributor of articles on Roman law to *Smith's Dictionary of Greek and Roman Antiquities*, the author of the five-volume *Decline of the Roman Republic*, and the editor of the *Biblio-theca Classica* series, the first substantial edition of classical texts with English commentaries.

The year of Bagehot's matriculation to University College, 1842, was a year of economic depression—hunger, political upheaval, and sharp-drawn ideological controversy. In February, some five hundred struggling manufacturers from the northern shires descended on London. Arm in arm, they marched down the Strand and Parliament Street roaring, "Down with monopoly" and "Give bread and labor." The prime minister, Sir Robert Peel, driving to the House of Commons, saw the respectable men before he heard their angry chants, at first mistaking the roars for cheers.[6] In fact the voices raged against him— and against the Corn Laws, the tariffs on imported grain that raised the price of bread in the service of protecting British farming ("corn," a generic term, encompassed the grains that, like wheat and barley, can be ground into flour). Opponents contended that British agriculture needed no protection and that the laws, besides constituting an offense against the principle of free trade, were promoters of state-sponsored hunger.

The barons and the squires replied that what the Corn Laws protected was the stability of British institutions. The owners of acres ruled by right and tradition, and slightly elevated grain prices were a small price to pay for political continuity and good government. The Reform Act of 1832, which had enlarged the franchise and proportionally reduced the authority of the landed interest, was a necessary concession to the tumultuous times, but it was enough—more than enough. Factory hands would have to learn to adapt to higher-priced bread, and manufacturers to deal with higher wages and lower profits. It did not sweeten the terms of debate when the Duke of Norfolk, presiding at an agricultural dinner in Steyning, Sussex, in December 1842, suggested that starving workers might allay their hunger with a pinch of curry in hot water.[7]

The Anti-Corn Law League was prepared to accept none of these arguments. The sons of Adam Smith spurned compromise with a system that advantaged the well-fed over the hungry. There could be no concession to an injustice so monstrous. Among the most persuasive spokesmen for the principles of free trade was a thirty-seven-year-old Scotch hat manufacturer named James Wilson. He happened to be Bagehot's future father-in-law.

NOBODY HAD TAUGHT WILSON political economy; he imbibed it from the pages of Smith, David Ricardo, and Edmund Burke. Wilson was the fourth of fifteen children, ten of whom survived to adulthood; his mother died in childbirth. Wilson's father, a Quaker, was a well-to-do wool manufacturer in Hawick, in the east southern uplands of Scotland. Young Wilson played the flute and had an eye for pictures, and, like the young Bagehot, excelled at his books but not at games. His schooling complete, and after an unhappy false start as a teacher, he pointed for the law. This, too, came to naught—Quaker doctrine was against the legal profession—and the thwarted lawyer turned to business. His father set him up in the hat-making trade with another one of his sons.

Wilson did well enough in business to amass £25,000. This small fortune he proceeded to lose on a speculation on indigo in the panic year of 1837. By then, the hat maker, who had married the beautiful Elizabeth Preston of Newcastle-upon-Tyne and left the Society of Friends for the Church of England, was the father of five girls under the age of eight. He lived with his family in the leafy London suburb of Dulwich in a big house with large grounds. He owned another residence in London.

Righting himself from this financial debacle, Wilson paid off his private debts. His commercial creditors, accepting cash for half of what he owed them, took the balance in an assigned interest on a foreign property. Wilson was under no obligation to make his creditors whole when that earmarked asset failed to realize its expected value. He rather did so as a point of fair-dealing.

It was in the throes of his crisis that Wilson began to devote himself to the repeal of the Corn Laws. In 1839, he wrote and published his first essay in persuasion, a pamphlet entitled "Influences of the Corn Laws as Affecting All Classes of the Community, and Particularly the Landed Interests." Wilson's position was that everybody lost with high tariffs; not even the landowners gained. English farmers could compete with Continental agriculture perfectly well, he demonstrated with a characteristically daunting array of data and argument. He raised another objection: artificially high prices for grain contributed to Britain's violent economic cycles, the busts hitting the landowners just as they did the manufacturers and the working people.

Some of the Anti-Corn Law brethren cast their arguments in terms of a perceived clash between the commercial interests and the landed aristocracy, but Wilson would accept no part of that class-struggle dialectic: "nothing can possibly be favorable to the whole that is detrimental to a part, and . . . nothing can be detrimental to one portion that is favorable to another portion."[8]

In 1840, Wilson's pamphlet went into a second and third edition, and Sir Robert Peel quoted from it in the House of Commons. The newly-minted controversialist earned his highest praise from a pamphleteer who attacked the free-trade champions by name and by argument. The protectionist devoted three pages to one author, five to another, nine to a third, fifty-three to a fourth—and 114 to Wilson.[9]

Writing came hard to Wilson. He knew full well what he wanted to say; at first, he just couldn't say it. No one was more certain than he of the tenets of laissez-faire economics, of which free trade was a logical outgrowth. Wilson achieved journalistic fluency through hard practice: "the only source of certain success, whatever the undertaking may be, is steady, well directed and unremitting assiduity," he wrote.[10] He practiced in the columns of the *Manchester Guardian*, a Scottish newspaper or two, and the *Examiner*, a crusading weekly owned and edited by the celebrated journalist Albany Fortesque. Eventually, the sentences came so easily to Wilson that Fortesque was obliged to take scissors to Wilson's copy. The columnist chafed at the editing and resolved to do something about it: he would start a free-trade paper of his own.

What the mother of his young daughters—by 1841, there were six—thought of that scheme is unrecorded. The capital of the cash-strapped Wilson now consisted of knowledge, character, and his all-too commodious houses. To get ready money, he moved his family to London, reduced the staff of that residence to two, and rented the place in Dulwich. Having raised £800 in this fashion, he borrowed another £500. By late June 1844 he thought he could see the future. "I think," he wrote to Elizabeth, "with my great fund of commercial and statistical matter and very original articles on Free Trade and Political Economy, there is no danger but a good and attractive paper may be made. You know the facility with which I write on all these subjects, and with weekly practice that facility will increase, and my style will improve, although it is considered extremely good, clear and effective for such subjects at present." His paper would be "perfectly philosophical, steady and moderate;—nothing but pure *principles*."[11] The *Economist*,* he called it; vol. 1, no. 1 appeared on September 2, 1843.

BAGEHOT WAS AWARE OF these boiling public controversies;† he and his friends talked them to death. They heard the Chartist agitators flay the capitalists, and the Anti-Corn Law orators assail the protectionists. One evening in 1844, at Covent Garden Theatre, they heard Daniel O'Connell, the great Irish orator, mesmerize a houseful of Anti-Corn Law partisans. On the same occasion, they listened to the politely received remarks of James Wilson on the universal blessing of free trade.[12]

For a day or two, Bagehot could think of nothing but the spectacle and the speech-making. Then he thought of the crowds that had walked right by the theater. They apparently had something more important to do: "I had hardly ever so distinct a notion of the greatness of London, as when I came out, and saw how little interest all this great assemblage seemed to excite three streets off, and how little effect it had on either the numbers or direction of the throng of passengers."[13]

In Walter Bagehot, there was no gentlemanly fear of conveying scholarly effort. He reveled in reading and writing. Often falling asleep with his pen in his hand, he awoke like a stiff old man. He did fear failure, and so dreaded the exams at which he finally and predictably excelled. Stricken with some malady in the summer of 1843, he skipped

---

* The full birth name was a mouthful: the *Economist: or The Political, Commercial, Agricultural, and Free-Trade Journal.*

† As was his father. In Langport, in January, Vincent Stuckey, addressing his fellow bank directors, ordered the charge-off of £13,362 of "absolutely bad" debt and the making of a careful inventory of the bank's London-housed portfolio of government securities. The bank was sound enough, said Stuckey, but it must "of course partake of [the] general depression." The "middling rich people" whose youths would supposedly furnish the University College student body were certainly feeling the pinch. Stuckey's Banking Co. Ltd., *Director's Minutes*, Royal Bank of Scotland Archives STU2.1 (28 September 1858–26 July 1877), 146.

the autumn term to rest and recover on horseback in Langport, where a private tutorial in practical banking awaited him. A young clerk at the Stuckey's branch in the east Somerset town of Frome had made off with £420, covering his tracks with fake book entries. The sum was shockingly large, even if it failed to dent the bank's net worth of £126,000. What shook the confidence of the senior officers was that they were so long in the dark. The finance committee, on which Watson Bagehot sat, had failed to spot it.*

His health restored, Bagehot returned to London in 1844, quickly making the acquaintance of the litterateur, diarist, lawyer, Peninsular War *Times* correspondent, and inveterate networker Crabbe Robinson. A bachelor in his sixties, Robinson hosted famous literary breakfasts with good talk but no breakfast. Literature, for Bagehot, was a pleasure as much as a duty, and he distinguished himself in the University College debate society. Once he spoke to the topic of "Whether Government ought to interfere with the dissemination of blasphemous or seditious publications." He couched his reply—it was in the negative—in arguments so tightly wound and in authorities so apt that his speech would have done credit to an MP in the House of Commons. Reminiscing several years after graduation, Bagehot wrote that in his mind, the core of one's education consists

> not in tutors or lectures or in books "got up," but in Wordsworth and Shelley; in the books that all read because all like—in what

---

* The chairman, too, served on the finance committee. Vincent Stuckey, by now a banker-statesman, had been spending much of his time in London rather than visiting branch offices in the county of Somerset. The chairman reported to his fellow directors that he had met with Sir Robert Peel, as well as with the chancellor of the exchequer and the chairman and deputy chairman of the Bank of England. "And from all," Stuckey related, referring to himself in the third person, "he had received the most flattering Testimony as to the Principles on which the Company was originally formed, and as to the mode in which it has been conducted." Stuckey's Banking Co. Ltd., *Director's Minutes*, Royal Bank of Scotland Archives STU3.2, 154.

all talk of because all are interested—in the argumentative walk or the disputatious lounge—in the impact of young thought upon young thought, of fresh thought on fresh thought—of hot thought on hot thought—in mirth and refutation—in ridicule and laughter—for these are the free play of the natural mind, and these cannot be got without a college.[14]

Travel, too, was in the teenager's curriculum. On a tour of the Continent in the summer of 1844 with his aunt and uncle Reynolds, Bagehot marveled at the beauty of the Catholic Church. "[As] I tried to enter into the conception of the painter, the tears came too fast to my eyes to let me look any longer," he reported of a devotional painting at the Antwerp Museum. As for a statue of Jesus and the Virgin, attributed to Michelangelo, in the Cathedral of Notre Dame, Bagehot could find no words to describe its beauty. Yet how curious it was, the Protestant youth reflected, that these great achievements of the human mind "should be at the service of a system, which sets with denying the right of private judgment in matters of religion—that is, the right of exercising the highest of its powers on the noblest of subjects."[15]

It was a sore point with his mother that her young genius had his head in the clouds. He had always chosen the most difficult coursework in school, though his spelling, for all his learning, was barbarous. The work had taxed his health—his delicate chest recalled the "hereditary consumption" on her mother's side. Then, too, she observed, "many a mathematician is certainly a learned booby."

Bagehot had been contemplating a career in the law, but his mother pressed him to return to the family bank instead. "[T]urn your attention a little to business when you are home," she wrote him in 1845, his twentieth year:

try to understand Papa's cleverness in it, and if very or totally inferior at first, do not be depressed. If he were to die now, which

God forbid! I am sure I should at once wish you to understand *what business is.* I have often told dearest Papa, it was a fault more of his habits than his intentions, that he had not, as a matter of course, made you better acquainted with its practical details and mysteries; but all paths are open to good sense, good feelings, good intentions and industry, and, as deep and abstract study is now so bad for you, you must seek to apply the stores already acquired in lighter converse and associates, and in more of the practical details, friendships and usages of daily life, and not be so much of the studious, mawkish scholar any longer.[16]

Yet in November 1846, Bagehot astonished himself, if no one else, by securing first class honors in his final examination and becoming a Bachelor of Arts. It seemed he would become a lawyer after all.

Preparation for this career entailed a program of directed reading and clerical drudgery in one of London's four Inns of Court. Preceding all would be two years of study to earn an MA, also at University College. In February 1847, the newly-minted college graduate secured rooms for himself at No. 6 Great Coram Street—a nice, quiet street, full of nice, unassuming houses. Thackeray's Mr. Todd lived there in the pages of *Vanity Fair.*[17]

Elsewhere in London, statesmen clashed. Britain's serial monetary and banking upheavals set up a cry for reform. Restoration of the gold standard in 1821 had solved some of the problems with paper currency, but it had not procured peace and quiet, let alone unchecked prosperity. Something about British finance seemed to need fixing: Peel's government focused first on the stock market, second on the Bank of England.

In 1841, a committee of the House of Commons investigated the phenomenon of joint-stock companies. Its report, three years in the making, was produced under the guiding hand of the demonically energetic William E. Gladstone, the thirty-one-year-old vice president of Peel's Board of Trade. Readers bypassed the dry legal preface for the true-crime taxonomy of shady dealing, invitingly entitled "Modes of Deception." Gladstone proposed a law to streamline the process of incorporating a business. No more would an entrepreneur have to seek a royal charter or a private act of Parliament; he could pay £5 to a government registrar instead. A requirement to disclose essential corporate information would protect the investing public against fraud. Gladstone's labors bore fruit in the Joint Stock Companies Act of September 1844. "The principle of non-interference has its limits," applauded *Law Magazine*.[18]

The Bank Charter Act, also enacted in 1844, was the Peel government's attempt to fortify the pound by controlling the issuance of bank notes. Peel's Act, as the landmark law was also known, centralized monetary power in the Bank of England, even as it sundered the Bank in two. The Issue Department would emit notes in a predictable and semi-mechanical fashion, every pound of issuance above £14 million to be matched by its equivalent in gold in the Bank's vaults. As to banks like Stuckey's, their note-issuing powers would be circumscribed, while note issuance by new provincial banks would be prohibited. The Banking Department, the Issue Department's fraternal twin, would take deposits and make loans, much like any other London bank. No more would it operate chiefly in the nation's interest. It would, rather, be managed in the interest of the stockholders.*

Assure the gold value of the paper, control the issuance of pound notes by the country banks, and all would be well, reasoned the authors of what was intended to be—and what indeed proved to be—the most significant banking legislation of the Victorian age.

•   •   •

---

* "The Bank directors are said to be now free from all responsibility as regulators of the currency, and to have no other duty to perform than to do the best they can for their shareholders, the same as other banking establishments," commented the *Morning Chronicle* in January 1845.

A BANKER'S SON WOULD not have failed to notice that a great bull market* was raging in railroad shares. The punters' roll call—the official roster of people who had committed to buying railroad shares—included 157 members of Parliament, 257 clergymen, and two and a half pages' worth of people named Smith. By 1845, 20,000 Britons had subscribed £2,000 or more to purchase railroad equities. Perhaps not many of these individuals had the cash needed to pay full value for their subscriptions, but they didn't have to stump up the funds—so little was initially required. Calls for additional capital would come after business plans were successfully translated into action. Pending that rendezvous with reality, the price of the "scrip"—as in subscription—bounded higher.

Rarely before or since have so many speculative stars been so perfectly aligned as they were for the railway mania of the mid-1840s. Harvests were plentiful and money was cheap. Steam power and the telegraph were technologies just as wondrous as the promoters avowed them to be: horse-drawn coaches, even while zipping along on Macadam's newly paved roads, averaged no more than five miles an hour, while George Stephenson's steam locomotives were achieving speeds of fifteen miles an hour. Messages moved still faster on the humming wires of the telegraph: in 1844, *The Times* was on the streets of London with news of the birth of Queen Victoria's second son, Alfred Ernest, within forty minutes of the royal announcement. For this journalistic feat, the editors credited "the extraordinary power of the Electro-Magnetic Telegraph."

Visionaries invited the earthbound to imagine how the railways would draw nations together in trade. Cities would be emptied of surplus populations, the liberated excess happily resettled as commuters in the now accessible suburbs. The railway era would be one of redrawn

---

* In investment language, "bull market" means rising prices, "bear market," falling ones. The terms are thought to allude to the ways that the two animals attack: bulls with an upsweep of their horns, bears with a downward swipe of their paw.

maps, of thriving new businesses, and of vaulting real estate values. And really, how could nations wage war in a world so intimately twined as theirs would shortly be?

Neither would a banker's son have failed to mark a steep decline in interest rates, nor the Bank of England's role in bringing them down. Standard doctrine held that the Bank's administered rate should hover slightly above the rates that private actors agreed to accept in the open market. Yet, from the passage of Peel's Act through the end of 1846, market rates averaged 3.24 percent, the Bank's rate, 2.93 percent.[19] Low interest rates were not the Bank's only contribution to the speculative frenzy. With the new commercial latitude that Peel's Act accorded to it, the Old Lady lent more freely than she had previously done, at longer maturities and against a more eclectic range of collateral. And to supplement her holdings of government securities, the Bank purchased railroad debentures (not mortgages but unsecured loans), a lapse of judgment that a committee of the House of Lords would later condemn for giving "a high sanction and an effective stimulus" to a stock market that needed no official encouragement.[20]

The first railroad bubble was a kind of starter, warm-up mania. It popped in 1837, and burnt investors did not immediately return to the market to duplicate their errors in a new upswing, though the railroads lived up to their operational billing by earning a profit in the economically depressed years that followed the bust.[21] A bigger and gaudier boom was in full swing by 1844. In previous bull markets, promoters might float a few hundred new companies; more than 450 joint-stock railroad lines entered their names in Gladstone's company registry in the single month of September 1845. Honest and crooked promoters both judged the £5 registration fee eminently manageable.[22]

Sober observers thought it strange that the shares of nine or ten competing lines could each appreciate, though only one would win the coveted right of way. "It will be a matter of marvel and pain to discover the universality of the character of this speculation," prophesied

Wilson's *Economist*—by now producing its own nine-page "Railway Monitor"—about the certain denouement. "From domestic servants, footmen, and butlers, to titled spinsters and church dignitaries, running through all ranks and professions, the suffering will be more general than on any former occasion. It will be like a universal domestic affliction."[23]

Still, by the end of October 1845, more than 1,200 railway companies were on the drawing boards with an aggregate projected cost of more than £560 million, a sum of money slightly greater than the national income of the time. Promoters were floating a dozen new schemes a week.[24] Logic makes as poor an argument against a boom as it does against a love affair. A measure of the intensity of the speculators' ardor was their willingness to pay borrowing costs of as high as 80 percent[25] at a time when the Bank of England, lending against first-class commercial bills, charged 2.5 percent.

The boom was cresting as Bagehot entered the home stretch of his undergraduate studies. Share prices came under pressure late in 1845 as railroads began to call for actual capital from their not always liquid, committed, or well-endowed scrip-holders. Some £40 million was thus summoned in 1846. Not all of it obediently appeared.

These were real demands on scarce resources: "As construction got under way," related the historian Edward Chancellor, "money was diverted from the normal channels of business to pay for land, iron, timber and, above all, labor. These costs had to be shouldered by railway speculators, who were forced to reduce their employment of domestic servants, consumption of wine and sporting activities in order to meet their ongoing railway calls."[26] In January 1847, a short harvest and drain of gold pushed the Bank of England to raise its discount rate to 4 percent from 3.5 percent. Railway capital calls continued, to the tune of £5 million a month.[27] In the upswing, credit had been available at a price, even if a usurious one. It was available no more. In March, depositors staged a run on the Stuckey's branch in Bath: "constant, and at times severe, pressure" now characterized the money market, as the directors of the Bagehot family bank were apprised in April.

Well did the Stuckey's directors know it. The embarrassment at Bath, at least one of their number believed, was traceable to their own credit policies. Vincent Stuckey had died in 1845 at the age of seventy-four. When he was running things, the first words spoken— or, at least, recorded—at directors' meetings were the price of gold and the state of the foreign exchanges. It is unlikely that Stuckey would have ignored the flapping red signal pennants of 1847, and an entry in the directors' minute book in April of that year rebuked the board for its inattention. The expansive course of Stuckey's Banking Company "is much to be regretted," wrote the anonymous critic, almost certainly a fellow director, "being contrary to the example set by the stringent course adapted at present by the Bank of England and by all the London Bankers, as well as being contrary to right principles."[28]

It BOOSTED NO ONE'S confidence, in August, to learn of the failure of thirteen grain merchants, including the firm led by none other than the governor of the Bank of England, W. R. Robinson.[29] This plague of bankruptcies, a knowledgeable contemporary recorded in October, went "beyond all precedent in the commercial history of the country." Now the Bank itself was in trouble: low on gold, it refused to lend even against public securities, the prices of which duly plunged. On October 23, a deputation of City merchants and bankers implored the chancellor of the exchequer to suspend the restrictions on the Bank's issuance of notes that Peel's Act had imposed only three years before. The chancellor assented, the Bank resumed its lending, and the panic stopped in its tracks.

James Wilson now allowed himself the pleasure of reminding his readers how right the *Economist* had been. It had warned against the railroad mania and against the government's attempt to regulate it; Gladstone's registration protocols provided no protection against fraud and, by seeming to lend official approval to any and every railroad promotion, arguably facilitated crooked dealing.[30]

In banking, too, the *Economist* had proved prophetic. It had opposed Peel's Bank Charter Act, arguing that the government's narrow attempts to regulate the supply of bank notes ignored the growth in checks and credit instruments. It was fanciful to believe, as some of the more enthusiastic friends of the legislation suggested, that the certain and unquestioned convertibility of the pound would of itself protect lenders and borrowers from gross miscalculation. There was, besides, the correct and principled objection, as the *Economist* put it, "that people, resting satisfied and relying on the self-action of the new law, may consider themselves entitled to act with less private circumspection and caution than they otherwise would."[*]

Peel had long defended the Corn Laws; the Tories he led regarded them as sacrosanct. But the Irish famine of 1845–46 brought Peel into the fold of Richard Cobden, John Bright, the Anti-Corn Law League— and the *Economist*. Wilson celebrated the prime minister's conversion at the close of January 1846: "To the abstract science propounded by Adam Smith, Sir Robert Peel is the first minister who has given a full and unqualified practical application." The *Economist* could confer no higher praise.[31]

In this flush of journalistic vindication, Wilson published between hard covers a collection of *Economist* articles on the topics of money, banking, Peel's Act, and the late financial crisis. The volume appeared

---

* The article continued, "The railway share market might conceivably have got out of hand even if monetary factors had been comparatively unfavorable; but there is no doubt that the 'secondary' speculation, and the actual railway building, were very largely fostered, if not literally created, by the ease with which accommodation could be obtained at the Bank and in Lombard Street." W. T. C. King, *History of the London Discount Market* (London: Frank Cass, 1972), 134.

in 1847, along with a new installation of Thomas Tooke's *History of Prices* and a lengthy pamphlet in defense of Peel's Act by Colonel Robert Torrens.

The editor of the *Prospective Review*, the leading Unitarian journal of the day, commissioned Walter Bagehot to review all three titles. Readers of the resulting essay, entitled "The Currency Monopoly," might have surmised that the unsigned author belonged to a banking family. They probably would not have guessed his age (twenty-two), his credentials in economics (slight),* or the number of his previously published works (none). From the certitude of his judgments and the fluency of his style, they could have formed the opinion that Bagehot was a man to be reckoned with.

The stated purpose of Peel's Act was not to foreclose the possibility of financial panic, but to reduce the chances of a crisis by ensuring the convertibility of the pound. Wilson and Tooke judged the act a failure, while Torrens defended it. The underlying question was one of political philosophy: what was the proper role of government in coining money and regulating banks, including the central bank? Precise technical issues likewise presented themselves. Bagehot masterfully dealt with all of them.

The novice critic self-confidently began with a declaration of his own political prejudices. They were neither Tory nor radical but rather moderate and Whiggish. Laissez-faire had much to recommend it when confined to "its legitimate function," said Bagehot, "viz. when watching that government does not assume to know what will bring a trader in money better than he knows it himself; but it is a sentiment very susceptible to hurtful exaggeration." As an example of a proper function of government, the critic cited the enforcement of "a compulsory sanitary

---

* At University College, he read—in a lively, thoughtful, and critical way, to judge by the notes he took—the work of Adam Smith, David Ricardo, John Stuart Mill, and John R. McCulloch.

reform." Wilson, reading him, might have winced; the *Economist* was on record opposing the creation of a board of health.[32]

Bagehot was full of admiration for the work of the man he was soon to know very well, though he observed that Wilson's writing (and copy-editing) left something to be desired. The *Economist*'s position on the substantive monetary question was that bank notes, if carefully managed, could never be issued to excess. Bagehot brushed aside that contention with a banker's worldly awareness of the propensity for error on both sides of the teller's cage. It is curious, the young writer allowed, "that a distinguished practical man of business like Mr. Wilson" should fall into such an error, and he quoted David Ricardo as his authority—"a still greater authority" than the founder of the *Economist*.

Bagehot's essay was a tour de force. It anticipated some of the errors of modern monetary economics, as in the common-sense observation, sunk in a footnote, that the mere quantity of money tells you less than you think; no less important than the volume of pounds sterling in existence was the rate at which they move from hand to hand. Bagehot concluded that money was the government's business. A twenty-first-century reader, borne down by central banks, may quarrel with that contention—though perhaps not with the critic's charge that the monopoly power conferred on the Bank of England at its 1694 founding was a colossal historical mistake.

CHAPTER 3

"VIVE LA GUILLOTINE"

Was there anything more "hazardous or discouraging" than an apprenticeship in the law? William Blackstone posed the question to an Oxford audience a century before Walter Bagehot completed his work for a master of arts at the University of London, in 1848. "A raw and inexperienced youth," continued the great legal scholar,

> in the most dangerous season of his life, is transplanted on a sudden into the midst of allurements to pleasure, without any restraint or check but what his own prudence can suggest, with no public direction in what course to pursue his inquiries, no private assistance to remove the distresses and difficulties which will always embarrass a beginner. In this situation he is expected to sequester himself from the world, and, by a tedious lonely process, to extract the theory of law from a mass of undigested learning.[1]

Bagehot concluded his formal education with a flourish, taking the gold medal in intellectual and moral philosophy, a branch of knowledge then encompassing political economy. To receive his award, the winner was obliged to rise from his seat and walk the distance to the head of the convocation. The exertion was more than Bagehot's strength would allow—his exact illness is unclear—so he leaned on a friend's arm. His health restored after a visit to Langport, he returned to London later that year to study for the bar in the chambers of Sir Charles Hall.[2]

Very quickly, Bagehot noticed how little had changed since Blackstone. One hundred years on, an aspiring barrister still applied for admission to one of the only four Inns of Court. He dined at that imposing institution—in Bagehot's case, Lincoln's Inn—but took no classes there, as virtually none were offered, and prepared for no examination, as he was not, and never would be, examined. He worked in a law office by day, not in "reading" the law, exactly, but in copying documents about which he understood nothing.

"A heap of papers is set before each pupil," Bagehot recalled of his days of drudgery,

> And, according to such light as he possesses, and with perhaps a little preliminary explanation, the pupil is set to prepare the document for which these papers were sent . . . A precedent is set before each pupil, out of which he is to copy the formal part, which is always much the same in such documents, especially in the easier ones set before the younger pupils. As to all the non-formal part, the firm precept given to a beginner is one not so much of deep jurisprudence as of simple practice. He is told to "write wide," which means that the lines of the pupil's writing should always be at so great a distance from each other that the preceptor should have ample room to strike them out if he pleased, and write his own words in between them. And of this room he largely avails himself.[3]

Bagehot acknowledged the possibility that one might absorb useful legal information in this fashion. A superb student himself—to study had been his one and only job in life—he could learn almost anything he set his mind to. But he presently came to doubt that the law was one of those things.

On a visit to Langport in March 1851, the family put Bagehot to work researching an obscure point of ecclesiastical law. The issue touched on a troubled £1,000 loan that Stuckey's had extended to a church on the security of future taxes, or "rates," on the congregation. The transaction was by now a source of regret all around: Stuckey's had gone unpaid for five years, as the vestrymen and wardens quarreled about how to raise the funds with which to service the debt. The bank wished it had never lent the money, and the encumbered church surely regretted that it had ever borrowed it.* Bagehot, though he was coming to wish that he had never picked up a law book, contributed such advice as he could.

At the age of twenty-five, the reluctant barrister-in-training knew he could not live at home. Then again, what awaited him in London was more of the work he wanted no part of. What were the alternatives for a brilliant former student? Church, army, navy, teaching, trade, banking were among the few, and none appealed to Bagehot. There was a bank in his family, of course, but joining it would entail living under his parents' roof. He could write as few others could write, but he had seemingly rejected—if he had even considered it—a life of professional authorship.

He unburdened himself to his friends. William Caldwell Roscoe, another reluctant law student, was one of these soul mates, Richard

---

* In January 1853, Stuckey's settled for two-thirds of its claim on the Kingsbury church—Bagehot's father informed the board of directors that there was a problem in the loan documentation. The forgone one-third of the principal was given over to compensating the church faction that had opposed the mortgage. Another £50 was presented to the estate of the late churchwarden, who had led the side that had unsuccessfully fought to enforce payment of the debt. Stuckey's Banking Co. Ltd., *Director's Minutes*, Royal Bank of Scotland Archives STU3.2 (28 September 1848–27 January 1854), 190.

Holt Hutton another. The three of them criticized one another's writings ("Yours ever speaking plainly," Bagehot signed himself to Roscoe at the end of an uninhibited critique of the other's play, "Violenzia"), and exchanged notes on religion and God. Hutton had upbraided Bagehot for his arrogance* while they were students together at University College, but there was nothing supercilious in Bagehot's professions of faith and Christian devotion: "the highest life is an imitation of Christ's," he had written to Hutton in their undergraduate days.[4]

Hutton had begun to study at Manchester New College with the intention of following his father into the Unitarian ministry. For Roscoe, too, religion was at the center of life—"I have a profound conviction that to be in all things a child of God is the highest and ultimate object of life," he told Hutton.[5] Concluding that the law would require him to shade the truth rather than to profess it, he resolved to throw over his legal studies. Roscoe and Hutton were friendly cousins and more: in 1851, Hutton married Anne Roscoe, his friend's sister (and also, necessarily, his own cousin).

In August 1851, Bagehot did Roscoe one better. He not only quit the law, but also—pulling up such stakes as he had—moved to Paris.

It was not the most obvious thing to do at the time. England had at last put the "Hungry 40s" behind it. Crops were abundant, the banks were repaired,† and the operational promise of the railroads, as distinct from their speculative razzle-dazzle, was well on its way to being real-

---

* In his 1848 review of John Stuart Mill's *Principles of Political Economy*, Bagehot seemed to concede Hutton's point: "The admirable qualities of mind displayed in it, and the extensive research out of which it has sprung, make it necessary for the critic to practice a humility to which he is perchance but little accustomed."

† At mid-year 1851, Stuckey's showed year-over-year growth in earnings and assets in excess of 12 percent. The accounts, commented the directors, "will be found to be of a very satisfactory nature." A small persistent concern was the dwindling outlook for the bank's investment in the Bridgwater & Taunton Canal Company, then encountering stiff new competition from the Bristol & Exeter Railway. For a creditor, progress is not always a net benefit.

ized. The 1848 revolutions that had convulsed Europe had passed over
the British Isles. Drunkenness, crime, and poverty had peaked years
earlier. Many noticed that, by the early 1850s, the workmen were dressing like gentlemen, or—as the French painter Delacroix put it—the
gentlemen were dressing like workmen.[6]

The first world's fair, the Great Exhibition, opened in the Crystal
Palace in London on May 1, 1851, to celebrate "the works and industry of all nations"—and arts, too, especially those of Great Britain and
the British Empire. More than 40,000 people a day paid their shilling
to enter Joseph Paxton's astounding 990,000-square-foot temple of
glass and iron, a structure conceived in June 1850, built in less than
a year, and completed on budget and on time for the opening-day
walk-through by Queen Victoria and Prince Albert. The Crystal Palace and the 100,000 objects it displayed, including high-speed printing presses, sculptures, a cigarette-making machine, finely engineered
machine tools, locomotives, Colt's repeating firearms, "tangible ink" for
the blind, and a folding piano, were a tribute to invention, ingenuity—
Paxton's ingenuity, not least*—and the optimism of the age. To James
Wilson, the Great Exhibition was a symbol of the triumph of peace over
war, enterprise over barbarism. The *Economist* predicted that opening
day, May 1, would go down as "one of the most memorable days in the
history of Great Britain, and of the whole human race."

Why a high-achieving Englishman would exchange this splendor
for an indefinite stay in Paris was a question for which Bagehot had a
ready answer. To learn French, he would reply. Luckily for the future
journalist, he arrived in Paris on the eve of a coup d'état.

Bagehot settled in the home of the Meynieux family, once friends
to his mother. To Madame Meynieux, Edith Bagehot was no crazy lady

---

* And not exclusively Paxton's. "Sparrow-hawks, Ma'am," was the Duke of Wellington's succinct advice to Queen Victoria on how to remove the sparrows that had
nested in the roof of the Crystal Palace.

but a person of radiant charm, as her son had the pleasure of reporting back to Langport. His hostess claimed the honor of being the greatest of Edith's "idolateurs" and "idolatrices." Hearing this "heathenish" praise, Bagehot playfully told his mother that he was at a loss for a "Christian" reply. "[7] Neither could the visiting Englishman waltz. This fact, he said, he had proved to the satisfaction of innumerable bruised dancing partners ("It's very amusing running small French girls against some fellow's elbow, it's like killing flies years ago").

His talents lay instead in the art of journalistic observation.

The president of France, Louis-Napoleon, the unprepossessing nephew of the late Napoleon Bonaparte, was living in exile in London when France erupted in revolution in 1848. "I'm going to Paris," Louis-Napoleon announced to his cousin Marie, "the Republic has been proclaimed. I must be its master." "You are dreaming, as usual," Marie replied.[8] But his cousin was not the last person to underestimate the man whom Adolphe Thiers, a political adversary to the would-be master of the Republic, would call "that cretin."[9] Defying the predictions of France's political elite, Louis-Napoleon won the presidential election of December 1848 with 74.2 percent of the vote. "The nephew of the great man, with his magic, will give us security, and save us from misery," ran one of the victor's campaign slogans.[10]

The new French constitution allowed the president one four-year term, but the new incumbent had other plans. He lobbied the lower house of Parliament, the National Assembly, to amend the constitution to allow him to continue in office. He instituted controls on speech, free association, and the press. His administration placed eight departments under martial law.[11] Bagehot had not been very long in Paris before it became evident that the scheduled 1851 presidential contest would be conducted without the ballot box.

The radical left, the principal target of Louis-Napoleon's emerging police state, countered repression with muttered threats to finish the work left undone by the Terror of 1793. "Vive la guillotine!" some roared. Many conservatives judged that there were worse alternatives for France than the statism of Louis-Napoleon.

The incumbent, unable to imagine any acceptable alternative to himself, gathered loyal elements in the army and police. It was no ordinary coup d'état they were plotting—Louis-Napoleon was already the president—but a kind of self-coup against the constitution and the National Assembly as well as an anticipatory stroke against the socialist left, the *spectre rouge.*

The conspirators moved in the early morning of December 2. They dissolved the National Assembly, arrested the likely leaders of the resistance, seized the semaphore telegraph system and deployed 30,000 troops in Paris alone. Some of the soldiers fired indiscriminately into dwelling places on the Boulevard Montmartre.[12]

Alexis de Tocqueville, author of *Democracy in America,* apprised that the coup met with the approval of important segments of English public opinion, composed a lengthy dispatch pleading the righteousness of the conservative resistance. Unsigned, it ran in *The Times* of London on December 11. "If the judgment of the people of England can approve of these military saturnalia," de Tocqueville concluded,

> and if the facts I have related, and to the accurate truth of which I pledge myself, do not rouse its censures, I shall mourn for you and for ourselves, and for the sacred cause of legal liberty throughout the world; for the public opinion of England is the grand jury of mankind in the cause of freedom, and if its verdict were to acquit the oppressor, the oppressed would have no other resource but in God.[13]

For Bagehot, the coup d'état was a tonic. He thrilled to the drama, to the action in the streets, to the political spectacle, and to such small physical risks as he personally bore in the role of freelance onlooker. On December 4, two days after Louis-Napoleon's self-elevation, the young Englishman sallied forth into the Boulevard Saint-Martin to lend a hand in the barricade-building. He tried to rent a window from which to observe the imminent *guerre des rues*, but the worldly-wise Parisians shooed him away—they knew enough to close the shutters. "I therefore retired," as Bagehot told his father, "though not too quickly. It is a bad habit to run in a Revolution, somebody may think you are 'other side' and shoot at you, but if you go calmly and look English, there is no particular danger." He could hear the cannon and the musket fire, and he could see the blood in the streets—"a good deal of it."[14] Twenty-seven soldiers and 380 Parisian insurgents were killed, either in fighting, spectating, or summary executions.

Nassau Senior, Oxford's first professor of political economy, happened to be in Paris, too. Seeing things much as de Tocqueville did, the economist recorded his condemnation in a diary. Bagehot boldly wrote for publication.

Signing himself "Amicus," the tyro foreign correspondent addressed seven letters from Paris in January and February 1852 to the editor of *The Inquirer*, an English Unitarian weekly. The first paragraph of the first submission set the ironical tone: "Sir—, You have asked me to tell you what I think of French affairs. I shall be pleased to do so; but I ought perhaps to begin by cautioning you against believing, or too much heeding, what I say." A foreigner, Bagehot deprecated what he could possibly know or understand. Yet 60,000 words followed.

Bagehot proceeded to defend Louis-Napoleon, to explain away the executions and deportations, to scorn the heroic assemblymen (among whom was de Tocqueville), and to attest to the popularity of the usurper among the "inferior people." He argued that the imminent threat to civil order justified the coup and all that went with it. The overexcitable French were incapable of governing themselves in a parliamentary system; their national character did not allow it. "My reasons for so believing I shall in this letter endeavor to explain," Bagehot promised, "except that I shall not, I fancy, have room to say much on the moral defensibility or indefensibility of the coup d'état." Utilitarian-fashion, he would rather focus on the facts, leaving "ethical speculation" to "Printing-house Square," that is, to *The Times*, which had already printed de Tocqueville's impassioned plea to the English people to take sides with the liberty-loving French. "You will, I imagine," Bagehot addressed his readers, "concede to me that the first duty of a government is to ensure the security of that industry which is the condition of social life and civilized cultivation."[15]

Probably, as Bagehot well knew, the high-minded readers of *The Inquirer* would concede no such thing. The paper's own coverage of the coup was anti-Louis-Napoleon. Nor, likely, would *The Inquirer*'s audience have sympathized with Bagehot's arch tone, nor with his grating fondness for paradox. It had been reported, "Amicus" reminded his readers, that Louis-Napoleon had squandered his youth at the racetrack, but—the correspondent insisted—there could be no better practical training in probability and statistics than that which Boney's nephew had wisely given himself among the horse players at Newmarket and the cardsharps at the London clubs.[16] Then, too, Bagehot mused, Louis-Napoleon had the virtue of his ignorance: "he has never been a professor, nor a journalist, nor a promising barrister, nor, by taste, a littérateur."[17] Not a few of *The Inquirer*'s readers pursued those very occupations, as indeed did the ironic and literary correspondent himself.

To his intellectual audience, "Amicus" praised the virtue of stupidity. You can do without clever newspapers—as Louis-Napoleon was daily demonstrating—but not without dull commerce. "By the sound work of old-fashioned generations," Bagehot posited,

> by the singular painstaking of the slumberers in churchyards—by dull care—by stupid industry, a certain social fabric somehow exists; people contrive to go out to their work, and to find work to employ them actually until the evening, body and soul are kept together, and this is what mankind have to show for their

six thousand years of toil and trouble. To keep up this system we must sacrifice everything.[18]

A playful fellow was "Amicus." Though a professed partisan of Louis-Napoleon, he had, so he related, helped to direct the construction of barricades. He made it seem a bit of a lark. He was at the barricades until one of the deadly earnest revolutionaries—"sallow, stern, compressed, with much marked features" and armed to the teeth besides—chased him away: "it was not too slowly that I departed, for I felt that he would rather shoot me than not."[19]

By this point, the Unitarians must have wondered what had become of their *Inquirer.* "Amicus" was actually contending that France needed a tyrant because business was more important than liberty. In posing this problematic argument, Bagehot was inclined to make light of the suffering of the poor: "Starvable classes"[20] and "ruinable persons"[21] were among his memorable phrases. These phrases—the paradoxes, aphorisms, provocations—jostled one another in his fast-flowing sentences. It was not so easy to dismiss such a writer out of hand, nor was it soothing to read him.

Perhaps the subscribers had not marked the true measure of the French left, including the anarchist Pierre-Joseph Proudhon, who famously equated property with theft. As the leftist press had been gagged, there was no telling if all the stories about socialist atrocities were true. But if even a quarter were on the mark, the "new reformers" menaced civil society in ways that the autocrat Louis-Napoleon had scarcely dreamt of. "That is what people here are afraid of," Bagehot went on, "and that is why I write such things,—and not to horrify you, or amuse you, or bore you—anything rather than that."[22]

There was certainly no intent to bore in Bagehot's discussion of national character and racial stereotypes. "The Jews of today are the Jews in face and form of the Egyptian sculptures," he lightly remarked; "in character they are the Jews of Moses—the negro is the negro of a thousand years—the Chinese, by his own account, is the mummy of a million." You couldn't change these things; they just were: "There are breeds in the animal man just as in the animal dog. When you hunt with greyhounds and course with beagles, then, and not till then, may you expect the inbred habits of a thousand years to pass away, that Hindoos can be free, or that Englishmen will be slaves."*

Few of Bagehot's Protestant readers likely fancied themselves inferior to the average Catholic priest. "Amicus" proceeded to disabuse them of that misconception. Suppose, Bagehot addressed both the Unitarian intellectuals and the French radicals, "you succeed—what you call succeeding—your books are read; for three weeks or even a season, you are the idol of the salons; your hard words are on the lips of women; then a change comes—a new actress appears at the Theatre Francais or the Opera—her charms eclipse your theories; or a great catastrophe occurs—political liberty (it is said) is annihilated . . . Anyhow, you are forgotten—fifty years may be the gestation of a philosophy, not three its life—before long, before you go to your grave, your six disciples leave you for some newer master, or to set up for themselves. The poorest priest in the remote region of the *Basses Alpes* has more power over men's souls than human cultivation; his ill-mouthed masses move women's souls—can you? . . . Consider the hundred volumes of Aquinas—which of you desire a higher life than that? To deduce, to subtilise, discriminate, systematise, and decide the highest truth, and to be believed."[23]

French businessmen tended to take Louis-Napoleon's side in 1851,

---

* Compare William Hazlitt in his essay "Hot and Cold": "I should say then that Northern people are clean and Southern people dirty as a general rule, because where the principle of life is more cold, weak and impoverished, there is a greater shyness and aversion to come in contact with external matter." And: "The dirt of the Italians is as it were baked into them, and so ingrained as to become a part of themselves." Or Disraeli, in *Coningsby*, who has his hero and alter ego, Sidonia, declare, "All is race—there is no other truth." If Bagehot has shocked posterity with his racial musings, he very likely upset few of his contemporaries.

as did many English residents in France.[24] In London, the *Economist* was inclined to give "the usurper" the benefit of the doubt—evidence pointed to the existence of a "great socialist conspiracy" that would coalesce in 1852. As between the fractious, troublemaking National Assembly and the tyrant who slapped the politicians in jail, Wilson's paper leaned toward the oppressor.

No one leaned—either one way or the other—with such verve as Bagehot. His words raced along on the page. You can read widely in contemporary English-language reporting and commentary on the French coup and find nothing half as scintillating as the letters of the still callow twenty-five-year-old. And if this maiden effort in weekly journalism made him no friends among *The Inquirer*'s influential readership,* it at least proved that he had a calling outside the law. Upon his return to England in the summer of 1852, Bagehot informed his father that he at last had made up his mind. He was renouncing the legal profession "utterly and forever." He would be a banker after all.[25]

---

* Richard Taylor, proprietor of Britain's largest scientific publishing house, wrote to the editor of *The Inquirer* to protest "Amicus's" decision to ignore the morality of the coup (ostensibly because there wasn't room to fit it in): "As to the speculations of any one who would leave out of question the morality of an atrocious stroke of statesmanship and only advert to its supposed beneficial consequences, and present adaptation to the wishes of certain classes, I confess that I hold such speculations very cheap . . ."

CHAPTER 4

THE LITERARY BANKER

"Mr. Bagehot, having requested that his son, Mr. Walter Bagehot, might be allowed to attend at the Bank at Langport, with a view to making himself acquainted with the business, his wish was acceded to."

—Minutes of Stuckey's Banking Company, June 17, 1853[1]

Walter Bagehot's father showed more confidence in his son than Walter did in himself. In preparation for joining the family bank, the refugee from the law* lived in Langport to make a study of double-entry bookkeeping. He admitted that the theory of accounting "is agreeable and pretty, but the practice perhaps as horrible as anything ever was."[2] The student who had kept up with the pyrotechnical intellect of Augustus De Morgan at University College could not seem to add or subtract. "If only," Bagehot playfully moaned to a school friend, "my relations would admit that sums are matters of opinion."[3]

The elder Bagehot's request was granted; his fellow directors could

---

* Bagehot had not abandoned his studies before being "called to the bar," that is, becoming certified to practice, which he never did.

hardly refuse him the courtesy. Besides, talent like Walter's did not walk in the door of a country bank every day. Rare in banks of any size was the trainee who had already written a penetrating article on English monetary affairs and filed masterful dispatches from strife-torn Paris (the ability to think straight in a crisis is always a desirable quality in a banker).

Walter was as lucky in his employer as his employer was in him. Solvent, profitable, growing, and well-managed, Stuckey's was an ideal place to begin work, even if that work entailed life under the roof of his unbalanced mother and a father who doubled as his daytime boss.

Happy, too, was the timing of Bagehot's arrival. Gold strikes in California and Australia in 1849 and 1851 gave his career a monetary tail wind: English prices had been sinking since the close of the Napoleonic wars, but presently started to rise. The downward creep in interest rates, too, soon reversed. As recently as 1852, Stuckey's had been overwhelmed by deposits; there seemed no place to invest them. But by 1853, the demand for money was catching up with the ample supply.

Money is the measure of capital. It's capital—a train, a factory, an idea—that creates wealth. Capital springs from invention and enterprise, and as those things flourish, so may wealth grow.

Take, for example, a Victorian epitome of that invention and enterprise, the resplendently named Isambard Kingdom Brunel, former chief engineer of the Great Western Railway, designer of Paddington Station, builder of the Clifton Suspension Bridge in Bristol—and consulting engineer in the construction of the Great Bow Bridge in Langport. In 1852, aged forty-six, Brunel made a doodle in his diary, underneath which he jotted, "Say 600 ft x 65 ft x30 ft." The dimensions described a seagoing ironclad six times larger by volume than anything then afloat. The naval architect John Scott Russell, whom Brunel had met at the Great Exhibition, declared that Brunel's conception could swim. Plans for the *Great Eastern*—or, as Brunel affectionately dubbed his creation, "Great Babe"—moved forward.

Not in just any age could a man like Brunel find the ideas, capital, and liberty with which to mobilize imagination. Reasons not to reach too far ordinarily appear more persuasive than the case for untried action—certainly so in private enterprise. What set the 1850s apart was the confidence that something wonderful was about to happen. "Good luck to the new world citizen!" effused Karl Marx to a private correspondent in 1852. "There is no more splendid time to enter the world than the present. Australia and California and the Pacific Ocean! The new world citizens won't be able to comprehend how small our world was."[4]

If the factory hands were happy "beyond what we have ever before witnessed," or so claimed a Manchester cotton merchant in 1852,[5] stock-market bulls were transported. A 2 percent Bank Rate—as the Bank of England's principal interest rate was, and is still, called—posted in April 1852, as well as rising Australian gold imports, went far to explain how the once sedate shares of the Australian Agricultural Company rose twenty-fold on the strength of one errant report of a gold strike on the corporate sheep pasture. Shipbuilders could hardly keep up with the demand for vessels to accommodate the thousands of eager Britons seeking passage Down Under.

Commodity prices, stock prices, ship prices, train traffic, interest rates, and wages were all on the hop. In the first six months of 1853, average wages climbed by 10 to 20 percent, gains that, as some contended, were little more than incomplete restitution for the pay forgone in the Hungry 1840s. Even so, not all enjoyed these improvements. In October 1853, in Preston, Lancashire, 20,000 unionized laborers[6] went on strike for a 10 percent raise. They returned to work on May 1, 1854, not one penny better off than before.*

---

* The ugly factory city of Coketown in Charles Dickens's anti-Utilitarian *Hard Times* owed some of its inspiration to Preston, which Dickens visited in January 1854; the first serialized installment of the novel appeared that April. Thomas Tooke and William Newmarch, *A History of Prices*, vol. 5, 1848–1856 (London: Longman, Brown, Green, Longmans, & Roberts, 1857), 296.

As for that golden influx, it was not Britain's to keep: relatively high prices and relatively low interest rates sent the bullion packing to more attractive destinations. As there were imports to pay for and a granary to stock, English interest rates rose to assure that the outflow did not become a torrent. Bank Rate stood at 3.5 percent at the end of August 1853. It rose to 4 percent on September 1, 4.5 percent on September 15, and 5 percent on September 29.

Even so—strikes, emigration, volatile interest rates, and short crops notwithstanding—1853 was a standout year in a singular decade. In Britain between 1850 and 1860, pig iron production climbed by 53 percent, coal production by 62 percent, cotton imports by 109 percent, installed horsepower of the British textile manufacturing industry by 21 percent, and railway mileage by 49 percent.

Such wonders of production did not come out of nowhere: population growth, technological progress, a stable currency, and intellectual ferment crystallized them. Free trade (the *Economist* sometimes reverentially capitalized the initial letters "F" and "T") had proved every bit the boon that Richard Cobden, John Bright, and James Wilson had promised.* In the span 1815–45, between Waterloo and the final year of the Corn Laws, the value of British exports had grown at a crawl, from £51.6 million to £60.1 million. In 1853, they weighed in at £98.9 million. By 1860, they would reach £136 million.

"Astonishingly rapid now is the progress of society," the *Economist* marveled at the start of 1853. "Railroads, electric telegraphs, free trade, the gold discoveries—each of which is enough to have immortalized an age—are all crowded in the space of a boy's life; what may be the equal or greater discoveries in the next twenty years is not given to us to know. We are only privileged to suppose that they will be equaled

---

* Nor were these apostles the most zealous. "Jesus Christ is free trade and free trade is Jesus Christ," declared Sir John Bowring, the polyglot member of Parliament, man of letters, failed entrepreneur, and governor of Hong Kong. Ben Wilson, *Heyday: The 1850s and the Dawn of the Global Age* (New York: Basic Books, 2016), 240.

or surpassed; and of the wonderful progeny the year that has now begun with great activity will no doubt bring forth its share. We fear no retrogression; but whither the progress is to lead, and where it is to end—except in the bosom of the Almighty, where it began—human imagination cannot conceive."[7]

All was well at Stuckey's, too. Profits hit a new high in the first half of 1853. It fell to the directors to apportion this bounty among the bank's various constituencies: the balance sheet (in the shape of a larger reserve fund), worthy officers and employees (the heavy volume of business at Bristol and Bath earned the managers of those branches raises of £100 a year), and the stockholders. A payment of £2 a share every six months was the customary Stuckey's dividend, one the board had adhered to even during the depression of the 1840s. Now that profits were flush, the directors voted a temporary £1 per share bonus. Addressing their fellow owners, they allowed themselves an understated note of self-congratulation: "The proprietors will see from the statement of assets and liabilities now on the table that they have the best grounds for being satisfied with the state of the concern."

Stuckey's conducted a conventional banking business with the progressive flourish of a large branch network in its home county of Somerset. The bank took in deposits and issued negotiable notes, that is, currency that bore Stuckey's own name. The depositors earned 2 percent per annum or so on savings accounts, nothing on checking accounts. Deposits and equity capital were the twin sources of funding. Some banks enhanced their returns by borrowing against their assets at the Bank of England—i.e., "rediscounting," as that mildly aggressive technique was known. It was not the kind of thing that Stuckey's did.

Stuckey's made loans, discounted commercial bills (i.e., farmers' or merchants' IOUs, typically of 90 days duration), invested in bonds, and laid up cash in neighboring banks and at the Bank of England. It avoided mortgages, for which there was no liquid market. Loans and discounts yielded in the neighborhood of 5 percent to 6 percent, government bonds half of that.

Vincent Stuckey saw clearly the benefits of decentralized banking within the framework of a tautly managed holding company. Local managers, informed about local circumstances, would make credit decisions; the home office would manage the disparate operations.

There was nothing fancy about those operations. To the millennial banker, heavily taxed and regulated, juggling lines of business in what are broadly termed "financial services," Stuckey's may hardly seem like a bank at all. It earned virtually no income outside of the interest it derived from discounts, advances, and fixed-income investments. It did no trading, conducted no arcane hedging or derivatives operations, obtained little income from fees. As for technology, Vincent Stuckey marveled as late as 1841 at how the check, in use since 1659, continued to transform the banking business.*

It is unclear which financial time traveler would be more uncomprehending of the sights at his temporal destination, a Bagehot-era visitor exposed to the regulatory and monetary mores of the twenty-first century or a twenty-first-century visitor set down in the self-regulatory, gold-standard system of the mid-nineteenth century.

Walter Bagehot's uncle had laid it down that, while bankers were mortal, banks should live in perpetuity. To that end, some capital was essential, and Watson Bagehot, for one, pressed his fellow directors to

---

* On its June 30, 1853, statement, the bank showed assets of slightly over £2 million; it had exceeded the £2 million mark six months earlier, having reached £1 million in December 1835. Loans against a variety of collateral, including securities, constituted 38 percent of those assets. Bonds and other interest-bearing obligations amounted to 30 percent, commercial bills 22 percent, and cash equivalents 10 percent. The stockholders' capital represented on the order of 5 percent of the assets—by no means a large proportion, judged either by the standards of the Britain of Bagehot's time or the America (or Britain) of our own.

raise more of it[8]—that is, visible capital, the funds on the balance sheet. The latent kind, callable in case of emergency, likewise furnished support. There was, of course, no deposit insurance.

Of non-interest-bearing gold and silver, Stuckey's held the bare minimum. In testimony before a parliamentary committee in 1819, Vincent Stuckey said that he and his bank—and his customers, too— wanted no part of gold coin, prone as it was to fall short of the legal weight and unhandy as it was to transport. As to who should bear the cost of keeping the nation's store of monetary gold, the banking community was more than happy to cede that unremunerative job to the Bank of England.

In 1846, the monetary commentator Richard Page, signing himself Daniel Hardcastle Jr., drew attention to the paradox behind these ideas. Without gold, there could be no gold standard, an institution the bankers believed in even as they chafed at the obligation to hold the metal itself. Beautiful as it was, it paid them nothing. Far better, for them, to hold credit instruments—bonds, loans, notes—which paid them a great deal and cost them little to store and move. Gold, under the gold standard, had come to resemble the Old Maid in the game of cards:

> Every recent improvement in Banking has gone upon the principle that we should retain gold as a standard, but bring it forward as seldom as possible, and scarcely ever touch it. Such improvers would make it "small by degrees, and beautifully less," until it had vanished altogether . . . They would exceed the art of the modern cabinet-maker, who makes twenty tables out of one log of mahogany which formerly only made one, and goes on veneering and veneering, until it has become a matter of doubt whether there is an inch of solid mahogany in any well-furnished house in London."[9]

For fifty years, Hardcastle contended, England had been trying to shift the cost of managing its monetary metal "from one shoulder to another."[10] He had a plan to fix it—as, later on, would the author of *Lombard Street*.

FOR ALL INTENTS AND purposes, Stuckey's had nothing to do with the British government. It paid a direct tax of less than 1 percent of its 1853 income. It submitted to no regulatory oversight but that of its auditors and customers. Proof of the trust that the customers reposed in the management was their willingness to hold the notes issued by Stuckey's itself. An elderly lady once presented herself at a Stuckey's branch to clean out her account—she had heard that the bank was in trouble. When the teller asked if she would like to be paid in notes of the Bank of England, she replied, "Certainly not," and demanded the scrip of the bank she had come to leave—Stuckey's.[11] The Stuckey's financial records give no indication of public refusal of the bank's currency even in the sweat of a panic. (The ranks of the private banks of issue grew thinner with the passage of time, as the authors of the Bank Charter Act of 1844 intended, and by 1909, when Stuckey's merged with the larger Parr Bank, the volume of the Stuckey's note issuance was second only to that of the Bank of England.[12])

Attentive to the quality of their assets, the Stuckey's directors were equally mindful of the solidity of their fellow stockholders. The shares were listed on no stock exchange; you acquired them as you would membership in a club. You might ask to be admitted, though it was better form to wait to be asked—and even Walter Stuckey, a family member, only just made the grade, as he was merely a cashier. The directors reasoned thus: "although much caution should be expressed in admitting cashiers and other clerks to hold shares, it would not be advisable to preclude their doing so by any positive and general rule—that, having

regard for Mr. Walter Stuckey's long and faithful services, and his zeal
for the interest of the business, and looking also to the respectability of
his family and connections, his admission as a shareholder [should] be
approved of."[13]

Respectability was the very quality that John and Ann Collier
lacked. The brother and sister wanted to invest in Stuckey's, and their
mother made the request on their behalf. The directors refused her
because, as they agreed among themselves, reputation was the bedrock of credit. Stockholders had to be "well known in their respective
neighborhoods, as persons of property, respectability and fair standing in the class to which they belong." The Colliers were too young
to have earned the requisite position, nor had their mother succeeded
in imparting it to them. To grant them permission to purchase shares
would not only tend to "lower the tone of respectability of our proprietary, but lead to the assumption that the directors had no power to
reject undesirable persons, or refused to exert it, it would lessen the
present reputation of the bank, and would affect its future stability,
by creating a disinclination of men of good standing in their respective
classes to join it."[14] A hard judgment, but not, after all, a snobbish one.
The directors were sorting not by social standing, or even social class,
but by character and financial strength.

To sell his or her stock, a Stuckey's shareholder had to find a suitable
buyer, an arrangement that anticipated the protocol and rigmarole of a
modern New York City cooperative apartment building. Then again,
not many Stuckey's holders would have wanted to sell: at £60 each, the
price offered when Walter Bagehot joined the bank, a share of Stuckey's delivered an annual dividend yield of 6.67 percent at the regular
£4 per share dividend. The Bank of England's common shares, which
did trade in liquid fashion but only with the permission of the directors,
were priced to yield in the neighborhood of 3 percent. Stuckey's was a
superlative investment.

The opulence of the second half of 1853 seemed to surprise even

the directors. "Notwithstanding the prosperous results of several preceding half years," the year-end minutes recorded, "that for the half
year ended December last is considerably in advance of any former
one." In the first six months, the bank had earned £19,383, in the second half, £24,826,* for a combined £44,209. As a return on year-end
equity capital, it amounted to 40.4 percent—nowadays, 15 percent is
rated excellent. As against year-end assets of £2,103,279, it came to 2.1
percent—1.5 percent at this writing is judged handsome. Counting a
second £1 per share bonus, duly declared at year-end, the £6 per share
payout delivered a dividend yield of 10 percent—three times what a
good bank pays now.

Such returns were astounding. The directors, mindful of both the
constructive conservatism of Vincent Stuckey and the panic years of
1825, 1837, and 1847, proceeded to trim sail. From the head office came
instructions to boost deposit rates; that is, to check the migration of
funds out of the bank and into alternative investments, and to restrict
advances and other loans "in the present state of the money market."
The management was of a single mind that trees did not grow to the sky.

At Stuckey's, as in most institutions, people created problems.
Some employees excelled, others disappointed, and a few gave offense.
What to do, for instance, about the intemperance of Reynolds Wood-
land, an officer at Bridgwater, frequently drunk and disruptive, almost
as frequently remorseful? Remove him from his managerial position,
the board decided, but—in view of his efforts to reform—offer him a
clerk's position at Bristol "at a salary proportional to the position allotted him." Trouble, too, was the overbearing Mr. Salmon, also of the

---

* This was gross profit. Of income tax in the second half of 1853, Stuckey's paid the
grand total of £114 2s 17d. The bank earned what might be termed operating income
of £40,459, out of which it set aside £3,000 for bad debts, £2,000 for the construction
of new offices in Bristol, £4,424 for deferred expenses, £7,672 for the regular dividend, £3,836 for the bonus, and £3,894 for the reserve fund. Earnings—£24,826—
were what remained. Stuckey's Banking Co. Ltd., *Director's Minutes*, STU3.2, 529.

Bridgwater office, and the hotheaded Mr. Caines, of Wincanton. For each, the directors prescribed a good talking-to.[15]

Walter Bagehot was two years at his post when the board took up the question of facial hair. Beards had become de rigueur during the Crimean War. They signified manliness, and expressed solidarity with the deployed British troops who wore them for warmth and convenience. Some civilian Englishmen stopped shaving to make a political statement against the unbearded aristocracy who had bungled the management of the war.[16]

Stuckey's refused to allow it: "The directors express their decided objection to the wearing of mustaches or beards above the chin by the employees of the company, and request all of them to comply with their wishes in this respect." The one and only portrait for which Bagehot ever sat shows him fully bearded, possibly in his mid-forties, by which time the war was long over.

ON THE ONE HAND, the chairman's son missed his London friends. On the other, he was never far from his most steadfast friends, the great writers. Literature was the love of Bagehot's life, and to share that love he wrote long literary essays; reprinted in books, some of them span thirty pages. Writers can be sorted by their affinity for the act of composition—some like to write, others only to have written—and Bagehot almost certainly belongs in the first happy cohort. His prose has the cadence of brilliant talk; reading him, you wonder how his pen kept up with his mind.

In 1847, when he was twenty-one and completing his master's degree, Bagehot published his first essay, "Festus," a critique of a popular poem by Philip James Bailey. The article appeared in the *Prospective Review*, which, like *The Inquirer*, served a mainly Unitarian readership. The piece was unsigned, though Bagehot, who had only just earned his bachelor's degree from the University of London, seems almost a physical presence on the page. The bounding style, youthful piety, moral earnestness, and disdain for fact-checking are Bagehot's watermarks.*

He judged that the poem, which retold the story of the man who sold his soul to the devil, was worthy to stand in the company of the great *Faust*s by Marlowe and Goethe. Bailey's signal shortcoming was his failure to acknowledge the all-important workings of "the Law of Retribution." Sin demands punishment, a cardinal truth that Bailey had astonishingly "mislaid." Just as he would in his Paris letters a few years later, Bagehot made a bow to the Catholic Church, either not realizing—or perhaps more likely, realizing full well—how little it would please his non-Catholic readers. He shocked them with a provokingly broad-minded view of the sale of indulgences: he granted there was a certain measure of superstition in paying the Church to effect the early release of a soul from purgatory, "but surely it should come home to the hearts of a money-getting generation, that three centuries ago men were willing to give hard cash to save themselves from the pains of sin. We suspect that a priesthood in [ancient] Greece would have got little by putting up to auction the fee simple of the Elysian fields." Here was a glimpse of an adult emerging from his university chrysalis.

The young critic condemned Bailey for creating not one, not two, but six love interests for his hero's enjoyment, a scandal of imaginative promiscuity. Expounding on the necessity of punishment, Bagehot took a swipe at the penal reformer Alexander Maconochie, dismissed as warden of the brutal British prison on Norfolk Island, New South Wales, Australia, for administering fewer beatings than his predecessors. "Only if we can bring it home to the hearts of men," he wrote, "'that the wrath of God has been revealed from heaven upon all unrighteousness and ungodliness of men;' that he has ordained its punishment; that human

---

* The world was unaware of Bagehot's authorship until it was revealed by William Haley and Robert H. Tener in a letter to the editor of the *Times Literary Supplement* in the issue dated February 8, 1963.

legislation is but a feeble and coarse endeavor to make his will in this respect be done now as it will be done hereafter—then, and not until then, shall we induce an enlightened and sympathizing people to bear without repining the wholesome severity of just laws."[17] Observant readers, noting that Bagehot had cast a stone at sinners, would have marked him down as a saint or a youth.

In writerly terms, he was not a youth for long. Proof of Bagehot's early arrival at the age of wisdom is his magnificent essay on "Shakespeare—the Man" in the July 1853 issue of the *Prospective Review*.

Ostensibly, the purpose of the piece was to review a pair of recent works on Shakespeare's times and texts, but Bagehot's real objective was to intuit Shakespeare's character. In a work of the purest amateurism, the author wrote not one footnote. He scarcely quoted from any book, even the ones he was supposedly reviewing. He didn't have to: delving into his own deep storehouse of reading, he offers compelling insights about Shakespeare's personality, drawn from Shakespeare's writing.

The essay proceeds by quoting the well-worn claim that Shakespeare is a mystery man. (Whether that man might, in reality, have been Francis Bacon, Edward de Vere, the 17th Earl of Oxford, or Christopher Marlowe, Bagehot didn't choose to address.) Someone writing under that name produced sublime poetry—and that is as far as our knowledge extends. But Bagehot then flicks this contention away: the works themselves constitute a trove of Shakespearean autobiography, he proposes. Only consider some lines from "Venus and Adonis":

> *And when thou hast on foot the purblind hare,*
> *Mark the poor wretch, to overshoot his troubles,*
> *How he outruns the wind, and with what care*
> *He cranks and crosses, with a thousand doubles:*
> *The many musits through which he goes*
> *Are like a labyrinth to amaze his foes.*

It's absurd, Bagehot goes on, "to say we know nothing about the man who wrote that; we know that he had been after a hare." The aspiring banker himself chased hares, behind a pack of hounds.

Like Shakespeare's hare, Bagehot the essayist "cranks and crosses, with a thousand doubles." Digression follows digression. The reader is like a man lost in beautiful countryside. He doesn't know where he is or where he's going, but he's not unhappy to be there.

"Shakespeare—the Man" takes an early detour from the Bard to the character and physical bearing of François Guizot, the former French premier driven from power in 1848, a historian and author of one of the books ostensibly under review. William Pitt, the long-serving wartime English prime minister, next comes into focus, he and Guizot being examples, Bagehot contends, of the kind of person who experiences nothing and notices nothing of the world around him. Then come Sir Walter Scott and John Milton, each providing contrapuntal insights.

Like Scott but unlike, for instance, Guizot and Pitt, Shakespeare had an "experiencing" nature, Bagehot writes. He loved the world and the world loved him back. Dealing, as the playwright did, with actors, audiences, and the theatrical box office, Shakespeare bore no resemblance to the cloistered literary man, of which Robert Southey was an avatar. "He wrote poetry (as if anybody could) before breakfast," says Bagehot of the long-serving Poet Laureate, not saying how he came by this intimate information;

> he read during breakfast. He wrote history until dinner; he corrected proof sheets between dinner and tea; he wrote an essay for the *Quarterly* afterwards; and after supper by way of relaxation composed the "Doctor"—a lengthy and elaborate jest. Now what can anyone think of such a life—except how clearly it shows that the habits best fitted for communicating information . . . are exactly the habits which are likely to afford a man the least information to communicate.

Bagehot next reverts to the bluff, open-faced, gregarious Scott, the shining exception to the rule about study-bound authors: "If you will describe the people—nay, if you will write for the people—you must be one of the people," he writes of the author of *Rob Roy*; "you must have led their life, and must wish to lead their life."[18] Shakespeare wrote from the same wellspring of human wisdom. He acquired it, as did Scott, Bagehot approvingly relates, by living his life among the common people. Had Shakespeare lived otherwise, there could have been no Falstaff: "all great English writers describe English people, and in describing them, they give, as they must give, a large comic element; and speaking generally, this is scarcely possible, except in the case of cheerful, easy-living men."[19]

Bagehot's authority for this generalization was his own eyes and ears. What follows is one of Bagehot's most elegiac passages, as he pauses to observe that Shakespeare was not all hearty "flowing enjoyment":

> Thus he appeared to those around him—in some degree they knew that he was a cheerful, and humorous, and happy man; but of his higher gift they knew less than we. A great painter of men must (as has been said) have a faculty of conversing, but he must also have a capacity for solitude. There is much of mankind that a man can only learn from himself. Behind every man's external life, which he leads in company, there is another which he leads alone, and which he carries with him apart. We see but one aspect of our neighbor, as we see but one side of the moon; in either case there is also a dark half, which is unknown to us. We all come down to dinner, but each has a room to himself.[20]

Bagehot never presumes to compare himself to the greatest English writer. But the aspects of Shakespeare's writing—and intuited character—of which Bagehot most heartily approves are the ones that seem also to apply to himself. For instance, the quality of "boyish buoyancy."[21] Or the quality of "a certain constitutional though latent melancholy."[22] Or Shakespeare's inferred reading habits: "He was a natural reader; when a book was dull, he put it down, when it looked fascinating, he took it up and the consequence is, that he remembered and mastered what he read."[23] How much like the brilliant young aspiring literary banker.

HOW DID BAGEHOT RECONCILE his life of the mind with his life in the bank? Another essay, "The First Edinburgh Reviewers," which appeared in the *National Review* in October 1855,[24] provides autobiographical clues. It describes the founders of the influential Whig quarterly journal the *Edinburgh Review*, and through these superb portraits, the twenty-nine-year-old essayist likewise sketches himself.

The cast of featured characters—besides, inferentially, Bagehot—includes Francis Jeffrey, Henry Brougham, Sydney Smith, and, as a Tory foil, Lord Eldon. Bagehot traces their literary and political contributions to English life while ruminating on the nature of mysticism. He comments on the ostensibly shortening attention span of the English reader, the weaknesses inherent in the very kind of essay that Bagehot had written, and the indescribable something that dies along with a vivid character—his "air or atmosphere." There is Bagehot's trademark hyperbole and condescension ("the multitude" need instruction), as well as his equally characteristic insights into the human condition.

The reader early on encounters a sentence astounding in its length, virtuosity, and incongruity. It is one of the greatest Bagehotian sentences, 213 words in length, written in support of the contention that "short views and clear sentences" are the imperative new thing in English letters. In its entirety:

There is exactly the difference between the books of this age, and those of a more laborious age, that we feel between the lecture of a professor and the talk of a man of the world—the former profound, systematic, suggesting all arguments, analyzing all difficulties, discussing all doubts—very admirable, a little tedious, slowly winding an elaborate way, the characteristic effort of one who has "hived wisdom" during many "studious years," agreeable to such as he is, anything but agreeable to such as he is not; the latter, the talk of the manifold talker, glancing lightly from topic to topic, suggesting deep things in a jest, unfolding unanswerable arguments in an absurd illustration, expounding nothing, completing nothing, exhausting nothing, yet really suggesting the lessons of a wider experience, embodying the results of a more finely tested philosophy, passing with a more Shakespearian transition, connecting topics with a more subtle link, refining on them with an acuter perception, and what is more to the purpose, pleasing all that hear him, charming high and low, in season and out of season, with a word of illustration for each and a touch of humor intelligible to all—fragmentary yet imparting what he says, allusive yet explaining what he intends, disconnected yet impressing what he maintains.

"This is the very model of our modern writing," Bagehot adds. "The man of the modern world is used to speak what the modern world will hear; the writer of the modern world must write what that world will indulgently and pleasantly peruse."[25]

No reader had far to look for a sterling example of a "writer of the modern world." One had produced the essay itself.

In the first decades of the nineteenth century, the Whigs opposed the Corn Laws and the slave trade. They sympathized with the French Revolution, or at least with its ideals, and supported the emancipation of the Catholics. They opposed the brutal laws to punish free speech, crush delinquent debtors, hang shoplifters, and maim poachers.[26]

These were Whiggish doctrines, but Whiggism is not a creed so much as "a character," Bagehot maintained. The Whigs are men "of a cool, moderate, resolute firmness, not gifted with high imagination, little prone to enthusiastic sentiment, heedless of large theories and speculations, careless of dreamy skepticism . . ."[27] The legal reformer Sir Samuel Romilly, whose writings Watson Bagehot read aloud to his household at Langport, was an archetypical Whig, as was Francis Horner, who pressed for the early resumption of gold convertibility after the Napoleonic Wars. Horner's death, at the age of thirty-eight, was everywhere mourned, Bagehot recounted, a fact that produced a memorable digression: "It is no explanation of the universal regret, that he was a considerable political economist: no real English gentleman, in his secret soul, was ever sorry for the death of a political economist: he is much more likely to be sorry for his life."[28]

Bagehot's portrait of Sydney Smith, a contributor to the first number of the *Edinburgh Review* and to many that followed, reads, again, like a description of a certain new hire at Stuckey's: "There is as much variety of pluck in writing across a sheet, as in riding across a country. Cautious men have many adverbs, 'usually,' 'nearly,' 'almost': safe men begin, 'it may be advanced': you never know precisely what their premises are, nor what their conclusion is; they go tremulously like a timid rider; they turn hither and thither; they do not go straight across a subject, like a masterly mind. A few sentences are enough for a master of sentences; a practical topic wants rough vigor and strong exposition. This is the writing of Sydney Smith."[29]

Smith was an Anglican cleric, yet, Bagehot judges, he missed his mark in theology. The Whiggish divine forgot that religion "has its essence in awe, its charm in infinity, its sanction in dread; that its dominion is an inexplicable dominion; that mystery is its power."[30] This was the blind spot of the Whig character. Bagehot took it as a guiding principle that "Taken as a whole, the universe is absurd." There was

an unbridgeable gulf between the sacred and quotidian, between "the human mind and its employments." "The soul ties its shoe; the mind washes its hands in a basin. All is incongruous."[31]

In the course of the essay, Bagehot demands, "How can a *soul* be a merchant?" As for his soul, it was housed in the body of a banker. Bagehot's father, who saw no especial incongruity in a soul that held a job, had pressed his fellow directors to raise capital to support the bank's bounding growth. In October 1854, the board assented, voting to issue up to 1,250 new shares on top of the 4,000 already authorized and, for the most part, issued. Existing shareholders, invited to buy one new share for every four they owned, would pay the prevailing price of £60 per share, while new shareholders would henceforth pay £70. If all went according to plan, the capital of the bank would expand by slightly more than half.

The directors thought it reasonable to suppose that the current semiannual dividend rate of £3 per share would continue to be paid. The reserve fund, soon to be £50,000, no longer required topping up: interest earned on its investments would provide adequate future growth. Future profits would therefore flow to the bottom line, thence into the pockets of the dividend-earning stockholders. All of this, naturally, was "dependent on the general trade and business of the country," and on the "many contingencies to which that trade is exposed."[32]

The stockholders fairly leapt at the directors' offer, as well they might have. Among the new investors recorded at the start of 1854 was Walter Bagehot; his father had given him 25 shares. With a payout of £6 per share per year, Bagehot would earn more in dividend income than many senior Stuckey's clerks did in salary. Secure in his vocation, virtuosic in his avocation, Bagehot was a most fortunate young man.

CHAPTER 5

"THE RUIN INFLICTED ON INNOCENT CREDITORS"

There was, however, something missing. Precocious as he was in literature, Bagehot was reluctant in romance. He seemed to want nothing to do with it. At University College, in correspondence with his friend Richard Hutton, he invoked St. Paul to contend that celibacy was "essential to an absorption in the highest end of human action." To his mother, he quipped that while a man's mother "is his misfortune, his wife is his fault." Whether from fear, unfamiliarity, or misogyny, Bagehot tended to speak slightingly of women, when he mentioned them at all.

He was a decade out of college—the date was January 24, 1857—when the still-confirmed bachelor presented himself at the door of the country seat of James Wilson. The founder and owner of the *Economist* was now member of Parliament for Westbury and the financial secretary to the Treasury in the Whig government of Lord Palmerston. Wilson had heard good things about the literary barrister and West Country banker; the time had come to meet him.

Wilson's six daughters were politely curious. Not catching his last name, they judged their father's guest to be singular, if not exactly handsome. "He was," one of them recalled, tall and thin with rather high, narrow, square shoulders; his hands were long and delicate and the movements of his fingers very characteristic. He held his fingers quite straight from the knuckles and would often stroke his mouth or rub his forehead when he was thinking or talking.[1]

At dinner, the eldest, Eliza, twenty-four, insisted on hearing his unpronounceable name spelled out so that she wouldn't forget it. "Headache" was the excuse for her nonappearance at breakfast the next morning. Disappointed, Bagehot sat with her three younger sisters in the family schoolroom. "Your governess is like an egg!" he announced, and yes, the delighted bevy of Wilsons realized, she exactly resembled an egg. "He became one of us," remembered Emilie, the youngest. "We were six sisters without a brother. It was something strangely new, delightful and nutritious that he brought into our lives."[2]

The visitor felt much the same way about his hosts. Numerous, cheerful, petticoated, and sane, the Wilsons presented a happy contrast to the sparse and complicated Bagehots.

James Wilson, confined to his bed by a riding injury, was sizing up Bagehot for a contributor's role at the *Economist*. Hutton, to whom Wilson had offered the editorship of the paper, swore by the genius of his friend. Wilson must have taken Hutton's point, as Bagehot's work soon began to appear in his paper. The new correspondent signed his opening essay, on February 3, "A Banker." It ran out under a headline that nobody could have called sensational: "The General Aspect of the Banking Question."

The essay's thesis was indeed very general. Credit grows as civilization advances, Bagehot propounded: "certain individuals, of whom the world thinks better than it does of others, induce those who have dealings with them to take their promise of payment instead of actual payment." The creditworthy required fewer gold coins than the uncreditworthy mass—the promises of substantial people were a kind of weightless gold which they alone could spend. The bullion thereby conserved represented a savings for rich and poor alike. It would be wrong, then, to tax the IOU-worthy minority, who "obtained their credit, I do not say by the practice of all the moral virtues, but by decency, regularity, by being always seen in the same place every day, and never failing in pecuniary engagements when called on to discharge them. This 'respectability' may not be the highest of virtues, but I do not perceive why it should be mulcted of its natural profitableness."[3]

It soon became clear that the moral bar for obtaining a loan was not so high as "A Banker" believed it to be. Many had borrowed without suitable collateral, and many had lent, or guaranteed the payment of others' lending, without adequate capital. Such financial malpractice was not confined to England but was prevalent in America and Europe as well.

Perhaps the lenders and borrowers had forgotten the lessons of the railroad mania of 1847. Financial crises had occurred in 1825, 1837, and 1847, as *The Times*, peering ahead in a New Year's Day 1857 essay, reminded its readers. On form, the outlook for the next twelve months was guarded; so it seemed to the German diplomat Klemens von Metternich, on whom Henry Reeve, longtime writer on foreign affairs for *The Times*, went calling in August 1857. The eighty-four-year-old eminence of the long-ago Congress of Vienna talked first about the rebellion in India, then switched subjects. "After all," said Metternich, "what alarms me most in the present state of the world is not a Hindoo revolution or a Sepoy mutiny, but the consequences pending over us from a false system of credit and from the speculation which this system has encouraged both in Germany and in France."[4]

The August failure of the Ohio Life and Trust Company—the news reached London in early September—proved the crack of the starting pistol of the Panic of 1857.

It was a worldwide event, with mutiny in India—a general nationalist uprising against the rule of the British East India Company—complementing the bank runs, industrial distress, and commercial failures in America and Britain, and on the Continent. There was no particular novelty in transatlantic financial difficulties—the United States and Britain had suffered together in 1819 and 1837. What was new in 1857 was the connective tissue of telegraph wires, railroads, and steamships, though not yet a transatlantic cable: "so closely united now are the monetary transactions of all the great commercial countries in the world, that whatever affects one less or more affects the whole," as the *Economist* put it.[5]

Gold, the international money, likewise connected the advanced financial nations. It imparted information as it shunted back and forth between gold-standard countries. Nations lost gold when they over-issued bank notes and other paper claims against that treasure; they regained gold by restoring themselves to competitive trim. Naturally, moneyed people preferred to hold their wealth in countries where prices and wages were low, banks sound, and interest rates attractive. Central bankers who knew their business therefore tightened credit in response to the earliest signs of a gold exodus, in particular, a foreign or "external" drain.[6]

The contest for gold was a test of national determination. To compete in times of monetary pressure, Britain had to tolerate high interest rates. Lord Overstone, the monetary moralist of the age, writing as "Mercator" in *The Times* in January 1857, posed a challenge: "Is England, then, the country which is unable or unwilling to pay the rate of interest which in a temporary emergency may become requisite for retaining the amount of capital proportioned to the extent of her engagements . . . ? [W]eakness and irresolution in the hour of trial always prove false friends to those who foolishly place reliance in them. They lead not to honor or to safety, but are the fatal guide to disgrace and danger."[7] The Bank of England exhibited no weakness or irresolution as the crisis unfolded; correctly anticipating the arrival of the American hurricane, it raised its rate to 6 percent from 5.5 percent on October 8.

A timely rise in the rate of interest is "the only means" of keeping panic at bay, the *Economist* judged.[8] Still higher interest rates were imminent. Mitigating this fact was the abundant harvest; there would be no need to ship gold abroad to pay for imported grain. Then, too, said the *Economist*, the blessings of the earth went far to "repair much of the mischief to which folly and inordinate cupidity have exposed the trading community"—for there had been premonitory financial rumblings in 1856.[9] The Bank of England's next move, then, could hardly have shocked the City of London, though the bankers and the brokers were evidently not expecting the full-percentage-point hammer that fell on October 12. The *Economist* called for calm. No feature of the situation, certainly not a 7 percent discount rate, justified panic.[10]

Another percentage-point rise in the discount rate, to 8 percent on October 19, moved the *Economist* to remark on the "calmness and confidence" with which the country was meeting the highest interest rates in ten years. "Everybody," the paper contended, "feels that the general trade of the country is sound, and that a pressure which arises almost exclusively from foreign influences cannot be of prolonged duration." Nor was the distress—such as it was—without its compensations. When tightening credit forced speculators to unload the sugar and tallow that they had been withholding from the market in hopes of higher prices, consumers were the gainers. Wilson believed that monetary panics and commercial crises sprang from human nature; public policy could only do so much to allay them. There had been crashes and crises under systems of both protection and free trade, under paper money and gold, and both before and after passage of the Bank Charter Act.*

Wilson's journal was predisposed to take a confident and constructive editorial line. The founder and publisher, a rich man, was a member of the government, the right-hand man of the chancellor of the exchequer, Sir George Cornewall Lewis. Before taking up the seals of office in 1855, Sir George had edited the *Edinburgh Review*. He was an accomplished philologist and author of books including *An Essay on the Influence of Authority in Matters of Opinion* (1849) and the two-volume *An Inquiry into the Credibility of the Early Roman History* (1855).

In April 1857, Wilson asked his counsel: Would Sir George deem it useful for the *Economist* to publish some critical articles on the 1844 Bank Charter Act, now that that law was up for parliamentary review? Yes, please, Lewis replied—and "A Banker" promptly went to work on a three-part series exposing the weaknesses and fallacies of Peel's prize monetary legislation.†

---

* True to his laissez-faire convictions, Wilson advocated less regulation of the banking business, not more. He positively rejected, for instance, suggestions that British banks should be put under a government audit. In 1856, he wrote to G. C. Lewis: "Interferences with trade of this kind are mischievous not only inasmuch as they give to the community a false security and induce them to carelessness and laziness, but also inasmuch as they impose upon Governments responsibilities for which it is impossible they can do justice, but for which, in the event of failure, they will be called to account, and will become objects of popular discontent. They add one more and most difficult and odious element to the task of governing." The chancellor replied that he agreed with Wilson's "every word." Emilie I. Barrington, *The Servant of All* (London: Longmans, Green and Co., 1927), 1:322–24.
† Karl Marx would later do the same for the *New York Daily Tribune*. The difference between his monetary critique and Bagehot's—the difference, in general, between Marx's and the *Economist*'s coverage of the 1857 crisis—is that the co-author of the *Communist Manifesto* seemed to cheer on the crisis as if it were a racehorse on which he had put down a large bet. Thus, Marx on December 15: "While on this side of the ocean we were indulging in our little prelude to that great symphonious crash of bankruptcy which has since burst upon the world, our eccentric contemporary *The London Times* was playing triumphant rhetorical variations, with the 'soundness' of British commerce as its theme." Marx was, of course, no member of the Palmerston government, as was Wilson. Nor was he a stock-holding executive of Stuckey's Banking Company, as was Bagehot.

More than just the principal monetary measure of Victorian Britain, Peel's 1844 law was the most controversial. Proponents and detractors, Lord Overstone among the former and Wilson and Lewis notable among the latter, debated it throughout Bagehot's lifetime and long after his death. If we consider the ideas central to the debate—discretion versus regulation in monetary management, the problem of moral hazard—the battle has raged to this day.

To secure the gold value of the pound was the monetary desideratum of the age. One might have supposed that the pound needed no such protection, as it was defined by a weight in gold. The wild card was credit, the promise to pay money, and here there was no such clarity. True, the law required that each and every issuer of bank notes, whether the Bank of England or private banks like Stuckey's, stand ready to convert paper into gold and vice versa at the demand of the holder. What the law could not secure was coordination between the growth in paper claims, on the one hand, and the volume of gold with which to collateralize those claims—notes, bills, deposits—on the other. So the pound was as good as gold, provided that the banks of Liverpool or Glasgow or Langport or Bristol did not issue more paper claims than they had metal with which to make the required conversion. Most of the time, most Britons were happy with paper; only in a crisis did some of them clamor for the precious metal. As crises were relatively rare, the temptation was ever-present to lend and borrow beyond the limits of the metallic collateral.

It was the fearful drama of 1839, when only a timely loan from Paris saved the Bank of England from having to suspend gold payments, that had convinced Sir Robert of the need for reform. To safeguard the pound, he urged the House of Commons to control the emission of bank notes and to curtail the discretion of the directors of the Bank of England. Britons had had their fill of what Sir Robert described, in the peroration of his speech of May 6, 1844, as "the reckless speculation of some of the Joint Stock Banks, the losses entailed on their shareholders, the insolvency of so many private banks, the miserable amount of the dividends which have in many cases been paid, the ruin inflicted on innocent creditors, the shock to public and private credit . . ." To stop these recurrent spasms, as we have seen, the act split the Bank in two. In the Issue Department was vested authority to produce and distribute Bank of England notes and to exchange those notes for gold and vice versa; in the Banking Department, responsibility for conducting an everyday banking business. The division of the Bank was no mere administrative shuffle but a long and deeply considered monetary reform.

Samuel Jones Loyd, later Lord Overstone, was a strong and reasoned advocate of Sir Robert's ideas (or Sir Robert of his, though Overstone insisted that he had never spoken with or even met the prime minister). Like Bagehot, thirty years his junior, Overstone was born above the premises of his family's bank, Jones, Loyd & Co., which had been founded by Overstone's father, Lewis Loyd, whose early training in the Unitarian ministry somehow put him on the path to becoming one of the richest men in Europe. By the 1820s, Jones, Loyd was generating annual profits exceeding £200,000, as much as ten times those of Stuckey's.[11] Overstone became a City nabob, far richer than Vincent Stuckey, let alone Stuckey's brilliant nephew.

Overstone and Bagehot both wrote authoritatively on money and banking, often in opposition to each other; testament to the power of literary style is that posterity recalls only one of these forceful intellects. Overstone's manner of speaking and writing was as dry and severe as Bagehot's was conversational and epigrammatic. Reading the transcripts of Overstone's voluminous parliamentary testimony, his pamphlets, or his cerebral "Mercator" letters to *The Times*, you can hardly imagine him smiling, even in the privacy of his grand estates (though some did attest to his lively wit). Bagehot's bouncing essays might lead the reader to imagine that the man who wrote them could hardly stop smiling.

Overstone—like Bagehot, a clarifier of complex ideas—was among the first to identify the cycle of boom and bust, which he described in these words in 1837: "First we find it in a state of quiescence—next improvement,—growing confidence,—prosperity,—excitement,—overtrading,—convulsion,—pressure,—stagnation,—distress,—ending again in quiescence." Later, in 1862, he elaborated:

> Prosperity will generate excess, over-trading and over-production will cause a fall of prices, accompanied by temporary depression and despondency; this fall of prices will, in turn, check production, increase consumption, augment the exports, cause the precious metals to return to the country, the quantity of money will be thus increased, prices will again rise, and the country will in the end find itself very far removed from the verge of utter bankruptcy. Such is the "constant rotation of the unwearied wheel that Nature rides upon."[12]

Overstone, once more like Bagehot, was a political Liberal, contending that the world, led by England, was ever improving in thought and material condition. Not least was the progress of the age apparent in monetary matters. The 1821 restoration of gold convertibility was one such mark of advancement; in Overstone's mind, the 1844 Bank Charter Act was its companion piece. Under Sir Robert's system, rules replaced discretion. The Issue Department of the Bank would run like a machine. It could circulate up to £14 million of notes against the collateral of British government securities. Beyond that sum, pound for pound, every note would be secured by gold. Of course, the Bank had competition in the note-issuing business; banks like Stuckey's circulated their own. The act prohibited newly formed banks from copying the Stuckey's business model, capped the amount that the grandfathered banks of issue might circulate, and ensured that a private bank would lose its note-printing privilege in case of a merger with another bank. All of this started the countdown to a future day on which the Bank of England would occupy the position of Britain's sole bank of issue. Speed the day, said Overstone, who contended that the creation of money was the government's business alone.[13]

Peel's Act would redirect the Bank to its public obligations, unwritten though they were. The loss of gold to the Issue Department would set in motion a reciprocal contraction of the note issue. To protect its gold reserve, the Bank would be forced to raise its discount rate. By denying the management of the Bank its accustomed discretion in deciding when to act, the Peelites hoped to force early action—to nip a panic in the bud. "It is always wise," said Overstone, "to submit to the inconvenience of early preventatives rather than incur the risk of a more distant but greater evil."[14] And indeed, in 1844, Peel broadly hinted that the changes would do more than protect the convertibility of the pound. They would, he said, spare the country future shocks "to public and private credit."

Sir Robert foresaw neither the railway mania nor the Irish potato famine. It was to relieve the pounding pressure on British finance during the Panic of 1847 that the government of Lord John Russell suspended the 1844 Act; Sir Robert's opponents gloated. But Overstone, called upon to defend the Act, conceded nothing. The convertibility of the pound had never been in doubt, even in the worst of the crisis, he was pleased to observe. Whether the bankers and the speculators had managed their affairs well or badly was beside the point.

Ten years later, Walter Bagehot joined the still-fierce debate. As "A Banker," on the attack in Wilson's pages, he charged Overstone with a failure to keep up with the times—"the enormous importance attached to the convertibility of the bank note, as distinguished from the stability of banks, is a relic of past times. The deposits are in truth the growing element in banking; they were very small in importance years ago . . ."[15] The very rigidity of the rule that tied the hands of the Bank's directors was problematical. "Where," posed Bagehot, "are the rigid statesman to enforce the rigid rule?"[16]

In that autumn of 1857, America's crisis was fast becoming Britain's. British investors held an estimated £80 million of American securities; American consumers absorbed between a fifth and a quarter of British exports.[17] So shoulders sagged in the City of London on receipt of news in mid-September that sixty-two out of sixty-three banks in New York City had stopped paying gold to the depositors who had every right to demand it.*

The "foreign influences" to which the *Economist* was prepared to assign blame for the autumn's financial disturbances could explain only so much of the mismanagement at the Borough Bank, Liverpool, and the Western Bank, Glasgow. Those were home-grown British disasters. The Borough's losses would absorb every pound of its £940,000 capital. The Western Bank, likewise defunct, had the largest branch network in Scotland.[18]

The Western was a disaster long in the making. It had almost come to grief in 1834, two years after its founding, and would have failed in 1847 except for a £300,000 credit from the Bank of England. For the next ten years, it lent as if it were positively determined to fail. This it achieved in 1857, when it showed paid-in capital of £1.5 million and £5.3 million in deposits. *How to Mismanage a Bank: A Review of the Western Bank of Scotland*, an early example of the business case study, appeared in 1859.[19]

The Bank of England had wisely refused to lend to the Western, but, anticipating the too-big-to-fail doctrine of the twenty-first century,

---

* By refusing to join in the citywide default, Chemical Bank earned both the resentment of the New York banking fraternity and the doughty honorific "Old Bullion," on which moniker it traded into the early part of the twentieth century. Having absorbed Chase Manhattan, Chemical became a component of JPMorgan Chase in 2000.

the wounded giant formulated a scheme to beg the government's help anyway. The chancellor could hardly believe the bank's presumption. It was an absurdity, Sir George wrote to Wilson: "If you hear of any such extravagant idea, pray put an immediate extinguisher upon it. The Government have no means of providing funds for banks which cannot pay their creditors."*

It wasn't only the Scots who had overextended themselves: on October 28, the largest and seemingly most substantial of the London bill brokers, Overend, Gurney & Co., applied for accommodation to the Bank of England in the highly unusual form of a request for a blank check. Would the Bank furnish Gurney's with anything and everything that it might presently require?[20]

Up went the Bank Rate to 9 percent from 8 percent on November 5. No more did people borrow because they needed money—they borrowed because they feared that there would soon be no money to borrow.[21] George W. Norman, a director of the Bank, advised Overstone on November 5 on the developing crisis: "Exchanges are still unfavorable [i.e., gold continued to leave the country]—The pressure on the Bank heavy, and our Reserve uncomfortably low."[22]

On November 9 came one final turn of the interest-rate screw, to 10 percent. It was an unprecedented and shocking rate for the City of London, but—so said *The Times*—hardly a ruinous one, nothing at all like the panic-induced lending rates of 24 percent or even 60 percent which were on offer in the United States. Indeed, the monetary system of Great Britain was nothing less than "perfect," *The Times* contended,

---

* News that a delegation of frightened Scottish mill owners and merchants was coming to London to plead for emergency government relief elicited a more-in-sorrow-than-in-anger reproof from the *Economist*: "We thought that our countrymen north of the Tweed had formed too sound opinions as to any influence which the Government can exercise in matters of trade, to have come to such a resolution." Emilie I. Barrington, *The Servant of All* (London: Longmans, Green and Co., 1927), 2:61–62.

taking Overstone's side of the argument, "and has upheld us in a position to command the admiration of the world."[23]

Still, the structure of British credit bore every hallmark of human
frailty. To a certain kind of reckless management, the protections that
the law put in place to encourage sound practice and penalize incompetence and criminality—for instance, stockholders were at risk to the
extent of their entire personal fortunes for their pro rata share of the
debts of the firm in which they invested—seemed to have no effect.
November 11 brought news of the failure of the City of Glasgow Bank,
another supposed Scottish pillar, with capital of £1 million and ninety-
six branches, as well as the fall of Sanderson, Sandeman & Co., a leading London discount house.

Bagehot had asked from whence the "rigid statesmen" would
come to enforce Peel's Act. They were not to be found in London. On
November 12, Sir George C. Lewis signed a letter to suspend the Act
of 1844 for the duration of the emergency; now the Bank could issue
notes without regard to the adequacy of their gold cover. Relief was palpable, though it lacked the immediate curative power of the joy that had
instantly greeted the signing of a similar letter ten years earlier. Still,
the main force of the crisis was spent.

Eighty-five large firms, apart from banks, had failed in the two
months preceding the suspension of Peel's Act, and another fifty would
fall before the end of the year. Employment, prices, and profits all bore
the marks of what had begun to seem a crisis of morals as well as of
judgment. The parliamentary committee that conducted the post-panic
inquest fixed blame on "excessive speculation and abuse of credit."[24]
Witnesses testified to cases of banks and merchants operating on next
to no real capital. One failed merchant reportedly incurred liabilities of
£900,000 on capital of less than £10,000.[25] It galled Overstone and his
friends to see the lucky, imprudent ones rejoice at their escape from
the jaws of financial justice.[26] The law had protected the integrity of
the pound. It had not promoted the integrity of banks, discount houses,

and bill brokers. "Is not this," demanded Overstone, "as much as can be reasonably expected from any monetary system?"*

Peel himself had agreed when his act had first been suspended, in 1847—as, indeed, had Overstone. As for this second abrogation of the law, a confidant of Overstone's, the economist J. R. McCulloch, put the best face on it: "The Habeas Corpus Act has been frequently suspended, but still it is the best act in the Statute Book."[27] Neither did Bagehot and Wilson see anything to regret in the government's action. As far as they were concerned, Peel's Act served no useful purpose in tranquil times. In a panic it only incited the fear that the chancellor would refuse to sign a letter to suspend it.

Benjamin Disraeli, now a Tory MP, rose in Parliament a month after the suspension of the Bank Act to raise the question of moral hazard. "If," he asked, "the House be prepared to sanction the exercise of this dispensing power at the arbitrary will of the Minister of the day, how does it propose to reconcile the difference of position between those firms who fall victims before the dispensing power is exercised and those, who, holding on a favored twenty-four hours, struck upon the clock of the Royal Exchange of London, are enabled to dominate over those with whom they ought to be fellow-victims?"[28]

---

* Few were so provoked as the unsigned commentator in *The Times* who condemned the abusers of bank credit: "The speculator in produce, without capital or talent, assuming to be a millionaire, certain of a large fortune if the market advances, and trusting to the fears of his banking accomplices to uphold him if his game goes wrong—the bank with its 'wealthy proprietary' (irrespective of a score or two of widows and orphans) gambling by means of re-discounts to ten times the extent of its available resources, so as to make large dividends and surplus profits to cover the most disgraceful losses—the popular manager to whom everything is entrusted, usually an upstart, proud of his power to crush the business of any respectable house by backing up with unlimited loans a set of penniless protégés to counter-act its operations—and the money firms who assist the process only so long as it is thoroughly safe; all alike are conscious that between them and the Bank Charter Act there can be no quarter." *The Correspondence of Lord Overstone*, 2:807; "Money-Market and City Intelligence," *The Times*, November 12, 1857.

BAGEHOT PRODUCED A REVIEW of the autumn upheaval almost before it had subsided. "The Monetary Crisis of 1857," which appeared in the January issue of the *National Review*, featured the themes on which "A Banker" had harped in the pages of the *Economist*. The inadequacy of Britain's gold reserve was one of these ideas,* the inadvisability of the concentration of that treasure in the basement of the Bank of England was another, the trouble with Peel's Act a third. As was his wont, Bagehot advised against tilting at windmills. Yes, the Bank of England had thrown its weight around—overbearing monopolies usually did—but there was nothing to be done about that.[29] "The use of parliamentary eloquence is not to bewail fixed habits, but to improve improvable habits."[30]

Who was to blame for the shambles of English finance? Bagehot denied the very premise of the question. The joint-stock banks had sailed through the crisis. Compared to Hamburg, say, or New York, London was almost an island of calm. Even so, the City was not invulnerable: "Our hard capital is clothed in a soft web-work of confidence and opinion; on a sudden it may be stripped bare, and with pain to our prosperity," he wrote.[31] And it required no deep study of economics to follow his description of the intermediation of credit: "In its essence, the system is this: a man in the north is trustworthy and wants money; a man in the south has money, but does not know who is trustworthy; a middleman in London knows who is trustworthy, and lends the money of the south to the man in the north."

Could Bagehot suggest any improvements for an already functional

---

* A mark of Bagehot's coming of age in journalism was his facility in the labor-saving device of self-quotation. "A correspondent of *The Economist* who writes under the signature 'A Banker,'" he wrote in preface to a self-plagiarizing line on the paucity of cash reserves at British financial institutions. *The Collected Works of Walter Bagehot*, ed. Norman St John-Stevas, vol. 10 (London: the Economist, 1978), 53.

system? He proposed that, come a crisis, the Bank and the government jointly share responsibility for suspending Peel's Act, rather than the government alone signing off on the emergency policy. This, in turn, raised a question as old as central banking. Should the directors of the Bank of England be bound by rules, or should their judgment be their guide? Bagehot favored judgment: "it may be an evil to have discretion; but the events of the last few months prove . . . the evils of a rigid rule which admits no discretion."[32]

Hutton wasn't the only critic who applauded Bagehot's essay. Sir George Lewis told Wilson, "I have read several articles on the money crisis in reviews—all bad, except one in the *National Review*."[33]

"IN A GREAT COUNTRY like this," Bagehot coolly wrote, "there will always be some unsound banks, as well as some insolvent merchants."[34] Resignation in the face of human error was not Overstone's approach. The crisis left him desolated. He fastened on the bankers and brokers who paid interest on demand deposits, the kind of liabilities that the depositors might remove on a whim. "It is an unsound and dangerous form of credit," Overstone wrote to Lewis at the end of November; "it cannot permanently coexist with an honest and well-regulated Monetary system—One or other must succumb—If the credit system be too gigantic, and too powerful to be grappled with—we then only waste our time and labor in endeavoring to establish a sound Monetary system."[35]

How much worse might things have been without the 1844 Act? Only look to America, Overstone bitterly charged, "the monetary cesspool from which the pestilence of inflated Credit has diffused itself over the trading world."[36] In this, Overstone made analytical common cause with, of all people, President James Buchanan, who would devote the opening paragraphs of his first annual message to Congress to an attack on "our extravagant and vicious system of paper currency and bank credits, exciting the people to wild speculations and gambling in stocks."

For his part, Overstone prophetically speculated on the remote consequences of that breach in monetary discipline. He singled out Overend Gurney for its massive draw on the Bank and its lobbying to suspend Peel's Act:

> Gurney's, I am confident, will persist, with increased confidence, in their present course, in consequence of what has now occurred. Govt, they now know, will not allow them to declare their inability to discharge their debts *at call* to the trading world, when they amount to many Millions—and therefore they will have no misgiving or fear in again incurring such dangerous obligations—and the public also will be without the salutary lesson which should teach them not to rely upon such security. As it is, this system will be continued, and upon a more enlarged scale—The final, and not distant, result must be, a tremendous crash.[37]

Bagehot was not so wise as the old banker—at least, the younger man saw no cause to warn about the distant consequences of extraordinary government interventions in finance. In his rage and disappointment, Overstone might have exaggerated, but he didn't entirely miss his mark.

CHAPTER 6

"THE YOUNG GENTLEMAN OUT OF MISS AUSTEN'S NOVELS"

W ell might "A Banker" have taken a hopeful view of life, and monetary life among its other aspects, in that year of panic. The bank that employed him survived very nearly unscathed. It required no assistance from the Bank of England—far from it—and continued to pay its regular £3 per share dividend along with the by now customary £1 per share bonus.

Bagehot was a part of the enlightened management that delivered those results. He might have owed his job to his father, but he advanced on merit. In 1856, the directors named him secretary to a new permanent committee of management, at a salary of £200 a year; he likewise formed half of a two-man committee to investigate problems at the branch in Bristol.[1] Promotion to the position of secretary of the board of directors quickly followed.[2] In 1857, it was Walter Bagehot whom the directors selected to appear on behalf of Stuckey's at the Parliamentary Bank Act hearings, though it appears that Bagehot was never called to testify. At the end of the year, he was named co-manager of the Bristol branch; he would work there three days a week, the other days at Langport. His salary leapt to £500 a year.

There was more than money on the mind of the rising financier. Eliza Wilson had made fast work of the woman-scorning bachelor. He found that he could not erase the image of her loose hair flying in the wind. Naturally cheerful, he had never before been so discombobulated—nor, in alternating moments, so joyous. When he was apart from her, he read, reread, and kissed her letters, "till I begin to get wild."[3] If a Victorian courtship resembled a pair of simmering kettles, Bagehot's had come to a boil.

The Wilsons encouraged him. After that first meeting in the country, Eliza's mother, Elizabeth, urged him to visit their London home at 15 Hertford Street, Mayfair. Early on, the sisters called him "the young gentleman out of Miss Austen's novels," though Bagehot, at thirty-one, was not so very young.[4] There were poetry readings, chaperoned walks, sightseeing parties including an expedition to Millbank to view the immensity of the *Great Eastern*, and dinners with literary and political celebrities.

George Ticknor, a Boston scholar of Spanish literature, was one of these visitors. The American described "a very luxurious table as far as eating and drinking are concerned," and Eliza and two of her sisters, he recorded, spoke French "as few English girls can." After dinner, "de Tocqueville came in . . . and we all changed language at once, except the Master [Wilson] who evidently has but one tongue in his head, and needs but one, considering the strong use he makes of it." Ticknor remarked, too, on the presence of "a barrister whose name I did not get." The name was Bagehot.[5]

When Parliament disbanded for the summer, Bagehot visited the Wilsons at Claverton, their rented country home, with its twenty bedrooms and paintings by, among others, Sir Joshua Reynolds. When the sun shone, the young people picnicked on the Wiltshire Downs, Eliza mounted on the back of a donkey. She was not up to walking, she believed. "On wet days," recorded Emilie, the youngest Wilson sister, "there would be games of battledore in the picture gallery, Walter's characteristic eyeglass floating about in the air on its black string as he ran hither and thither after the elusive shuttlecock."

The pace of the courtship was unhurried—to the younger sisters, hoping for a wedding, it was drawn out exasperatingly. On September 27, Bagehot solemnly took Eliza aside to make a clean breast of something that he felt she had to know. Eliza describes the moment in her spare and quotidian diary: "Sat in the conservatory where Mr. Bagehot told me his mother was mad." On October 3, Eliza records, "I took Mr. Bagehot to see the view and lost the donkey." On October 8: "Mr. Bagehot read us Morte d'Arthur and Ulysses in billiard room, seated on stove. He is going to publish his essays."[6]

Her narrative continues:

Oct. 28th. I walked with Mr. Bagehot before the house. Beautiful moon. Fall of Delhi [a reference to British forces retaking Delhi during the Indian Mutiny].

Oct. 31st. Papa received a letter from Mr. Bagehot with an enclosure for me and invited him to come here.

Nov. 2nd. Mr. Bagehot came at 2.30. He gave Papa a letter detailing his affairs and Papa sent him out riding with me, Julia and Mr. Greg. Papa and Mr. Bagehot had a long talk before dinner, and settled that he would speak to me next morning. Papa quite ill. Mr. Bagehot and I played at Beggar my Neighbour, and he gained a queen's head from me.

Nov. 4th. Mamma held a consultation with Mr. Bagehot in the library before breakfast, and then he got me in there under the pretext of looking for a book, and proposed to me.

Nov. 5th. Talked over my proposed marriage with mamma and went to bed at 9, but did not sleep till 3.

Nov. 7th. Mr. Bagehot came at 10 for my answer. I was in the dining room and engaged myself to him then and there.

Ten years earlier, Bagehot had recorded his thoughts on the institution of marriage in a letter to Hutton: "To those who have to lead a secular life, marriage is, I suppose in the majority of cases, an assistance in the performance of duty . . ."[7] A very different Bagehot now sallied forth to tell Hutton, still his best friend, the happiest news in the world.[8]

The financial position of the prospective bridegroom was promising. No longer a mere staff officer, "A Banker" was about to become an actual lending officer. His Stuckey's shares yielded him £210 a year in dividends. All told, including salary and £50 a year from his interest in the *National Review*, he brought in (or would soon bring in) roughly £1,000 a year, a comfortable living. On a promising path to earn money, Bagehot also liked to save it. Hutton said that he had the "anti-spending instinct."

Not Eliza: in a sense, spending was her occupation. The Wilsons consumed conspicuously. When they made their seasonal migration from Claverton to Mayfair, they took, by Eliza's actual count on January 31, 1852, fifty-seven pieces of luggage. When they entertained at Mayfair, dinner guests could number eighty.[9] It was not cheap to move in Mayfair society. Preparation for being presented at court required the extensive services of Miss Rutherford, the dressmaker, and a month's worth of instruction in the art of the curtsy, under Madame Adelaide.[10] There were theater tickets, Italian lessons, Queen's balls,[11] and Continental travel, including visits to the famous Paris salon of Madame Mohl.[12]

Wilson was fond of Bagehot, but he doted on his daughter. Once he knew of Bagehot's intentions, he took her aside, not exactly to dissuade her from marriage, but to remind her of how happy she was at home.[13] And when she finally decided to accept Bagehot's proposal, the father of six took to his bed.

In mid-November, as the financial panic was beginning to subside, Eliza and her sister Sophie, along with their mother, set out for Edinburgh. Like their mother,[14] the Wilson sisters suffered from headaches— Eliza had borne them since the age of eleven. What awaited them in Scotland was state-of-the-art phrenology under a certain Dr. Beveridge. He would massage the flesh, crunch and "grind" the bones. A friend of the Wilsons, the beautiful Lady Kinnaird, vouched for the doctor's efficacy: he had cured her. Bagehot was suspicious—"rubbing," he called the doctor's technique. Prone to headaches himself, he wondered why Eliza couldn't be rubbed in London.

James Wilson wasn't long in his grieving bed. He and Bagehot put the three Wilson ladies on a train for Edinburgh and dropped into the British Museum to inspect the antiquities of Halicarnassus, just arrived from Greece. Dining together, they talked about currency. Returning from dinner, they stood on the Hertford Street doorstep till half past one discussing bimetallism in France.* As for Dr. Beveridge, Bagehot wrote to Eliza, "I hate him. He will try to keep you in Edinburgh under pretense of curing you."[15]

For her part, Eliza was trying to get used to addressing "Mr. Bagehot" by his Christian name. She told him that she loved him and asked him to thank his mother for the friendly message that Bagehot had passed along at his mother's request. Wrote Eliza: "Please give her

* In which two metals, usually silver and gold, jointly serve as the standard of value. French law assigned a fixed exchange rate between silver and gold in the shape of a ratio of 15.5:1. When Wilson and Bagehot were discussing the phenomenon, the French were busily exporting silver to India and, with those proceeds, importing gold. Wikipedia contributors, "Bimetallism," *Wikipedia, The Free Encyclopedia*, https://en.wikipedia.org/w/index/index.php?title=Bimetallism&oldid=820858049 (accessed February 8, 2018).

my 'respectful love,' if you think that the proper thing." He replied that it was futile: his mother would not be shaken from the belief that Eliza had broken off the engagement—why else would she fly off to Edinburgh?[16]

"My dearest Eliza," he wrote on November 22,

> I fear you will think the answer I wrote yesterday to your most kind and *delicious* letter, was very superficial, but I wrote it at once while people were talking and bothering me. I have now read yours over and over more times than I should like to admit. I awoke in the middle of the night and immediately lit a candle to read it a few times again. It has given me more pleasure than I ever received from a letter, and infinitely more than I thought it possible I could receive from one.
>
> I fancy that it is not now an effort to you to write to me— at least it reads as if it was written without effort. Yet it tells me things which with your deep and reserved nature it must have cost you much to put on paper. I wish indeed I could feel worthy of your affection—my reason, if not my imagination, is getting to believe you when you whisper to me that I have it, but as somebody says in Miss Austen, "I do not at all mind having what is too good for me"; my delight is at times intense. You must not suppose because I tell you of the wild, burning pain which I have felt, and at times, though I am and ought to be much soothed, still feel, that my love for you has ever been mere suffering. Even at the worst there was a wild, delicious excitement which I would not have lost for the world.

He closed on a note of Wilsonian laissez-faire. "I hope the Doctor does not think there is anything seriously the matter with your sister. Do not let him do much to her. I am more afraid of remedies than diseases."[17]

In Edinburgh, Eliza was bored to tears. The doctor forbade his patients to read—it was bad for their eyes—though he did not prohibit writing by eye-straining gaslight. She wrote to tell Bagehot how glad she was that he had immersed himself in the currency question. "I have a strong feeling too that you will distinguish yourself on 'Money' somehow or other; I don't mean by making much of it—I care far less about that than about people knowing that you understand it. I fancy we have both a little ambition of the right kind; do you think so?"[18]

Bagehot admitted that he was already a little distinguished in the monetary way. He had just filed 3,500 words of page-one copy for the *Economist* on the topic of the inadequacy of Britain's gold reserve. Wilson had accorded this submission some of his highest praise; he said it was written in a "business style."[19] William Rathbone Greg, a family friend of the Wilsons, a manager of the *Economist*, and co-venturer, with Bagehot and others, in the *National Review*, praised the submission, too, after a fashion. "Better than any of your literary things, Bagehot," said Greg, who had every reason to be jealous of Bagehot's claim on the respect of his employer and the affections of the Wilson daughters. The recipient of Greg's comment observed to Eliza that it was "paying a compliment and spoiling it rather."

Bagehot did not deny that he was ambitious. He sought such reputation as accorded with his objective value—a wholesome kind of ambition. The wish to be appraised at more than one's value was the undesirable kind. "I am afraid I covet 'power' influence over people's wills, faculties and conduct," he told her. "I think this is a very good thing too in many ways, but I do not quite approve the intensity with which I feel it."[20]

By the end of November 1857, life was beginning to brighten in dull Edinburgh. The Wilsons had procured a piano, on which Sophie played Beethoven. In the evenings, a Wilson cousin came to read aloud from *Zanoni*, a popular occult novel by Edward Bulwer-Lytton, and Jane Austen's *Mansfield Park*. Dr. Beveridge was "rubbing" Eliza for two hours a day now—a ten-year-old spinal injury was the bodily insult that had caused her head and eyes to ache, or so he determined. Stuff and nonsense, replied Bagehot.

Her intended lightheartedly blamed her for his inability to concentrate—he would sleep past his stop on the commuter train. He owed the *Economist* another article, and he had promised the *Encyclopedia Britannica* a note on the French Credit Mobilier, a subject he had written about for the *Economist*. The clock was also ticking on the deadline for an essay on the autumn financial crisis for the *National Review*, and the proofs of his soon-to-be-published collection of biographical studies were still uncorrected. "All the soft relaxing time that I used to give to literature insensibly goes to meditating on one face, and it requires such an effort to turn my mind away from it."[21]

Her letters brought tears to his eyes; the "firm and stoical" front he showed to the world was fast breaking down. "Knowing you not only 'gives a new significance to life,' but has made a revolution in my whole being somehow. I must whisper these things to you: it is vain to try to write them."[22] Loving her, he became isolated from other people— "All the distracting world seems to be gone and we seem to be alone together in the sight of God."[23]

Eliza had expected to be released by Christmas, but the doctor commanded more massage (her body was "fibrous"). As she could not come to London, Bagehot packed his bags for Edinburgh. Could he arrive by her birthday, Wednesday, December 16? How she hoped so: "If you could manage it, it would be delicious . . . We would have a real Sunday talk to begin with, and then you would cheer me with your jests and nonsense, the more nonsense the better as far as I am concerned, and I think you like to talk what you call 'rubbish' to me. Do you know, I feel quite joyous at the bare possibility of having you here."[24]

"What nonsense it is about love being blind," Bagehot wrote to her. "It sees so distinctly or does not one mind overhear the other? After I have gone away from you I have passed many aching moments trying to overhear what you must have thought of what I said to you."[25]

.   .   .

THE NEW YEAR BROUGHT Bagehot's first publication between hard covers. *Estimates of Some Englishmen and Scotchmen: A Series of Articles Reprinted by Permission Principally from the National Review* incorporated his commentaries on Gibbon, Cowper, Shelley, "the First Edinburgh Reviewers," Sir Robert Peel, Hartley Coleridge, and Bishop Butler.

The book-buying public had come to like these anthologies of essays from the top literary quarterlies. Two such journals mattered most, the *Edinburgh Review* (for Whigs) and the *Quarterly Review* (for Tories). The *National Review*, which Bagehot had helped to found in 1855, had no particular politics, and disrupted that intellectual duopoly by the strength of its ideas and the pleasures of its writing, Bagehot's especially.

Eliza cut out the first review she saw, a lukewarm notice in the *Statesman* ("tolerable," the critic allowed). The *Examiner*, while "heartily" recommending the book, was disapproving of Bagehot's glibness, his attempts to achieve the "modern form of smartness that shall win the public ear, which in the essay on Shakespeare borders on impertinence."[26]

There was no such holding back in the *Morning Post*, which extolled the author for his possession "of qualities that entitle him to a foremost place among the essayists of our own times." Still less did the *Economist* stint. Hutton showered his best friend and journalistic stable-mate with superlatives: "There is true genius in these fascinating, and, perhaps, disrespectful estimates, and it is of a somewhat rare kind." The *National Review*, Hutton judged, "is fortunate having secured in its early days the contributions of a writer so fresh and vivid a genius. His audacity would often provoke rebellion if it were not for the depth of his thought, and his thought would often seem abstruse and dull if it were not for the brilliancy of his humor."

Bagehot brushed aside that tribute, well-earned though it was, as he did Hutton's subsequent praise of his *National Review* essay on the Panic of 1857. But Bagehot's literary work had also caught the eye of Matthew Arnold, the great critic, who praised it for "showing not talent only, but a concern for the simple truth which is rare in English literature as it is in English politics and English religion." Bagehot was not so quick to deprecate Arnold's opinion—he gave Eliza the letter in which Arnold had written it.

The book was a kind of love letter, Bagehot told her. "It never would have been put together, but from a floating idea that perhaps you might read it and perhaps you might like me better for it."[27]

The two lovers, getting to know one another from afar, told each other about themselves. He related that he was "cheerful but not sanguine." He could make the best of anything, "but I have a difficulty in expecting that the future will be very good."[28] He talked to himself. He needed his sleep, was prone to be late for breakfast, disliked the cold, would not live in suburbia nor sleep in four-poster beds. He was tone-deaf.[29] He was afraid that she overrated his mind (though "I do not mind being thought too well of").[30]

For her part, she was "decidedly sanguine" (too much so, her family thought); "I always expect things to turn out well."[31] She spoke German fluently (she had gone to school in Cologne for five years),[32] French and Italian more than capably. Her nature was "very womanly"; she loved to lean "on a stronger nature, though I may appear to be somewhat independent on the surface."[33] Her taste in female beauty was "severe," more so, even, than that of her appraising fiancé, and she would not accept his worshipful comments on her good looks ("though I have not the shadow of an objection to your thinking it, dear").[34] She had an ear for music (her father loved the way she sang "Annie Lau-rie");[35] parties bored her.[36]

She confronted him about his misogyny: "Are you not somewhat hyper-critical about women, dear? They must not be stupid; they must not talk and they must not be silent, and whatever else they are or are not, they must be pretty. I shall begin to fancy I must be a wonderful 'juste milieu' in everything to be right in your eyes, and I shall be get-ting vain in spite of myself."[37]

Misogynist though he might have been, Bagehot condescended neither to his mother nor to his fiancée. He wrote to her during the crisis about the paradoxical nature of financial faith. "All banking rests on credit," he said, "and credit is rather a superstition. At any rate it is adopted not from distinct evidence but from habit, usage and local cus-tom, and when there is panic floating in the air no one ought to feel so comfortable as usual."[38]

Suddenly, six weeks later, it was as if the Panic of 1857 had not hap-pened. "It is really a very ridiculous world," he told her from London:

The last few times I have been here everybody was on their knees asking for money, now you have nearly to go on your knees to ask people to take it. Neither of these two extremes is very pleasant. Being besought is not unagreeable intrinsically, but when a man is very earnest for money, you begin to suspect he is "in difficulties" and ought not to have it, and in the other case it seems demeaning the majesty of money to ask—or beseech— human beings to take it. You look at a hard-eyed billbroker and think what is this man created for, if *not* to take money. Still the present state of things has the advantage that there is no tension of mind in managing your business while it lasts. You need not follow a man with your eyes when he takes away your money and think "Will he ever pay me?"—I own I like the sensation of safety.[39]

Few better observations of the cycles of bankerly feast and famine have ever been written. Historians of economic thought may make of it what they will that these passages are found not in Bagehot's financial journalism but in his love letters.

.   .   .

ELIZA, AT LAST FREE of the clutches of Dr. Beveridge, returned to London in February 1858 to buy "the then de rigueur dressing case" and to order her trousseau.[40] The next stop was Claverton, where she was reunited with her fiancé and her sisters. Fully integrated into the family, Bagehot amused the Wilsons by reading aloud from poetry or the *National Review* and by competing in zestful games of cup-and-ball, a monocle stuck in his eye. He loved to play cards, too, especially with the one Wilson sister who actually cared—as did he—about winning and losing.

In the weeks leading up to the wedding, set for April 21, Bagehot wrote an essay on Sir Walter Scott and the Waverley novels, conducted his banking business in Langport and Bristol, and went searching for a house for Eliza and himself. Bella Vista, the final selection was called, which the new Walter Bagehots presently rechristened "The Arches." Set on a hill near Clevedon, a seaside resort and Bristol bedroom community, the house commanded a view that was everything its original name implied. Bagehot had loved visiting the town during his Bristol College days,[41] and the air, he exulted to Eliza, was "eager." They would pay an annual rent on the order of £120. Mitigating that cost was the fact that, in the country, a gentleman could "wear very cheap clothes."[42]

They were married not at the cathedral, or by the archbishop as Eliza had jokingly demanded, but in the old church at Claverton. The great day dawned warm and sunny. There was dancing on the lawn to the strains of a Hanoverian band and, of course, there were speeches.

Neither of the bridegroom's parents was present—she could not stand the excitement, and he remained home to watch over her—so Bagehot took time from his honeymoon to describe the enchanting event. "A Mr. Moffat (MP for Ashburton)," he wrote home, "proposed our health in a copious and eloquent manner, and spoke of the 'hundred of thousands' who had read my writings, whom I myself should wish to see particularly."

He signed the letter, and so did Eliza:

I am your affectionate daughter,
  Eliza Bagehot
This is the *first* time I ever signed my new name.

CHAPTER 7

A DEATH IN INDIA

Post-panic finance was quiescent, just as Lord Overstone's theory of the economic seasons predicted it would be. English politics were livelier. In 1858, the Conservative government of Lord Derby began to prepare a new parliamentary reform bill, the first since 1832. Bagehot responded to the Tory initiative with his own proposals for constitutional renovation, and "Parliamentary Reform," the resulting 43,000-word opus, appeared in the January 1859 issue of the *National Review*.

The 1832 Reform Act had established a uniform test of eligibility for voting: to exercise the franchise, a man had to be living in a house for which the annual rent was at least £10. Bagehot was all for a property qualification, but he proposed that the minimum be established locally rather than nationally, and that, perhaps, other kinds of property—debentures, shares, savings bank accounts—be considered as equivalents to land and rent in determining who might cast a ballot. He urged, too, some reapportionment of parliamentary seats to secure a stronger voice in the nation's political councils for the fast-growing, industrial North.[1]

His essay, soon expanded and published as a two-shilling pamphlet, proceeded from an optimistic view of the age. Free trade, an improved poor law, municipal reform, a more enlightened colonial policy, and the abolition of forced tithing to the Church of England were among the signs of progress. All had followed the expansion of the franchise with the Reform Act of 1832. The authors of that profound legislation had succeeded in transferring "the predominant influence in the state from certain special classes to the general aggregate of fairly instructed men." Not that you could prove the point with statistics, Bagehot allowed: "We must trust to our eyes and ears, to the vague but conclusive evidence of events."[2]

Among some of the free traders who had stood shoulder to shoulder with Wilson since the Corn Law struggles of the 1840s—John Bright was one—there was a strain of almost pure democracy. Bagehot was immune to it. The schoolboy who had characterized his classmates as "the mob" and the adult who—in this very essay—condemned the vulgarity of the U.S. Congress ("Men of refinement shrink from the House of Representatives as from a parish vestry")[3] had no sympathy for universal suffrage. Still and all, for society's own good, the "lower orders," too, must be heard:

> . . . in every free country it is of the utmost importance,—and, in the long-run, a pressing necessity,—that all opinions extensively entertained, all sentiments widely diffused, should be *stated* publicly before the nation.
>
> We may place the real decision of questions, the actual adoption of policies, in the ordinary and fair intelligence of the community, or in the legislature which represents it. But we must also take care to bring before that fair intelligence and that legislature the sentiments, the interests, the opinions, the prejudices, the wants of all classes of the nation; we must be sure that no decision is come to in ignorance of real facts and intimate wants.[4]

Publication of "Parliamentary Reform" made a sensation. Bagehot's admirers showered the essay with praise, some of which they conveyed to Wilson with the request that he pass it along to his new son-in-law. Wilson went a step further: he invited a dozen of these appreciative and prominent readers—"public animals," Bagehot called the members of the star-studded guest list—to toast the author at dinner.

William E. Gladstone, William Makepeace Thackeray, Lord Grey, Lord Granville, Sir George Cornewall Lewis, and Robert Lowe were among the eminences who gathered around Wilson's table at 12 Upper Belgrave Street on April 1, 1859.[5] Lowe, an Oxford classicist turned Liberal member of Parliament, had bypassed Wilson to praise Bagehot directly. The essay, wrote Lowe in a letter, "is beyond compare the best I have seen on the subject, and is indeed written with the insight of a statesman and the moderation of a philosopher."[6]

Emilie Barrington, Eliza's little sister, would often watch her brother-in-law pull a "very tiny" notebook from his waistcoat and jot down fleeting thoughts. One such entry said this: "Living really in the political world is the greatest possible gain in a political country; knowing at first hand what others know at second hand only."[7] On April 4, three days after the Wilson-hosted dinner to honor the author of "Parliamentary Reform," the Walter Bagehots attended a party at the Gladstones' home.[8] The inside world of politics had a new member.

ELIZA HAD EXPRESSED THE hope that her fiancé would make a name for himself "on Money," and Bagehot presently tackled the subject head-on. The outpouring of gold from the mines in California and Australia prompted concern about a new inflation: as a superabundant harvest would tend to reduce the price of food, so, the argument went, would the recent gold strikes in California and Australia likely depress the value of money. Michel Chevalier, a French economist, free-trader, and friend of Wilson's, took that tack in a new book entitled *On the*

Probable Fall in the Value of Gold. He projected depreciation in gold coin of as much as 50 percent.

Bagehot, with a courtly bow to his father-in-law's friend, chose the other side of the argument. He reminded readers of the *Economist* that nobody knew the size of the existing stock of gold, and, absent this critical information, there was no telling what effect the addition of new bullion—between 1851 and 1857, it was surely immense—might produce. There was, in fact, persuasive evidence that the channels of commerce had swallowed the new gold without any noticeable disturbance to the level of prices. For inferential proof, Bagehot cited the ratio of the prices of gold to silver during the decade of the bullion bonanza: it had hardly wavered. It would surely have moved in silver's favor if gold had, in fact, become depreciated through a glut in new supply.*

Wilson challenged Bagehot's reasoning, especially on the technical point of whether the growth in quasi-money credit instruments like bank checks, convertible into gold on demand, ought to be weighed in reckoning the import of the new mine supply. Chevalier's concerns about the future stability of the monetary standard were ones that Wilson shared. It was a fond and friendly difference of opinion: "I wish I had you here to talk over this interesting point," Wilson wrote to his

---

* Twentieth-century research fixes the average rate of expansion in the world's above-ground stock of gold at between 1.07 percent and 3.79 percent per annum between 1839 and 1929. The single exception was the golden decade of the 1850s, when annual average production jumped by 6.39 percent. Chevalier's concern was hardly groundless, though, as Bagehot patiently demonstrated, it was debatable. The torrent of supply did not persist, contrary to the expectations of both Chevalier and Bagehot, but leveled off even as Bagehot was writing. Growth in the supply of the world's principal monetary metal reverted to its long-term trend (corresponding, more or less, to the long-term trend in population growth). The economist William Stanley Jevons, taking up the gold question in 1863, concluded that the purchasing power of gold had depreciated by at least 9 percent and perhaps by as much as 15 percent. Hugh Rockoff, "Some Evidence of the Real Price of Gold, Its Costs of Production, and Commodity Prices," in *A Retrospective on the Classical Gold Standard, 1821–1931,* edited by Michael Bordo and Anna Schwartz (Chicago: University of Chicago Press, 1984), 621.

son-in-law. "But go on with the articles. When shall we see you?" He sent his love to Eliza.

THE ONE-MAN-BAND PHASE of the *Economist* had ended in the late 1840s. In David Mitchell Aird, the paper had found a printer, manager, and occasional financial correspondent. In Herbert Spencer, the future author of *Social Statics*, it had had, for a time, a copyeditor. The anarchist Thomas Hodgskin was a regular contributor of fluent articles about politics, pauperism, economics, and capital punishment, which he abhorred. A kind of anarcho-socialist, Hodgskin propounded the doctrine that labor, and labor alone, was the true source of economic value. Such was his influence on socialist thought that Beatrice and Sidney Webb characterized Karl Marx as Hodgskin's "illustrious disciple."

William Rathbone Greg was another steady contributor to Wilson's pages. Born in 1809, the youngest son of a wealthy Cheshire mill owner, Greg set up in business with his father's help. The business failed and Greg turned his full attention to writing. He saw the world largely as James Wilson did, not least in his belief in free trade. His essay "Agriculture and the Corn Laws" won a prize from the Anti-Corn Law League in 1842. To support his wife and four children, Greg sold freelance articles to the *North British Review*, the *Westminster Review*, and the *Edinburgh Review*. In the early 1850s, he added the *Economist* to his string of journalistic outlets.

Greg was soon on more than professional terms with the Wilsons. In Julia, Wilson's twenty-year-old daughter, whom he met in 1852, Greg found his soul mate, though he was married and twenty-three years her senior. Greg's first marriage ended in 1873 with the death of his wife, who had long been insane. He and Julia married in 1874. Their only child, Walter Wilson Greg, born in 1875, was groomed by his parents for the editorship of the *Economist* but instead became a distinguished Shakespearean scholar.

Greg had a long nose, wide mouth, and close-set eyes. In a picture snapped during the phase of his life in which he encountered Julia, he leans on a cabinet with his right elbow as his left elbow juts akimbo. His mustache nearly connects with his lush side whiskers. He looks steadily into the camera, as if to affirm the judgment of a contemporary about his emphatic contributions to the discussions at the Political Economy Club, to which he belonged.*

Richard Holt Hutton, editor from 1857, likewise had a network of correspondents. Wilson himself wrote leaders in his not-abundant spare time—he was, of course, a member of Parliament and a Treasury official, besides, as well as a contributor to the *Manchester Guardian*—but not even this Hercules of labor could find the hours to write and electioneer simultaneously. In the final two weeks of April 1859, Wilson was called home to his parliamentary constituency to fight a contested by-election. He addressed an SOS to Bagehot: "Hutton will have to draw from all quarters this week and next. I cannot do anything for him. See what you can." Bagehot answered the call with a comment on the outbreak of war between France and Austria. The news had panicked the City and astounded Bagehot—he had never before seen a political event have such a violent financial effect. "It is like the panic the week we were engaged," he reminisced to Eliza.[9]

It could not have been lost on Wilson that Hutton cared little about money, banking, investing, or business. Nor did Hutton's discursive writing come close to achieving what Wilson meant by a "business style." On Saturday morning, the City men who subscribed to the *Econ-*

---

* Recalled Lord Courtney of Penwith: "Another clear and vigorous debater among us was W. R. Greg, author and reviewer—the W.R.G. of endless pungent paragraphs on topics of the day." Like Bagehot, who was also a member, Lord Courtney continues, "he had a very large knowledge of literature and of business, but whilst Bagehot went on refining Greg was prompt and decisive and, if his nail may not always have been the right one, he always hit his nail and hit it on the head." Ruth Dudley Edwards, *The Pursuit of Reason: The Economist, 1843–1993* (Boston: Harvard Business School Press, 1993), 281.

omist were likely to open the paper to discover reviews of, say, a new edition of the letters of the eighteenth-century English art historian Horace Walpole, or of a work entitled *Travels in Eastern Africa; with a Narrative of a Residence in Mozambique*, or of a collection of the *Biographies of Lord Macaulay Contributed to the Encyclopedia Britannica*. Hutton did not publish such material to the exclusion of business and financial news, or of the essential supporting statistics, the presentation of which the *Economist* pioneered. Nor did Wilson, no reader of books himself, object to book reviews per se. His daughters Eliza* and—especially— Julia were among the contributors of unsigned reviews to the family paper. Still, there was a great deal of material that a City stockbroker might have judged extraneous. Hutton's bookishness made him a more likely candidate for the editorship of a literary journal than a financial one.[10]

Bagehot's mind afforded him polymathic scope—not that he was alone, or even so very unusual, in the wide range of his interests. For many accomplished Victorians, curiosity seemed unbounded. As the engineer Brunel built railways, bridges, and ships, so did the statesman Gladstone translate Horace and Homer (in 1886, he was reading the *Iliad* for what he suspected was the thirty-fifth time), publish substantial works on religion and Neapolitan politics, and, while commissioner-extraordinary in the British protectorate of the Ionian Islands, address the Ionian assembly in classical Greek.† Linguists and amateur classicists were common in Bagehot's circle of friends. The parliamentar-

---

* Eliza took no great pains with her writing, but was content (as were many critics, then and later) to construct a review out of lengthy quotations from the work under scrutiny. In the case of Robert Von Mohl's *The History and Literature of Political Science*, which appeared in the *Economist* in 1856, even the copy-and-paste approach required considerable labor and not a little skill; Von Mohl wrote in German. Martha Westwater, *The Wilson Sisters: A Biographical Study of Upper Middle-Class Victorian Life* (Athens, OH: Ohio University Press, 1984), 41.
† "[P]erfectly orated but incomprehensible to his Italian-speaking audience," reads Gladstone's entry in the *Oxford Dictionary of National Biography*.

ian Robert Lowe was more than proficient in Sanskrit, and Sir George
Lewis was the author of *Survey of the Astronomy of the Ancients*. The
banker John Lubbock wrote prolifically on archeology and evolution-
ary theory. Henry Herbert, 4th Earl of Carnarvon, was a Fellow of the
Royal Society.

In 1859, Bagehot turned his attention—that part of it not occupied
by the gold controversy, Stuckey's, the *Economist*, and Eliza—to John
Milton. The newlywed banker was giving full vent to his literary avocation. His essay on Sir Walter Scott and the Waverley novels had appeared
in the *National Review* in 1858, followed by another on Charles Dickens. Now, in the July 1859 issue of the *National Review*, came a study of
the author of *Paradise Lost*. The Milton essay was, ostensibly, a review
article, though the publication of the works under review seemed more
pretext than catalyst. Bagehot pays his respects to the distinguished
authors of the Milton-themed works under his consideration—David
Masson, a professor at University College, and Thomas Keightley, a
scholar of folklore—but he no more defers to them on Milton than he
had to Chevalier on gold. "No one can wish to speak with censure of a
book on which so much genuine labor has been expended," writes the
amateur critic of the 780-page opening volume of Masson's projected
three-volume work, *The Life of John Milton*, "and yet we are bound, as
true critics, to say that we think it has been composed upon a principle
that is utterly erroneous." Not an academic, Bagehot was likewise not
a pedant. He goes on to complain about the biographers who shrink
before their scholarly critics: leave something—anything—out of the
narrative, and the professors will abuse you for it. So Masson leaves
nothing out, Bagehot writes, "in the production of a work at once over-
grown and incomplete." One trouble with the encyclopedic approach to
biography in this case is that Milton was a writing man: nothing much
happened to him. His wife left him, only to return to him, years later,
with the in-laws in tow. It was a happy reconciliation and, from Milton's
side, a generous one. Otherwise, events were few and far between, a

fact that removes the need for the kind of context with which Masson pads his pages: "A life of poetic retirement requires but little reference to anything except itself. In a biography of Mr. Tennyson, we should not expect to hear of the Reform Bill, or the Corn Laws."[11]

Thus disposing of Masson and all but ignoring Keightley, Bagehot proceeds to develop his own ideas on the poet and his works. Like Samuel Johnson before him, he concludes that Milton's "isolated and austere mind"[12] left him ignorant of the hubbub, the people, and the mores of the everyday life that swirled about him. Bagehot describes Milton, the ascetic; Milton, the author of a tract on divorce whose attitude is entirely and unapologetically pro-husband; Milton, the Puritan political partisan (without reference to the poet's magnificent defense of free speech, *Aeropagitica*, a curious omission for a writer and publisher); and, of course, the author of *Paradise Lost*.

The words that Bagehot expended recording Milton's height offer a window into the tempo of Victorian life and letters. The poet was neither short nor tall—that is the spare fact—but Bagehot does not simply assert it. He devotes most of a deep paragraph to quoting Milton, who seemed a little defensive on the subject, and the antiquary John Aubrey, Milton's contemporary, to establish the none-too-arresting datum that the great man was of middling stature. Nothing indicates that either Bagehot or his readers were in a hurry to move on to more substantive topics.

The next paragraph reveals something about the critic. Bagehot was given to frank appraisals of the personal appearance of people whom he encountered.* Here is what he had to say about Milton's reputed looks: "We are far from accusing Milton of personal vanity. His character was too enormous . . . for a fault so petty. But a little tinge of excessive self-

---

* His report to Eliza on a dinner hosted by the *Saturday Review* which he attended in July 1859 includes this: "I sat next to [The Rev. William Scott] who writes the little amusing politics in the middle of the paper, and is not unpleasant tho' he is ugly and unpopular." *The Collected Works of Walter Bagehot*, 13:550.

respect will cling to those who can admire themselves. Ugly men are and ought to be ashamed of their existence. Milton was not so."[13]

Bagehot draws a breath—perhaps, after those last jarring sentences, the reader, too, needs a pause—before taking up *Paradise Lost.* "No book, perhaps, which has ever been written is more difficult to criticize."[14] Milton's purpose was nothing less than to plumb the mystery of man's place in the universe.

Yet Bagehot stands unbowed before the masterwork. He enumerates its defects, the first being its foundation "on a political transaction." This undertaking assumes the form of the meeting of angels which God has called to announce his decision to appoint "My only Son" to sit at his right hand. "This act of patronage was not popular at court," Bagehot dryly comments; "and why should it have been? The religious sense is against it. The worship which sinful men owe to God is not transferable to lieutenants and vicegerents."

Which brings Bagehot to Milton's "great error": the poet makes Satan appear *"interesting."* Quoting Coleridge, Bagehot compares Milton's Satan to an Englishman's idea of Napoleon I. You may not root for Napoleon, Bagehot allows, but you are fascinated by him; so with Satan in books 1 and 2 of Milton's epic. You know that Satan will be vanquished, but you have no affinity with the "insipid" angels who oppose him. It therefore happens that "our sympathies, our fancy," are on the side of the devil.[15]

Satan's assault on God's first couple seems overwrought, Bagehot continues, unworthy of the power and majesty of the fallen angel: "Two beings just created, without experience, without guile, without knowledge of good and evil, are expected to contend with a being on the delineation of whose powers every resource of art and imagination, every subtle suggestion, every emphatic simile, has been lavished." Why, Bagehot remarks, "It is as if an army should invest a cottage."

Bagehot, never overawed by reputation, does at last give Milton his due. Every one of the poet's lines, he writes, "excites the idea of indefinite power."[16]

BAGEHOT WAS RIGHT ABOUT Dr. Beveridge of Edinburgh: his phrenological rubbing was all for naught. Eliza continued to suffer debilitating headaches. When stricken, which her diaries suggest was about once a week, she would spend most of the day in bed. Eye strain likewise troubled her. When she wanted to know what was in *The Times*, a servant read her the paper.

The Bagehots lived a pleasantly itinerant life. Residing at Clevedon, they made frequent visits to her parents' houses in London and in Claverton. After the wedding, at Langport, they submitted to the ancient ceremony called "sitting up," in which the bride surrenders herself to the inspection of her husband's friends and family.[17] Of an evening, or on Sunday, Bagehot might read aloud: the poems of Shelley or Matthew Arnold, the Psalms, Balzac's *Eugenie Grandet*, or Poe's "The Murders in the Rue Morgue." There were houseguests—her sisters, Mr. Greg—and they would play billiards or whist.

In February 1860, Bagehot and Eliza, along with Greg and Julia, took a holiday in Paris. It wasn't very successful, "at least to us soberer ones," Greg advised Eliza's sister Matilda. "It produced an enormous crop of bonnets and dresses—with which our room was absolutely *strewn*—but not much else—except that I had the stomach-ache en perpetuité, Emilie a sore throat and Julia influenza and measles." Greg's travelogue continued:

You never saw such people as Walter and Eliza for appetite and unpunctuality. They grubbed at 9, at 11, at 2, sometimes at 5, always at 6 and usually again at 11 or 12, with a snack in the interstices. The sofas and floor presented a most distracting chaos of newspapers, old and new, chocolate, gloves (—generally odd ones—) tea cups, lemonade, pats of butter, statistical returns and Blue books, physic bottles, fragments of bread, half-eaten pears, and the like . . .

Punctilious and unpunctual, Bagehot was a member of the first generation of English railway commuters. He would catch the 9:26 a.m. from Clevedon to Bristol to oversee the local Stuckey's branch. If London-bound, he would ride the Great Western express to Paddington. A late riser, he would sometimes, as the Victorians put it, "lose his train." Whichever train that happened to be was likely a spartan affair, though wondrous to those who had previously known only horse-drawn conveyances. Absent were heat, artificial light, food, beverages, lavatories. Passengers furnished their own refreshment and illumination. When the temperature dropped, they rented foot-warmers.

In his absence, Eliza paid endless rounds of social calls. She planned and executed dinner parties, attended to the servants, inventoried the linen, and doted on her husband's writing. She earned no money but ably helped to spend it—within a year of their marriage she calculated that they were spending at the rate of £1,400 a year while Bagehot was earning around £1,000 a year.[18] Just how Mr. and Mrs. Bagehot squared this particular circle is unrecorded.

Like many a young bride, Eliza discovered that it was useful to prompt her husband to do the things that he otherwise might have left undone. Thus, she wrote to him concerning the need for ponies to pull the phaeton: "I should be very pleased if you went and bought a pair of cobs tomorrow in your off-hand way." And, she adds, concerning a date she had planned for him at the photographer's, "Please go tomorrow at 11 (222 Regent St) and ask to sit with Mr. Scott. Remember to wear a blue tie and brush your hair with care, please, love."[19]

•   •   •

JAMES WILSON WAS MUCH in demand in 1859 within the Liberal government of Lord Palmerston. First came an offer to assume the vice
presidency of the Board of Trade. He accepted, and was also made a
Privy Counsellor. This last distinction required a visit to Windsor Castle
on June 18 to kneel on a stool before Queen Victoria, extend his right
hand toward her, palm up, take her hand lightly in his, and brush his
lips against it—"kissing hands," the ceremony is called.[20] A more dazzling invitation followed ten days later:[21] Would the newly-minted vice
president care to take up the duties of the Financial Membership of the
Supreme Council at Calcutta—functionally, to become the chancellor
of the exchequer of India? He would serve for five years.

Wilson liked his life the way it was. He could occupy a safe parliamentary seat for as long as he cared to have it. He enjoyed "the
best society in London," as he described it—because it was the most
intelligent—and the love of his large family. All of this he would have
to abandon. Then again, India promised adventure and fame. Wilson
had served as secretary to the India Board of Control and headed the
development of the Indian railway system;[22] well aware of the defects of
Indian finance, he had been of the view that nothing short of an emergency would present the opportunity to fix them. With the 1857–58
uprising against the rule of the British East India Company, India had
its emergency.[23]

Bagehot was the family member with whom Wilson was most eager
to discuss his future, and when the decision to go was firm and final,
it was his son-in-law with whom Wilson stayed up late one night to
review the details of his will. On the day before his departure, Wilson
dashed off a note to Sir George Cornewall Lewis: "My friend Bagehot
has undertaken a sort of general superintendence of the Economist and
Hutton remains Editor under him. Will you kindly allow Bagehot to call
upon you occasionally?"[24]

There were eighteen for dinner at Southampton on October 19,
the eve of the final leave-taking. Accompanying Wilson to India were

his wife, his daughter Sophia and her husband, the Indian civil servant William Halsey, and two unmarried daughters, Matilda and Zenobia, or Zoe. Eliza, Julia, and Emilie would stay behind. On the twentieth, the family and its well-wishers went together to say their goodbyes aboard the India-bound ship the *Pera*, moored three miles offshore. Emilie took her leave of her mother and sisters. Then she turned to her father:

> In an outburst of affection for him I threw my arms round his neck and kissed him; he did not respond, but stood quite still and looked beyond and away. A curious pained expression passed over his face . . . The thought perhaps that in a few weeks, half the world would be between him and his three children had struck his mind with painful vividness.

As Eliza paid endless rounds of social calls, Bagehot embarked on a whirl of professional ones. No small part of his superintendence of the *Economist* was searching for news to put in it. To this end, he traipsed from office to office and informant to informant, with Gladstone and Sir G. C. Lewis among his sources. To Zoe, by now in Calcutta, Bagehot described the life of a news supplicant:

> The great change of late to me is that having the Economist to look after. I come to London and call on public characters and sit (like Jet) with my mouth open hearing what they say. I do not say much myself, though I think if I was fifty and a cabinet minister, would not I talk platitudes?

Wilson and Bagehot wrote to each other almost every day. The son-in-law kept his father-in-law ("Dear Mr. Wilson") posted on political, financial, and journalistic developments at home. One such bulletin briefed the *Economist*'s absent proprietor about the launch of a new financial publication, the *Money Market Review*, whose maiden issue had alluded to a certain unnamed "journal of respectability" paying more attention to literature and politics than to business. Bagehot advised Wilson not to worry, "dull and feeble" as the upstart was. Ever inclined to take the gloomy side of an argument, said Bagehot, he was, with respect to the standing of the *Economist* in the suddenly growing market for financial and business news, decidedly "cheerful."[25]

The day following the Wilsons' arrival in Calcutta, November 30, was St. Andrew's Day. Wilson made his first public appearance in the strange new country at a dinner given by the Scottish diaspora of Calcutta. Then it was off to Meerut to meet Charles Canning, governor general of India, an overland journey of 800 miles. Wilson, the kind of person on whom nothing is lost, took in the scenery, the people, and the commercial tempo (gratifyingly upbeat). He was thrilled by the beauty and the promise of what he saw: "a flat, rich country teeming with people and the richest of crops of every description," he wrote to his daughters at home. "A goodly country to bear taxes."

The government was sorely in need of revenue. Before the Mutiny, the Indian government had owed its creditors £60 million, and the costs of suppressing the insurrection had pushed the debt to almost £100 million. To restore financial order, Wilson proposed an income tax—India's first—along with a license tax on traders, a tobacco tax, and a new paper currency.

At the close of December 1859, the Financial Member of the Supreme Council took his place at the Kashmere Gate, ceremonial entrance of the British rulers into Delhi and the scene of a bloody siege during the Mutiny. They entered on horseback, Wilson reported home, "I, as before, riding Lord Canning's English horse, Negus, a fine showy white horse. Lord Canning and Lord Clyde, with Lady Canning between them, headed the procession. Lines of troops with fine bands of music, our own Cavalcade, and the roadsides, streets and house-tops crowded with people: you may conceive how fine the sight was."[26]

The income tax sparked controversy, and not only from the Indians on whom the financial burden would fall. Charles Trevelyan, governor of the state of Madras, took the extraordinary step of issuing a public warning that Wilson's program would risk igniting a second uprising. Trevelyan soon found himself out of a job and on a ship bound for England. As for Wilson, he judged that the Indian people "are ready to submit to anything and to pay any taxes we impose; they are only astonished by our generosity and leniency after the deep offense we have received."[27]

As he had never failed to do in England, Wilson threw himself into his work. In February, he presented a budget that identified a massive deficit—of more than £9 million—and new taxes to fill the breach.[28] Public, political, and journalistic reception were favorable, not least in the pages of the *Economist*, but the hard work of collecting the taxes with which to bank the revenue remained. "It seems almost as if I had known nothing but India all my life," groaned Wilson, apologizing to Bagehot for his long neglect of family correspondence.[29]

No one was overly worried by the toll that this arduous labor exacted on Wilson's health, least of all Wilson, though he had been unwell since the start of the rainy season in May. He remained in Calcutta when old India hands, and the Wilson ladies, left the city in their annual migration to healthier summer quarters and the cooler mountain air. But on August 2, Wilson was felled by an attack of dysentery. He died on August 11. "Take care of my income tax," were among the final words he spoke; Halsey, Sophie's husband and Wilson's assistant, was at his bedside to hear them.[30]

British authorities sent word of his death to London by telegraph—they intended for the Wilson family to get the news through official channels. But it was Julia's cry at the Wilsons' Upper Belgrave Street home that sent up alarms. In her hands was a copy of *The Times*, which had scooped the government.

Bagehot instantly wrote to his parents. His father consoled him

with words that said much about the second father whom his son had
come to love:

> Hour after hour makes me feel more and more sad and my heart
> aches for you all more than I can describe. The loss of such a
> parent, and such a man is not easily borne, nor can its extent be
> at once comprehended. I think of you as a fellow sufferer quite
> with his own children. Your affection for him I know, and his for
> you was always shown in a way not to be mistaken, and the rela-
> tion of father to son seemed as complete as it could be. Your loss
> I cannot attempt to estimate. I will come to you whenever you
> wish. I feel almost that we have no right to intrude on sorrow so
> deep and trying.[31]

Bagehot could not come to grips with the fact of Wilson's death; the
older man's vitality seemed to preclude it. To Halsey, he confessed, "I
have never felt the shock of any event so much."[32]

Wilson was buried in Calcutta in what was described as the biggest
funeral in the city's history. Carriages bearing mourners made a two-
mile long procession to the burial ground.[33]

CHAPTER 8

THE "PROBLEM"
OF W. E. GLADSTONE

After the shock, death is a matter of details. Bagehot willingly dealt with the complications attending the distant death of his father-in-law. He was now, at the age of thirty-four, the patriarch of the Wilson family. In the company of Wilson's brothers, he was appointed an executor of his father-in-law's estate—indeed, the principal executor. He had formerly filled the temporary role as director of the *Economist*; now it became permanent.* To his sisters-in-law, he proved a godsend. "So completely one with us did we feel him to be, so naturally and unobtrusively did he at once take my father's place in managing all our family affairs and in settling all matters great and small in which our interests were concerned that perhaps, at the time, we hardly realized how much of the great blank he filled," Emilie testified."[1]

---

* Bagehot produced a fifty-page supplement to the *Economist* in tribute to its founder. In the early going, Wilson had put out the paper almost single-handedly, while simultaneously contributing to the London *Morning Chronicle*. "Long afterwards," Bagehot recounted, "he used to speak of this period as far more exhausting than the most exhausting part of a laborious public life. 'Our public men,' he once said, 'do not know what anxiety means; they have never known what it is to have their own position dependent on their own exertions.'" Walter Bagehot, *Memoir of the Right Hon. James Wilson* (London: Effingham Wilson, 1861), 23.

Perhaps, if Wilson had survived, Bagehot would have continued to live the balanced railroad-riding, banking, and literary life into which he had happily settled. It was pleasant to manage the Stuckey's branch at Bristol while writing odd pieces for his father-in-law's weekly newspaper, producing two or three long literary essays a year—his masterpiece "William Pitt" appeared in the July 1861 issue of the *National Review*—and enjoying the society that his marriage and literary reputation had opened up for him. But the old life was now impossible—there were not enough hours in the day to live it.

In May 1861, the Walter Bagehots quit their Clevedon home and moved to London, taking interim quarters in the home of Bonamy Price, professor of political economy at Oxford University and an adherent of a strain of such old-fashioned, high-purity laissez-faire as to have commended him to James Wilson.* The West Country was not entirely out of striking range from the couple's new London base and, in a staff capacity, Bagehot attended Stuckey's directors meetings at Langport, Bristol, Bridgwater, and Taunton. Now a Justice of the Peace for the county of Somerset, he attended his first meeting of the Petty Sessions at Taunton in January 1861. But it was out of the question for him to continue to work at Bristol, and Stuckey's allowed him to exchange that managerial position for lighter duties in London. By and by, he and Eliza, along with Eliza's mother and her two unmarried daughters, returned to the Wilson home on Upper Belgrave Street.

Once in India, Wilson had set in motion a chain of events that would place Bagehot in the *Economist*'s editor's chair. Instrumental in

---

* Gladstone later commented on how Price's uncompromising ideals contributed to a study of Irish agriculture: "the only man," he said of Price—"to his credit be it spoken—who has had the resolution to apply, in all their unmitigated authority, the principles of abstract political economy to the people and circumstances of Ireland, exactly as if he had been proposing to legislate for the inhabitants of Saturn or Jupiter." W. A. S. Hewins, "Price, Bonamy (1807–1888), economist," *Oxford Dictionary of National Biography*, 8 February 2018, http://www.oxforddnb.com/view/10.1093/ref:odnb/9780198614128.001.0001/odnb-9780198614128-e-22742.

this outcome was Meredith White Townsend, publisher of a respected English-language newspaper in Calcutta, *The Friend of India*. Tireless, enterprising, and accomplished, Townsend had worked in the country for ten years, not only producing—at times almost unassisted—his own paper, but also contributing to *The Times* and becoming fluent in Bengali. But now, his health failing, Townsend asked Wilson for advice on starting a newspaper in England. Possibly thinking of what a fine editor of the *Economist* his son-in-law would make, Wilson urged Townsend to hire the incumbent editor, Hutton. Townsend returned home to engage Hutton in what would prove to be a fruitful lifelong partnership at the *Spectator*, which Hutton and he revitalized and set on its course of distinction. With Hutton gone—and occupied in the literary work for which he was eminently suited—Bagehot added the editorship of the *Economist* to his previously conferred title of director.

Though not a father and destined never to become one, Bagehot was the paterfamilias of No. 12 Upper Belgrave Street. A late riser and no stickler for railroad time, he liked to linger over breakfast. It had been impossible in Clevedon, lest he miss his train. In London, with no train to catch, he would pace around the breakfast room long after the eggs had been cleared away, delighting his sisters-in-law with his fast and funny talk. He assured them that he preferred their company to that of the notables who crowded the Gladstones' breakfast parties.[2] It was not purely for social reasons that the Gladstones included Bagehot in these levees of the elite. They knew a rising journalistic and financial star when they saw one. Bagehot returned their good will.

IN 1859, GLADSTONE TOOK up the chancellorship for the second time, under Palmerston. It was customary for the chancellor of the exchequer to present the government's budget not merely in documentary form but also in a dramatic, sometimes hours-long speech—in Gladstone's case, on February 10, a four-hour oration on both the budget and a new French commercial treaty. To achieve this feat of stamina, he heaved himself out of his sickbed, arriving at the House of Commons at 4:30 p.m., began speaking at 5 p.m., and finished at 9 p.m.—"without great exhaustion," his diary recorded, "aided by a great stock of egg and wine. Thank God."[3]

The speech, the third-longest Gladstonian parliamentary stem-winder,[4] dealt with big themes as well as small facts, seasoned with pinches of Latin. As to the larger themes, the chancellor upheld free trade and attacked the idea that the best way to help the working classes was to reduce the tax they paid on the items they consumed. "This is good as far as it goes," he argued,

> But it is not this which has been mainly operative in bettering their condition as it has been bettered during the past ten or fifteen years. It is that you have set more free the general course of trade; it is that you have put in action the emancipating process that gives them the widest field and the widest rate of remuneration for their labor.[5]

As to the new commercial treaty, which provided for a deep reduction in the heavy British duties on French wine, Gladstone disposed of the canard that beer-loving Englishmen would drink no wine, even if you poured it down their throats. Of course they would—they had, once upon a time. "How was this consumption subsequently checked and discouraged? By the influence of prohibitive duties."[6] For the well-to-do, wine still served a medicinal purpose. And what of the poor, Gladstone demanded. He recounted a visit he had made to HMS *Scourge*, a British man-of-war. One of the seamen, recovering from an accident, was drinking wine under doctor's orders. What kind of wine, Gladstone asked his naval hosts. Why, the surgeon answered, wine from the officers' mess, the only potable supply on board. He urged Gladstone to taste the enlisted men's *vin ordinaire*, "and certainly," the statesman told the House, "it was with great difficulty that I succeeded in accomplishing the operation."[7]

Bagehot contended that, for anyone, the House of Commons was "the most severe audience in the world,"[8] though Gladstone might have quibbled that Bagehot himself was harder to please. In its coverage of the chancellor's speech, the *Economist* withheld all but the most measured praise: the fiscal plan was too ambitious for the short time allowed. Bagehot then followed up with one of his best biographical studies, a lengthy profile for the *National Review* titled "Mr. Gladstone."

Writers in the quarterly journals had an obligation to explore the personalities of the leading statesmen, Bagehot declared by way of preface. The politicians might not like it—indeed, many a reader might find it absurd. But "some deliberate truth should be spoken of our statesmen, and if Quarterly essayists do not speak it, who will?" Bagehot nominated himself for the task. Though his piece was unsigned, as such articles were until a dozen years later when the *Fortnightly* started to match bylines with headlines,[9] its style was no one else's.

Preliminaries out of the way, Bagehot sounded his theme: "Mr. Gladstone is a problem." What a piece of work: a great orator, of course, but likewise impulsive, frenetic, unanchored, mutable, unimaginative. Bagehot serves notice that he is about to perform a kind of journalistic vivisection, an act of courage: Gladstone was the second most powerful man in English politics, behind the prime minister. He was the leader of the majority party in the House of Commons and perhaps the most feared speaker in Parliament. Still, there was nothing else to do, no other way to speak some deliberate truth of this "singular man of genius."

One of the most enjoyable parts of Bagehot's essay is his attack on the pretensions of Gladstone's alma mater. "No one can deny to it very great and very peculiar merits," writes the University of London alumnus of Oxford University. "But certainly it is not an exciting place, and its education operates as a narcotic rather than as a stimulant."*

Yet he has to admit that Gladstone, so much the Oxford man, was anything but languid. He was the opposite: "He cannot let anything alone."[10] Even his literary criticism was frenetic, for the statesman was an amateur classicist: "His book on Homer is perhaps the most zealous work which this generation has produced."[11] Certainly, Gladstone had the "oratorical impulse"; on this alone the chancellor's friends and detractors could agree. He likewise had the "didactic impulse" and the "contentious impulse"—contentious, though far from bellicose; no politician hated war more than Gladstone or was more reluctant to finance it when hostilities became unavoidable. Moreover, he possessed a sixth sense about the English people: "He has the same sort of control over the minds of those he is addressing that a good driver has over the animals he guides: he feels the minds of his hearers as the driver the mouths of his horses."[12]

What the great man lacked was the anchor of principle, Bagehot goes on. In 1853, in his first tour as chancellor, under the prime ministership of Lord Aberdeen, Gladstone planned for the gradual extinction of the income tax, "an engine of gigantic power for national purposes," as he put it, only suitable in national emergencies. Reversing himself six years later, Gladstone declared that the income tax was a levy for all fiscal seasons. Bagehot said that he didn't fault the chancellor for shifting his position on the technical question; what troubled him was his about-face on the political principle underlying the tax.[13] Bagehot held

---

* The typical Oxford product, he continues, is the kind of languid critic who reviews a book in the *Saturday Review* (a stuffy journal to which Bagehot himself sometimes contributed). The book holds that a certain thing is correct, but that thing cannot, in fact, be correct, as the author "does not prove his case; there is one mistake in page 5, and another in page 113." Not that it matters much from the Oxford perspective. As Ralph Waldo Emerson satirized the Oxonian state of mind—Bagehot now quotes Emerson—"there is nothing true and nothing new, and no matter!" Walter Bagehot, *Biographical Studies*, 95.

that Gladstone did believe in truth—that is, he believed that there was such a thing as truth—but, like a clever lawyer, he was seemingly prepared to argue either side of a question of what constitutes that truth: "he has the soul of a martyr with the intellect of an advocate."[14]

Reservations aside, Bagehot ultimately concluded that Gladstone was fit to lead England. In Peel's time, the government's great work was the abolition of destructive laws—the Corn Laws, the Navigation Acts, and other such protectionist relics, for instance. Now comes the work of construction, a much harder task. "No one desires more than we do that Mr. Gladstone's future course should be enriched, not only with oratorical fame, but with useful power," Bagehot closes. "Such gifts as his are amongst the rarest that are given to men; they are amongst the most valuable; they are singularly suited to our parliamentary life. England cannot afford to lose such a man."

Gladstone's "oratorical fame" had seemed assured as soon as he spoke at the newly formed Oxford Union Society in 1830, at the age of twenty-one. Like the youthful Bagehot, he was a bit of a prig and no hand with the ladies. Unlike Bagehot, he won a seat in the House of Commons on his very first try, at the age of twenty-three (a seat, to be sure, in the close control of the young man's patron, the Duke of Newcastle).[15] An evangelical Anglican, Gladstone read the Bible every day, either in English or Greek. He read Dante, whom he revered, in the Italian, having taught himself the language, and he loved Homer—"Old Homer" to Gladstone—just as well. "German was still beyond him," biographer Roy Jenkins writes of the young Gladstone, "but he later acquired enough to be able in middle life to hold theological discussions with Ignaz von Dollinger in Munich."

Gladstone was, as charged, forever in motion. The Home Secretary who watched him execute his duties as a thirty-one-year-old vice president of the Board of Trade in 1841 recorded that "Gladstone could do in four hours what it took any other man sixteen to do and that he [nonetheless] worked sixteen hours a day." Nor was it only at work that he seemed a man possessed. He was a famous walker, sea-bather, feller of trees, train-traveler, reader (a lifelong total of 20,000 books), churchgoer (daily, when possible), author, and redeemer and counselor of London prostitutes. He wrote his first book, *The State in its Relations to the Church*—a work of 500 pages—in just over a month (it prescribed that the British government should employ none but communicating members of the Church of England).[16] His stamina was superhuman. One Friday evening in 1852, he made a late speech in the House of Commons, returned home after midnight, sat up all night to catch up on his correspondence, caught a 6 a.m. train to Birmingham, and walked 12 miles to his final destination. He was, he admitted, "sleepy enough" when evening rolled around.[17]

As Gladstone believed that he was put on earth to serve God, and as time was an irreplaceable resource, he husbanded minutes and hours. He called his diary, a seventy-year record almost as devoid of emotive color as Eliza Bagehot's, "an account book of the all-precious gift of Time."[18]

BAGEHOT DEALT WITH GLADSTONE in the many capacities of journalist, lobbyist, counselor, banker, and political candidate. Their journalistic relationship was, at first, a slightly awkward one, as Bagehot and the chancellor saw one another socially, sometimes at the Gladstones' famous political breakfasts. For Bagehot, as for any journalist in a similarly enviable position, a question arises: How to use the rich material that falls from the lips of one's knowledgeable host? Discretion is paramount, yet a precious quotation is never to be wasted. Besides, one's illustrious friend (let us call him) is a man of the world. He may wish that the words he chooses to utter should find their way into print, even, perhaps, attached to his name. Yet to request his permission to quote runs the risk of the dreaded reply that all is off the record—or, worse, a glance that conveys a rebuke for the impertinence of asking.

Perhaps some of these thoughts passed through Bagehot's mind as he wrote his finely wrought remembrance of Sir George Lewis, who died in 1863 while serving as Palmerston's Secretary of War. Properly proud of his essay, which ran in the July 1865 issue of the *National Review*, the author sent a copy with his compliments to Gladstone, an interested party in Sir George's career. He and Sir George had crossed swords over British policy toward America's Civil War, with Lewis successfully arguing against Gladstone for a policy of nonintervention.[19]

Gladstone approved of the article—"I think in every or almost every case your commendations of character as well as of his intellect are within rather than beyond the mark." He had, however, one question. Who was the unnamed authority that Bagehot quoted to draw a comparison between the formidable intellects of Lewis and Lewis's friend, the historian Thomas Babington Macaulay (who many years earlier had attacked Gladstone's *The State in its Relation with the Church* in the pages of the *Edinburgh Review*)?[20] Gladstone only wondered because he himself had drawn the same interesting comparison.

Bagehot hastened to apologize. He admitted that Gladstone himself was the anonymous source. Pleading creative necessity, he added, "It is very difficult in writing of recent persons not to allude to recent conversations—Half the life of a description is given by such details." Gladstone brushed the apology aside. "It was only that I aspired to the honor of having in whole or in part to do with the suggestion."[21]

Their professional acquaintanceship ripened. Bagehot earned the honorific "Spare Chancellor" for assistance tendered to Gladstone on many occasions. To judge by Gladstone's diary, that service was heavily concentrated in 1864–65 in the conceiving and drafting of legislation to regulate the circulating notes of the English country banks. The editor of the *Economist* and vice chairman of Stuckey's had a vital interest in the subject.

It was, indeed, in the multifaceted capacity of banker–lobbyist–editor–political aspirant that Bagehot visited the chancellor on March

3, 1864. Today, such an overlay of professional roles might set in motion
half a dozen ethics committees, but not then. Neither Bagehot nor
Gladstone seemed to find anything objectionable in a journalist who
pled his case—necessarily, an intermingled private and public one—
before a ranking politician, who would endorse that journalist for elec-
tive office just a couple of years later.

The question Bagehot raised now was whether banks like Stuckey's
should be allowed to continue to issue their own currency—a right that
the Act of 1844 had severely curtailed. And if so, should those issues be
taxed? Might the issuing bankers protest against such taxation less vehe-
mently if, in exchange for that exaction, there were relief from certain
regulatory restrictions? Gladstone set to work to draft a bill to resolve
these evergreen issues of Victorian banking policy.

In the days before checking accounts, private currency did yeo-
man's service in the English countryside. In exchange for his deposit, a
customer received his bank's own home-printed scrip in lieu of a credit
to a bank balance. It was money that he could spend or hoard. Under
law, the holder could convert the notes to gold coin or notes of the Bank
of England whenever he wished, but it fell to the issuing bank to manage its affairs as prudently as Stuckey's customarily did. Some banks fell
short of the mark, in which case the note-holder might come running to
convert his notes before his bank's gold ran out.

In general, the English financial establishment was hostile to the
country banks' ability to issue notes: the Bank of England's note issuance was taxed—not so the country issues. And the Bank of England's
note issue was adequately secured by gold and government securities—
not so, or, rather, not invariably so, was the country scrip. Nor were the
country bankers uniformly friendly toward the political and monetary
establishment. Seemingly arbitrary laws thwarted sound business practice: one forbade a country bank of issue from putting itself up for sale,
along with its note-issuing franchise; another barred a private bank,
organized as a six-man partnership, from bringing in additional part-

ners; still another barred joint-stock banks of issue from the lucrative London market.

There were many other anomalies in the crazy-quilt of English banking regulations. Gladstone, with Bagehot at his elbow, sought to begin the work of rationalization.

A committee of country banks of issue—in which Bagehot held an executive position—was only too happy to advise the chancellor on how to proceed. Between February and June 1865, the *Economist* produced five articles on the legislation,* and over the same period, Bagehot met with Gladstone on thirteen occasions; the banker-cum-journalist-cum-lobbyist advised by post, too. In one letter the editor acknowledged his personal interest, and wondered if Gladstone was perhaps not smiling at the thought that "those who are to pay the tax are not exactly the people to judge how great it should be." If so, said Bagehot in his own defense, "I can only say in answer that I *really* believe my reasoning to be true, and that hardly any one knows *all* the ins and outs of a trade who has not an interest of some sort or other."[22]

Bagehot counseled not only Gladstone but also a senior civil servant in the Treasury office, George Arbuthnot. Arbuthnot, in correspondence with Gladstone, praised Bagehot for his clear thinking and the fairness with which he approached the Act of 1844, the *Economist*'s longtime legislative punching bag. He mentioned Bagehot's "influence as the Conductor of an influential and ably edited Newspaper and withal his remarkable freedom from prejudice," and reported that the deputy governor of the Bank of England "talked of the *Economist*, and said that Bagehot was writing well and honestly, in constant communication with them."[23]

From Gladstone, via Arbuthnot, comes a historical revelation:

---

* The paper made no mention of its editor's interest in the outcome of the debate. Then again, it would be many years before the ethically sterilizing phrase "to declare an interest" became standard on Fleet Street.

Bagehot, the erstwhile advocate of minimal government interference in banking, broached a suggestion to Gladstone that anticipated the financial socialism of the twentieth and twenty-first centuries. He proposed that the government might guarantee the value of privately issued bank notes.

Bagehot floated this idea in a meeting with Gladstone on March 3, 1864. Gladstone relayed the gist of the discussion to Arbuthnot: "I have seen Mr. Bagehot. He thinks we might: 1 make the Notes a first charge [i.e., the senior-most liability of the issuing banks]. 2 require the periodical exhibition of a certain portion of Assets [i.e., demand more financial disclosure from the issuing banks]. 3 give State guarantees to the Notes."[24]

As it was, the country issuers had to bear the cost of providing collateral to support their outstanding note issues. Such collateral either earned no interest, as with gold, or minimal interest, as with government securities. A sovereign guarantee would be a boon to the profitability of banks that, like Stuckey's, funded a portion of their assets with circulating notes.[*]

Whether Bagehot was advocating for a reasonable policy or a wild, mind-expanding possibility, the chancellor did not say. Either way, in the context of the economic orthodoxy of Victorian Britain, it was a radical suggestion. One might well have asked, what gave a privately owned bank any claim to the credit of Her Majesty's Treasury? The question, long dormant, would rise up to torment the politics of the twenty-first century. A state guarantee of the bankers' notes in 1864 would have brought the taxpayers into the banking business several generations before deposit insurance, the too-big-to-fail doctrine, and the rest of the modern machinery of socialized financial risk came to fruition.

The legislative broth that these innumerable cooks prepared finally

---

[*] In the case of Stuckey's, as of June 30, 1864, 11 percent of the liabilities comprised notes, 78 percent deposits and other claims.

took the form of a proposition that the issuing banks could take or leave: they could elect to pay a tax of one percent of their circulation for fifteen years, in exchange for regulatory relief, and at the end of that period, Parliament could make new demands on them. Probably, Bagehot predicted in the *Economist*, Parliament would do just that, boosting the one percent tax on outstanding bank notes or requiring more collateral to protect note-holders against default.[25]

In the end, Bagehot's and Gladstone's hard work was for naught. On June 1, the chancellor withdrew the legislation, which had pleased no one. The proposed tax had especially displeased the bankers.[26]

BAGEHOT HAD ONLY JUST succeeded Richard Hutton at the *Economist* when the American secession crisis erupted in 1860. It was the biggest story in the world, and the *Economist* was bound to cover it, certainly its many financial and commercial facets. Whose side was Bagehot on?

The new editor had never visited the United States. He had said his piece against the vulgarity of American politics in 1859 ("men of refinement shrink from the House of Representatives as from a parish vestry"). As for Americans in general, he had conceived a general disapproval from his knowledge of a sample of the brash and thrusting Yankees who passed through London. He held a dim view of Abraham Lincoln and the politicians who remained in Washington after the southerners decamped: "How can men who have risen to power by low means be expected to use power for lofty purposes?" he demanded of the *Economist*'s readers in August 1861. "How can men who are where they are because they have truckled and temporized and cajoled and cringed and fawned upon the mob, now coerce the mob to do its duty, or overawe it into obedience and order?"[27] He opposed slavery, while clinically observing that the peculiar institution at least afforded the slave-drivers the leisure for cultural development.[28]

Editorial writers don the mantle of omniscience as judges do their robes. Standing over his desk—for he worked on his feet—the editor of the *Economist* wrote with the confidence of a man who had read the as yet unwritten history of the Civil War. Away from his office at No. 340 Strand, Bagehot would have had no quarrel with the observation that as human events are unforeseeable, the prudent forecaster must deal in probabilities, not certainties. At his post, attired in editorial vestments, Hutton's successor kept up professional pretenses.

The *Economist* had no correspondent in the United States. Its principal source of reportage on the war, like that of many Britons, was *The Times*, whose American reporter for the Northern states, Charles Mackay, a Scotch versifier, journalist, and anthologist,* sent home dispatches that confirmed the biases of his rabidly anti-Northern editors. Bagehot labored under the further disadvantage that the Palmerston government made him privy to official information. On the eve of the bombardment of Fort Sumter, Sir George Lewis, Palmerston's secretary of war, wrote to Bagehot to vent his frustration over the vagueness of the North's strategic aims. What would the Union do if it won, he asked:

> To restore the old Union would be an absurdity. What other state of things does that village lawyer Lincoln contemplate as the fruit of victory? It seems to me that the men in power in Washington are much such persons as in this country get possession

---

* In financial circles, Mackay is remembered for his 1841 production *Extraordinary Popular Delusions and the Madness of Crowds*, the story of alchemy, the South Sea Bubble, the tulip-bulb craze, and other such manias. It is cited to this day in opposition to the doctrine that the financial markets are somehow more coolly calculating— more "efficient"—than the people who operate in them. *The Times* recalled MacKay from his post late in 1863, substituting for him the more objective Antonio Gallenga Turin. "Now and then," dryly commented Charles Francis Adams, American Minister to the Court of St. James's, of the change in tone at *The Times*, "it goes so far as to admit a friendly article, correcting its own views." Allan Nevins, *The War For The Union: The Organized War, 1863-1864*, (New York: Charles Scribner's Sons, 1971), 505-6.

of a disreputable joint stock company. There is almost the same amount of ability and honesty.[29]

Bagehot took the argument to heart. He was still quoting from the letter in 1864: "After nearly three years of experience, it would be difficult to describe Washington more justly."[30]

It was Bagehot's view at the time that the Queen's ministers possessed "special information, long consultations, skilled public servants to guide them." No doubt Sir George, a devoted friend of Bagehot's late father-in-law, and Gladstone, the chancellor, whom Bagehot likewise consulted, knew things that others didn't. The trouble was that those things were often wrong.

The historian Hugh Brogan has shown how the *Economist* and *The Times* erred in lockstep. Evidently under the influence of the government, they were the purveyors of "fashionable English fallacy."[31] Each publication predicted a Southern victory; each asserted that, in any case, the North could never coerce the South back into the Union; each overestimated the human cost of the war, terrible as it actually was. Bagehot, an admirer of Lincoln's secretary of the Treasury, Salmon Chase, spared himself the embarrassment of duplicating *The Times*'s prediction that the North would spend itself into bankruptcy.

It rankled the free-trading *Economist* that the Union was raising its tariffs on English manufactures. Richard Cobden and John Bright, the *Economist*'s old comrades from Anti-Corn Law days, were similarly disapproving of the Union's insults to free trade. What the old radicals did not begrudge the North was the necessity of financing its war. It was a war—so Cobden and Bright saw it—against slavery. To Hutton, too, now happily settled at the *Spectator*, the war was as simple as slavery.

It was not so simple to Bagehot. In the *Economist* of August 17, 1861, which appeared shortly after news of the Federal defeat at Bull Run, Bagehot asserted that, really, the South was only fighting to choose its own government, something that no democrat—and the North, by its own estimation, was nothing if not democratic—could honestly deny it: "the abolition sentiment has nothing to do with the quarrel," Bagehot propounded, "and the Protection tariff a great deal, and the mere lust of dominion and of empire more than either."

Far from supporting slavery, as Bagehot argued early the next year, the *Economist* wished for emancipation. So did John Elliott Cairnes,* but whereas the rising Irish economist wanted to see the South defeated, the *Economist* hoped to see it victorious. "It is because," Bagehot tried to explain,

> we wish well to the Africans—because we are ardently bent upon their immediate improvement and their ultimate emancipation—that we wish for a dissolution of that Union which has hitherto crushed them down by its banded, undivided, and resistless might.

"Sometimes," notes the historian of the *Economist*, Ruth Dudley Edwards, "Bagehot's propensity for paradox led him down peculiar paths."[32]

AT 6 P.M. ON Monday, October 7, 1862, Gladstone stood before an enthusiastic dinner crowd of 500 in the Town Hall in the northeast English constituency of Tyneside. He addressed them, in part, on America's Civil War. "We may have our own opinions about slavery," said the chancellor; "we may be for or against the South, but there is no

---

* Cairnes, professor of jurisprudence and political economy at Queens College, Galway, and the author of *The Slave Power*, demolished Bagehot's argument in a letter to the editor which the *Economist* gamely printed two weeks later. The next year, Henry Ward Beecher returned to New York from a trip to England and addressed 2,000 of his admirers at the Brooklyn Academy of Music. Cairnes's name raised a cheer from the crowd when Beecher mentioned him among the many Britons who supported the North. Hutton and the *Spectator*, too, were named. Bagehot was not. "Mr. Beecher's Reception in Brooklyn," *New York Tribune*, November 20, 1863.

doubt that Jefferson Davis and other leaders of the South have made an army; they are making, it appears, a navy; and they have made what is more difficult than either, they have made a nation."[33]

Years later, Gladstone could hardly believe that he had said it—a ranking minister of Her Majesty's Government seeming to commit his Cabinet colleagues, whom he had not consulted, to the recognition of the Confederacy, a course of action that might have led to a diplomatic rupture with the United States, quite possibly war.[34] Others reached the same conclusion the moment they read Gladstone's shocking words. The *Spectator*, the *Morning Star*, and the *Daily News*, among other pro-Federal journals ranging from establishment to working-class, rushed to condemn them.[35]

Bagehot did not condemn. He excused Gladstone's intemperance— the chancellor was known to be "impulsive"—and, besides, "an orator, especially an eloquent orator, when on his legs is apt, unless he be cool as well as experienced, to say rather what he thinks and feels than what he intends." Sir George Lewis had quickly followed Gladstone's speech with a denial, on behalf of the Palmerston government, of any intention to recognize the Confederacy, and this position the *Economist* approved. But as for the political and strategic premises on which Gladstone based his ill-advised remarks, the paper was one with the chancellor:

> that the independence of the Southern Confederacy is a certain
> fact if not a *fait accompli*; that Jefferson Davis and his coadjutors
> have made the Confederacy a nation; that there is not the slight-
> est prospect of their subjugation or forcible re-annexation; and
> that both by the resolution they have shown, the strength they
> have put forth, and the victories they have won, they have shown
> that they can earn, if they have not yet fully earned the right to
> be admitted into the society of the world as a substantive and
> sovereign State.[36]

The *Economist* failed to reckon with the resolution and strength of Abraham Lincoln, who issued the Emancipation Proclamation on September 22, 1862, five days after Union Major General George B. McClellan checked the northern advance of Confederate forces at the Battle of Antietam. It was a controversial measure even within the Lincoln administration. The 1860 Republican platform had pledged only to contain slavery within the states where it existed, not to abolish it, and Lincoln himself was on record as saying that his "paramount object in this struggle is to save the Union." Freeing the slaves in the rebellious South—though in none of the loyal slaveholding border states—was fraught with risk. The slaves might refuse to work, which is what Lincoln had in mind. But what then? Would their masters not retaliate? Samuel Ward, brother of the poet Julia Ward Howe, author of "The Battle Hymn of the Republic," and a trusted and astute informant of Secretary of State William H. Seward, warned that the rebel leaders would kill their slaves, just as they had burnt their cotton. The Emancipation Proclamation raised questions strategic, legal, political, and moral. Perhaps the only result it was certain to achieve was intensifying the terrible fury of Southern whites.[37]

The news reached London shortly before Gladstone's ill-advised speech. Pro-Northern elements were jubilant: they had had little sympathy with Lincoln trying to hold together the fragile coalition of anti-slavery radicals, anti-abolition conservatives, and slavery-tolerant, pro-Union border states. Like American abolitionists, they yearned for the moral clarity of a complete, uncompromising break from the pestilential institution of slavery. Editorial comment followed its expected course: Hutton, in the *Spectator*, regretted that the proclamation did not apply to every state, loyal or rebellious, and to every slave; *The Times*, sneering at the strategic weakness of the Union cause, imagined blood-soaked reprisals and counter-reprisals between ex-slaves and former masters.

The emancipation order came as no real surprise. *The Economist* had anticipated something of the kind in early September. Bagehot was skeptical of what it might accomplish. "Is there, in fact," he wondered, "any grounds for assuming that, as a body, the negroes would prefer being their own masters with Northern treatment to being cared for and occasionally maltreated by their Confederate owners?"* He concluded, emphatically: "Our conviction is very strong, that the Southerners will never yield, that the Northerners will never subdue them, that no emancipation policy will materially influence the result."

Right or wrong, Bagehot was usually thoughtful, invariably serious. In the October 25 *Economist*, he sifts the "Meaning and Probable Consequences" of the now published text of Lincoln's decree. His essay is a model of lucid, taut, deductive reasoning. Journalism schools could assign it to aspiring editorialists to illustrate the myriad ways in which a brilliant and self-confident commentator can err.

Beginning with an acknowledgment of how little he knew, or could know, about the American war, Bagehot adopts a tone of quasi-omniscience. *The Times* has no business characterizing Lincoln's policy as "atrocious," Bagehot insists. The *Economist* is rather prepared to settle for a judgment of "dishonest and foolish." He objects to the Emancipation Proclamation on constitutional grounds—Lincoln had no authority to issue it, even in wartime—and on the grounds of humanity—"To arm savages against your antagonist is to make war like savages, and to descend to the level of savages."

---

* According to historian Eugene R. Dattel, in 1863–64 there was not much to distinguish slavery on an antebellum plantation, on the one hand, and work for hire under some Northern lessees of Southern plantations, on the other. Former slaves "were not allowed to leave the plantation without a pass." In 1864, two black wage-earners out of three were defrauded of their pay; they earned $10 a month. Then again, as the historian Adam Rowe observes, defrauding two-thirds of former slaves "still represents an unambiguous improvement for the one-third, and, at worst, a wash for the others." Eugene R. Dattel, "Cotton and the Civil War," *Mississippi History Now*, July 2008, http://mshistorynow.mdah.state.ms.us/articles/291/cotton-and-the-civil-war.

Savages? Bagehot clarifies: "The African race are not, as a rule, either bloodthirsty or vindictive. On the contrary, they are patient, most enduring, and usually contented and attached to their employers [sic] and their homes, though lazy and, above all things, not willing to labor unless they are laboring for themselves." How the editor of a London periodical came by this intimate knowledge of African-American ethnic culture, he does not let on.

Against the charge of racism it may be said in his defense that Bagehot was impartially contemptuous of the "lower orders" of all races. The educated classes should govern, he believed, although he made an exception of France and, for many years, of the United States. However, his warnings now that the Emancipation Proclamation would sink Americans into still deeper depths of "desperation and ferocity" were ones that many credited, including people in close touch with Lincoln's own Cabinet.

"How can a humane man," Bagehot wondered,

a thoughtful man, and a just man—and we believe Mr. Lincoln to be naturally all three—have ventured to urge a multitude of ignorant, helpless, excitable Negroes to revolt against their masters, when perfectly aware that he can afford them neither aid nor protection in their outbreak, and that he has been preparing for them only certain discomfiture and cruel punishment? This seems to us the very wantonness of unfeeling selfishness.[38]

And two years later, the *Economist* judged it "undeniable" that

Mr. Lincoln's administration has given satisfaction to no one. Its notorious and unprecedented corruption has disgusted the lovers of public purity and decency; its numerous acts of illegal and stupid tyranny have alienated the lovers of liberty and constitutional right; its military incapacity has disgusted all; while its inconsistent, timid, and tentative proceedings on the slavery question have alarmed and offended the Democratic masses, without having given confidence or satisfaction to the hearty abolitionists."[39]

JAMES WILSON'S PAPER WAS a business paper; if Hutton had been unaware of that fact, his successor had absorbed it from the founder himself. What the readers expected, and what Bagehot delivered, was analysis of the financial side of public events, including the American Civil War.

Interest rates were low and steady in London in early 1863, with long-dated British government securities priced to yield 3.25 percent. It was a good time to dangle a 7 percent coupon before the income-seeking public.

The Confederate States of America did even better than 7 percent: through the French firm Emile Erlanger & Co., the government in Richmond, Virginia, offered £3 million worth of twenty-year bonds bearing a 7 percent coupon. Priced at 90, i.e., 90 percent of face, or par value, they promised a yield to maturity on the order of 8 percent. Beyond that glittering rate of return, the bonds were exchangeable at par into a pound of cotton at the rate of 6 pence sterling, the equivalent per pound of 12.2 American cents (or, actually, in view of the discounted offering price, at 5½ pence, or 11.1 American cents, per pound). On March 19, as the bonds came to market, cotton in Liverpool fetched 20 pence a pound, or the equivalent of 42.5 American cents.

A buyer of the Confederate securities could elect to make the exchange for cotton at any time on sixty days' notice, though he would have to come calling himself for as long as the war dragged on. The cotton would be waiting for him "in the interior" of the Confederacy not more than 10 miles from a railroad or a navigable stream, thence to the ocean, and, perhaps, into the waiting arms of the United States Navy. The Union blockade was by no means impenetrable, but a would-be blockade-runner bore risks that a passive investor in British government debt did not.

One day, the war would end, possibly in Confederate victory—many in London expected it—or through an armistice brokered by concerned European powers—and not a few in London expected that. If hostilities ended and the Confederacy survived, the bondholder's cotton would be delivered free of charge to the ports of Charleston, Savannah, Mobile, or New Orleans.

Applying for bonds, a speculator was obliged to put down only 5 percent of face value. Another 10 percent was due upon allotment, with additional fractional payments of 10 percent or 15 percent falling due on the first of every month from May through October. As of October 1, the £90 pound purchase price would be fully paid.

Here was an imaginative, options-laden junk bond. Confederate partisans and cotton bulls alike rushed to sign on.* In early trading, the securities spurted to a small premium to the offering price.

How did the *Economist* appraise this unusual opportunity?

Bagehot wrote a good analysis whose shortcomings reveal less about his fallibility than the difficulty of financial forecasting.† He begins by observing that the Confederacy was borrowing money in Europe,

---

* W. E. Gladstone was one of these punters, as were John Thadeus Delane, the editor of *The Times*; A. J. B. Beresford Hope, proprietor of the *Saturday Review*; and J. S. Gilliat, a director of the Bank of England. A list of more than 300 English investors was published shortly after the war, producing much embarrassment and recrimination, along with many denials. See John Bigelow, *Lest We Forget: Gladstone, Morley and the Confederate Loan of 1863, a rectification*, New York: The De Vinne Press, 1905; for the original list of investors, see the John Bigelow correspondence and papers held in the New York Public Library's Brooke Russell Astor Reading Room for Rare Books and Manuscripts.
† This article from the March 21, 1863, *Economist*, which bears every mark of Bagehot's style and intellect, is omitted from *The Collected Works*.

"while the Federal Government has been unable to obtain a shilling from that usually liberal and enterprising quarter."

He describes the bonds, along with their potential risks. Could the Confederacy deliver enough cotton to satisfy its creditors? Bagehot demonstrates how relatively small the volume of cotton earmarked for the bond-holders—250,000 bales, or one-tenth of annual British cotton imports from those states in a prosperous year. Would the future price of cotton likely rise or fall? Bagehot makes a thorough and plausible case that the price would tend to fall but that 6 pence per pound would likely prove to be the floor. Would the Southern states repudiate this debt, as the state of Mississippi had done with its own in 1841? Unlikely: "No young State, with a character to make and a position to confirm, would commence its national existence by such a shallow and dishonoring blunder."

There was, finally, the risk that the Confederacy would lose the war. Nothing to worry about on that score, Bagehot judges: "as our readers know, we should be inclined to estimate very lightly. It is so slight that, of itself, it need not deter any man from sharing in an 8 per cent loan."

Yet the price of the cotton bonds was presently sawn in half; by year-end 1863, it had dropped to the low 30s. It rallied with the price of cotton in 1864 only to collapse, along with the Confederacy, in 1865. A flicker of interest persisted for years after the Southern defeat, even after the 1868 passage of the Fourteenth Amendment to the Constitution, which prohibited the United States or any individual state from discharging a debt incurred in the service of the rebellion.[40]

FOR FOUR YEARS, Bagehot had predicted a Southern victory. He had argued for the political, if not the moral, equivalency "of the continuance of slavery and the maintenance of the Union." Both were "injurious to mankind."[41]

In February 1865, nine weeks before Appomattox, rumors of peace swirled in the City of London. Bagehot called them premature: The Confederacy "have still large armies in the field; they have still the ablest generals of the Republic in their ranks," he said.[42] Not until the fall of Richmond did Bagehot confront the fact that the Confederacy was defeated and he was wrong.

With no acknowledgment of previous error, the *Economist* saluted the victorious North, adapting Gibbon for the occasion: "panic did not for a moment unnerve the iron courage of the American democracy." The editor did not linger long on the momentous historical moment, and instead, getting down to business, expertly speculated on the course of postwar prices and trade. In this piece he is measured, intelligent, epigrammatic. Of the complexities introduced by the "present vast and delicate division of labor," he wrote, "When everybody is working for everybody, everybody is injured by the mischances of everybody."[43]

Persevering readers of the *Economist* may not have recognized the Abraham Lincoln of Bagehot's post-assassination eulogy. It was a true and moving, if unexpected, portrait: "Power and responsibility visibly widened his mind and elevated his character. Difficulties, instead of irritating him as they do most men, only increased his reliance on patience; opposition, instead of ulcerating, only made him more tolerant and determined."[44]

A Scottish newspaper of no great pretension had reached much the same conclusion at the end of 1863. "President Lincoln," declared the *Caledonian Mercury* of Edinburgh,

> speaks of the attitude assumed toward the United States by European governments without irritation . . . He speaks without acerbity even of the rebels who have done so much to bring calamity upon the country . . . When we recollect the rancorous hate entertained in this country toward the Indian rebels

[a reference to the Indian Mutiny of 1857–58] we feel humili-
ated that this "village attorney," this "rail splitter from Illinois,"
should have shown himself so superior to the mass of monarchical statesmen.[45]

Superior to Gladstone, and, no less, to Gladstone's journalistic confidant, Walter Bagehot.

CHAPTER 9

"THEREFORE, WE ENTIRELY APPROVE"

Toward financial innovation, Bagehot kept an open and receptive mind. Though conservative in his approach to bank credit—as befitted an officer, and, as of 1856, a director, of Stuckey's Banking Company—he was hospitable to new ideas about finance and central banking alike. Some thought him a heretic.

One point of controversy was seemingly minute: was it advisable for London depository institutions to pay interest on checking, or demand, accounts? At savings banks, such payment was customary and unobjectionable—the depositors and their funds were presumably committed for the long pull. Stuckey's, a commercial bank, paid interest on demand deposits which it had reason to believe were at some small risk of being hastily withdrawn. (In forming this judgment, it helped that the managers knew the depositors personally.) Interest on millions of pounds' worth of impersonal checking, or "floating," balances—belonging to owners whom the managers of London banks could hardly be expected to know—was another thing, and the City's banks and bill brokers drew criticism for paying it. The depositors' money wasn't just lying around in the vault, but was out on loan or otherwise earning interest—as the depositors would readily discover if they came running for it all at once.

Bagehot welcomed these newfangled floating balances. They had financed the magnificent growth of British international trade, he pointed out, which would not have been possible without the inducement of interest payments to innumerable British capitalists large and small. It was no mystery why the growth in deposits had surged at such flourishing new institutions as the London and Westminster, the London Joint Stock Bank, and the Union Bank of London. Seeing an unfilled need in the money market, the pioneers had profitably filled it.[1]

Bagehot was likewise an adherent of limited liability in banking, though there was only one bank in the realm whose stockholders did not live with the threat of a ruinous contingent liability: the Bank of England. In the days before deposit insurance and the notion that some banks were too big to fail, the responsibility for a bank's insolvency fell squarely on the owners of the collapsed institution, and this was the rule for small private partnerships as well as the newer and larger joint-stock organizations.

Traditionalists had long contended that this was where the onus of insolvency properly belonged. Personal accountability correctly focused the owners' attention on the management of their own institution—certainly, that was the intent of the law. Bagehot, who dearly loved a paradox, denied that the intent secured the reality:

> The system of *un*limited liability is that which fosters the most *speculative* management. It is that system which makes bankers out of men who have nothing to lose—who do not object to subject all their property to liability, because they have no property—who are as reckless in the use of money as in the mode of obtaining it—who have never known the caution which the very possession of property teaches—who, like the directors of the Royal British Bank [which had failed in 1856], squander idly what they have acquired improperly.[2]

There was some truth to his argument, though the proprietors of many a profitable bank—Bagehot need have looked no further than his own—slept soundly in their confidence that professional managers were conducting the business as if it were their own.

In any case, the House of Commons saw the matter as the *Economist* did. Passage of the Companies Act of 1867 lifted the sword of Damocles of unlimited liability from any bank that wished to avail itself of the new form of organization, and it proved a powerful stimulant to new financial enterprise. To invest when one's entire net worth was at risk was, for many a thoughtful person, unacceptable. Limited liability defined the downside; it might be steep, but one could know it. "Thousands of men, who under the old system, would rather have invested their money at 3 percent at home than risk it abroad for 50, are now ready to place it abroad for 15, rather than keep it at home for 5."[3]

George Joachim Goschen, later Viscount Goschen, wrote those words early in 1865 while reflecting on the persistence of high interest rates in the United Kingdom. In 1864, they had averaged 7 percent. Though far from the highest rate on record, it was likely the highest average rate on record for a single year, and borrowers chafed at the cost. What, if anything, should the Bank of England do to reduce it? Goschen answered, nothing.

The eldest son and second of ten children born to a successful London banker, Goschen had assimilated the doctrines of pure laissez-faire from Bonamy Price, an assistant master at Rugby school when Goschen attended in 1845 who would later find an intellectual helpmeet in James Wilson. At Oriel College, Oxford, Goschen excelled at the classics and presided over the Oxford Student Union. Next came an apprenticeship at the family bank, Fruhling and Goschen, including a two-year posting to what is today Colombia. "Become a great merchant," his father counseled him; "a little one is but a poor beast." Upon his return to England from South America, Goschen joined the Court of Directors of the Bank of England in 1858, at the age of twenty-seven.* In 1861, he produced an influential book on the international money market, *The Theory of the Foreign Exchanges*, which explained what animates profit-seeking people in a self-regulating money market. Years later, a critic would say that the only other Victorian contemporary who could have written it was Bagehot. Goschen, a free-trading Liberal, entered Parliament in 1863. In the City of London, his parliamentary constituency, he earned the sobriquet "Fortunate Youth."[4]

So Goschen spoke with authority when he attributed the persistence of high interest rates to the progress of the age—to the broadening of the money market that had come about by passage of the new limited liability law. Dozens of new banks and finance companies were collecting formerly stagnant puddles of English savings "into large and available streams" (an observation with which Bagehot would have agreed).[5] One might have supposed that the opposite was true, that a glut of savings should depress the cost of borrowing. But the demand for savings was itself on the upswing, the argument went. It, too, was enlarged by the advent of limited liability banking. Indeed, the growth in demand was greater than the growth in supply; hence, rising interest rates.

No more, under the new system, did the prudent investor in a British financial institution confront a worst-case scenario of personal ruin. Potential loss was rather capped at the face, or par, value of the shares that he or she purchased. Investors in new flotations put down a percentage of par—perhaps a fifth or a quarter—with the understanding that another increment was callable later, in predetermined install-

---

* As it took a director twenty years or so to succeed to the office of governor, and as the governor's office could be physically and intellectually demanding, the court liked its new blood young. Walter Bagehot, *Lombard Street: A Description of the Money Market* (London: Henry S. King & Co., 1873), 209.

ments. There was a chance of an unscripted call from the directors in case of trouble, but a limited liability company had no further claim on its stockholders than par value.

Thus liberated from potentially limitless loss, financiers reconsidered the field of opportunity and found it to be bigger and more alluring than before, as Goschen observed. The British government borrowed at 3 percent with the assurance of absolute safety. The Turkish government, with no such assurance, willingly paid 12 percent to 15 percent; the Egyptian government, 8 percent to 9 percent; the government of the Confederate States of America, as discussed earlier, 7 percent—along with that option on the price of cotton.[6] Henceforth, Her Majesty's Treasury had to compete for funds against other riskier, and commensurately higher-yielding, sovereign borrowers. Similarly, British merchants and manufacturers faced financial competition from higher-yielding foreign businesses.

The 1860s were a time of upheaval. The Reform Act of 1867—enacted by a Conservative government over the protests of Liberals like Bagehot—ultimately granted the franchise to an estimated 830,000 new voters, a 61 percent expansion of the British electorate. A comparable extension of the financial franchise took place in the City of London. In the era of unlimited liability, financial institutions had been, of necessity, private clubs; not just anybody could join one, for not just anybody could meet an emergency call for capital. Private partnerships, operating behind closed doors, amassed private wealth. "The individual grew rich by a secret operation unintelligible to the masses," Goschen observed,

who had strange visions of occult and mysterious processes by which money was coined in the City, but how they hardly tried to guess. Now, on the contrary, trade is carried on before the eyes of the general public. The public itself is admitted to the secrets of the guild. Not only does it witness the process, but it is also invited to share in the profits. [7]

The new limited liability companies would operate in the open, or so the theory had it. They would admit new money, and a new class of investor, into British capitalism.

So 7 percent was a market-determined rate in a time of greater tolerance for financial risk. High rates of interest would persist for as long as foreign demand for English savings remained robust—and as long as the new financial intermediaries remained in place to channel those savings effectively. Goschen judged the chance that foreign demand for British capital would decline to be "very remote." Yet he ventured no odds on whether the new finance companies would survive—the ones that had proliferated in the bull stock market of 1863–64, such as the Egyptian Trading Company, the Australian Mortgage Land and Finance Company, the International Land Credit Company, the English and Foreign Credit Company, the International Financial Company, or the General Credit and Finance Company. Goschen did not imagine the collapse that duly ensued, and, with that wave of finance company failures, a plunge in British interest rates.[8]

Goschen had no claim to a literary reputation, but his long financial essays in the *Edinburgh Review* rose to the high standard set by Bagehot in the *National Review*. Both authors were bankers by trade and Liberals in politics. Both saw more good than harm in the flood of new limited-liability company formations. Lord Overstone, that most severe arbiter of financial and monetary rectitude, judged Goschen a "man of high standing as regards ability, education and integrity."[9] The same arbiter pronounced Bagehot a "fool."[10]

OVERSTONE'S AVERSION TO BAGEHOT'S view of central banking is easily explained. Under Bagehot, as under Wilson, the *Economist* opposed Peel's Act—which was, in good part, Overstone's act. He had championed it as the means to prevent the Bank of England from over-issuing paper money. The *Economist*, among other critics, contended that the

If Murder! murder! Rape! murder!
O you Villain! what have I kept my Honor
untainted so long, to have it broke up, by you at last?
O Murder! Rape! Ravishment! Ruin! Ruin! Ruin!!!

J.G! inv!

POLITICAL-RAVISHMENT, or The Old Lady of Threadneedle-Street in danger! Pub! May 22! 1797. by H Humphrey St James's Street

LOANS

BANK
of
ENGLAND

The Old Lady of Threadneedle Street, dressed in bank notes and perched on a double-locked
treasure chest, fends off the advances of the spindly prime minister,
William Pitt the Younger, in James Gillray's famous 1797 cartoon.

Walter Bagehot: the one and only contemporary likeness.

Benjamin Disraeli, novelist and prime minister, whose changeable views on trade and electoral reform incurred Bagehot's contempt—he possessed "the most ingenious and manipulating intellect of his generation."

William Ewart Gladstone, four times prime minister, four times chancellor of the exchequer, frequent seeker of Bagehot's advice and booster of Bagehot's run for Parliament—"your fitness must stand without dispute in the first rank."

Augustus De Morgan, the brilliant and fanciful mathematician who taught Bagehot at University College London: "We have been discussing the properties of infinite series, which are very perplexing."

James Wilson, founder of the *Economist*, champion of free trade, and father of six daughters, of whom the eldest married Bagehot. His new paper, vowed Wilson, would be "perfectly philosophical, steady and moderate—nothing but pure principles."

John Stuart Mill, economist,
philosopher, feminist, MP.

Richard Holt Hutton, editor of the
Spectator and Bagehot's fast friend
from college years. While chafing at his
"superciliousness" and "arrogance,"
Hutton saw that Bagehot really was
smarter than the rest of the class.

Isambard Kingdom Brunel,
the epitome of confident British enterprise,
pictured on the day of the attempted launch
of SS *Great Eastern* in 1858.

Sir George Cornewall Lewis, MP,
scholar and poor-law reformer, editor
of the *Edinburgh Review*, and
unmartial minister of war.

Samuel Jones Loyd, later Lord Overstone,
banker, monetary theorist, and a
sometimes bitter critic: "the muddy slime
of Bagehot's crotchets and heresies."

Matthew Arnold, poet and
critic, who praised Bagehot's
work for "showing not talent
only, but a concern for the
simple truth, which is as
rare in English literature as
it is in English politics and
English religion."

George Leveson-Gower, second Earl of Granville, foreign secretary under Gladstone, who called on Bagehot for a journalistic favor during the Franco-Prussian War.

Thomson Hankey, MP, longtime director of the Bank of England. No match for Bagehot in wit, he argued presciently against the doctrine of a lender of last resort.

Robert Lowe, later Viscount Sherbrook, half-blind classicist, lawyer, journalist, MP, and eloquent critic of democracy and reformer of public education.

Charles Pelham Villiers, MP, fighter against the Corn Laws and fixture of London society—"ill-dressed but witty, informed, civilized, at times mischievous."

John Lubbock, first
Baron Avebury,
banker, naturalist,
mathematician, and
author of a bill to create
the first secular holiday
in British history—"St.
Lubbock's Day," grateful
workers called it.

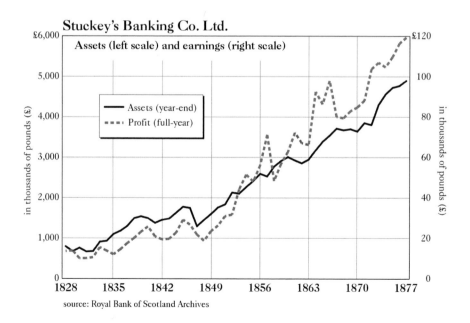

Stuckey's Banking Co. Ltd.

source: Royal Bank of Scotland Archives

Victorian money machine: the profits and assets of Stuckey's rose virtually
without interruption during Bagehot's lifetime.

act's rigidity contributed to the violence of the financial crises that seemed to recur every ten years.

Bagehot provoked Overstone in other ways. The older man, retired from an immensely successful banking career, bridled at Bagehot's taste for paradox. Neither did he share Bagehot's receptiveness to innovation. "Commercial and Monetary affairs again outrun my capacity," wrote Overstone to his friend G. W. Norman in 1863, Overstone's sixty-seventh year. "Joint Stock Banks and Limited Liability Companies— are the order of the day—and the boldest man seems the most likely to be prosperous—Has this state of things ever yet failed to end in a crash. The world is going up and down stairs, *without laying hold of the bannister*, and you too know well what the consequence of this must be. I hope they will only bruise their shoulder—and not break their necks."[11]

Since the 1850s, the French had been doing wonders with companies they called "Crédit Foncier" and "Crédit Mobilier." These were institutions that, like English banks, lent and borrowed; unlike English banks, they lent against seemingly anything, and would lend—and invest—for years, rather than months. From across the Channel, their success inspired envy at first, and later, following passage of the Limited Liability Act, imitation. Presently, the City of London was spawning "finance" companies.

The British versions of the Fonciers and Mobiliers did a little of what banks did and a lot more of what banks didn't do—or, at least, shouldn't do. A properly managed bank lent against prime securities and short-dated, self-liquidating trade bills, giving wide berth to loans or bonds of a speculative cast. It had nothing to do with mortgages, which, no matter how well secured, could not readily be turned into cash. Funding itself with deposits—most of them callable on demand— a bank had to be prepared to accommodate a sudden demand for cash, and thus liquidity was the heavenly banking virtue. Finance companies, by contrast, took no deposits, and instead funded themselves in the securities markets. Illiquidity held no terror for them; neither did

speculative-grade bonds or risky loans, as long as the yield was commensurate with the perceived risk. They had no depositors who might
demand their money in unison.

There was almost nothing that the new finance companies would
not invest in or lend against, relates W. T. C. King, historian of the London discount market, writing seventy years after Bagehot. They would

> build railways in any part of the world, finance every sort of pub-
> lic works (land development, sewerage, irrigation, road-making,
> swamp drainage, or even the building of museums), assist a
> Government, float loans, or make advances on fixed or floating
> property. Some were from the start, and others quickly became,
> concerns which hid under high-sounding titles every sort of
> "shady" or even fraudulent business, but a few were legitimate
> and substantial.[12]

General Credit and Finance Company of London, Ltd., was one of
the sturdier specimens of the new type, and its success inspired others
of less solidity. Notable among these dubious imitators was the Crédit
Foncier and Mobilier of England, an 1864 promotion of Albert Grant,
M.P., and the Mercantile Credit Association.

Grant, born Abraham Gottheimer in 1831, was destined to become
the model for the crooked financier Melmotte in Anthony Trollope's
1874 novel *The Way We Live Now*. He came to the attention of Trollope
and the British investing public through a long series of finance company promotions, each of them paying himself (and, at length, innumerable lawyers) much more handsomely than the public investors. In
some of these transactions Grant and his accomplice Henry John Barker
became entangled with the illustrious bill brokers and money dealers
Overend, Gurney & Co.

Overend Gurney, the "Corner House," occupied a place on Lombard
Street as lofty as that secured at a later date by J. P. Morgan & Co. on

Wall Street. Or a loftier position—"incomparably the greatest monetary house in London, and no doubt in the world," judged W. F. Finlason, barrister-at-law and author of the official summary of the litigation that followed the spectacular failure of this preeminent British financial institution in 1866.[13]

Never before had there been such a firm—and never such a bankruptcy. The Gurneys, Norfolk Quakers, were people of storied wealth and rectitude. Their stock-in-trade was turning English trade bills into cash: they accepted deposits, and with those funds they discounted prime commercial bills—essentially, lent against the collateral of business IOUs. It was a low-margin, high-turnover, and eminently profitable business.[14] In the 1850s, Overend Gurney generated average annual earnings in the neighborhood of £180,000.[15]

Distinguishing prime from second-class quality took knowledge and application, a point of pride for the firm, and so it broke the heart of senior partner Samuel Gurney when a negligent junior partner compounded a devastating commercial misjudgment with a bigger moral lapse. In 1853, upon discovering that the collateral pledged against a £200,000 advance was fraudulent, the subordinate, David Barclay Chapman, covered it up by extending further credit to the felonious pledgers. Before long, Gurney, seventy-one, was dead.

It was to D. W. Chapman, the disgraced Chapman's handsome son, that H. E. Gurney, another member of the founding family, unwisely delegated the sensitive work of appraising the securities presented as collateral against the firm's loans and discounts.[16]

To earn a profit, the business of bill broking required innumerable careful decisions on small amounts of money. Only the most painstaking credit analysis on the largest scale yielded a large profit. An alternative approach—more exciting, more potentially profitable, more risk-fraught and utterly alien to the old Overend Gurney—was to extend long-term speculative loans against illiquid collateral. It was to this line of lending and investing that the younger Chapman now committed the firm. H. E. Gurney, now the firm's chief acting partner, seemed unaware of it.[17]

Edward Watkin Edwards, an accountant whose experience as official assignee of the Bankruptcy Court afforded him intimate knowledge of the destination toward which Overend Gurney was hurtling, first gained access to the firm as a confidential adviser to Chapman. Edwards then made himself indispensable to his high-living sponsor when, in 1859, Chapman became heavily overextended. Now on Overend Gurney's payroll at a salary of £5,000 a year, Edwards accepted his first-year compensation in a lump sum, a lump he immediately slipped into Chapman's pocket. For all intents and purposes, Edwards now headed the firm's unconventional financing division, and just as H. E. Gurney had delegated the job of risk control to Chapman, so Chapman turned that critical function over to Edwards.

Yet—his experience in bankruptcy notwithstanding—never were man and work less congenially matched. "Within a few months," according to King, "Gurney's became grain traders and speculators, iron-masters, shipbuilders, shipowners, large-scale railways financiers, and partners in almost every kind of speculative and lock-up business." The phrase "lock-up" would resound over the next decade as Overend Gurney careered from phantom prosperity, to secret insolvency, to explicit failure, and ultimately to lengthy court proceedings. Having made its fortune in the most liquid kind of commercial collateral, Overend Gurney now plunged into the most fraudulent.

John Barker and Albert Grant, partners in previous financial calamities, now turn up in the Overend Gurney narrative. One Barker-initiated transaction, involving loans to the Galway steamship line, wound up costing the firm more than £1.4 million. Then, the case of the ill-starred Atlantic & Royal Mail Steam Packet Company, along with the associated construction of five large steamers—financing arranged by Barker and Grant—left the owners of Overend, Gurney & Co. poorer by another £1.4 million.[18]

How could a loan applicant, as opposed to a customer dealing in Overend Gurney's old specialty, trade bills, approach the eminent Corner House? Edwards had become the gatekeeper, Chapman his factotum. One customer described the negotiation for a sizable advance against the collateral of steamships as follows:

> After some little time, Mr. Edwards called us in, and then he informed me that Messrs. Overend, Gurney & Co. had decided on advancing me £80,000 for six months, to enable me to overcome my difficulties; but for that advance I should have to pay them a bonus of forty thousand pounds, and interest at the rate of 10 percent.
>
> "What! £40,000 and 10 percent interest?" I screamed rather than asked.[19]

This seeker of funds, Stefanos Xenos, the founder, chief executive, and owner of the Greek and Oriental Steam Navigation Company, was in no position to negotiate, though quibble he did. After some chaffering, he agreed to settle for a "bonus" of £30,000 and a 5 percent rate of interest.[20]

There was a final demand: Edwards told Xenos that he needed a little something for himself. Xenos, flabbergasted, asked if he was not in Overend Gurney's employ and, if so, whether the £30,000 "bonus" he had reluctantly agreed to pay was not enough? Edwards replied that he had "spoken to them about it, and that they had told him he must look to me for remuneration. He added that he would be satisfied with £500 a year." At least, Xenos reflected, the demand for an annuity, rather than a single payment, suggested some confidence in the solvency of himself and of Overend Gurney.[21]

As to Overend Gurney, there were recurring doubts. As early as February 1861, rumors had made the City rounds that this supposed Rock of Gibraltar was crumbling. In reply to an anxious correspondent, the governor of the Bank of England, Bonamy Dobree, deflected them. Yes, he acknowledged, Overend Gurney was said to have incurred heavy losses of as much as £400,000, and was engaged in a most "reckless" business with lock-up securities. Still, profits remained considerable, and "the capital is ample enough to meet any contingency. The uncertain mode in which the business is conducted is the subject of general censure."[22]

It had meanwhile dawned on Xenos that Edwards was not in the least curious about how he would repay his debt:

> He had advised the house to advance me the sum of £80,000, without even going himself or sending some competent person to inspect the steamers, a mortgage on which was to be the security for the amount lent. I was amazed at the facility with which this gigantic transaction was completed in the short space of eight-and-forty hours. Mr. Edwards, to whose name, as the nominee of Messrs. Overend, Gurney and Co., the steamers were to be mortgaged, did not even ask me, till several months after, for the policies of insurance on them; and it was a week after I had all the money that I signed the bills of mortgage. In fact, I received nearly all this large sum of money without having given any security in return.[23]

When not so constructively engaged, the new partners organized an attack on the Bank of England—or rather, by their lights, a counterattack, as the Bank had provoked them in 1858 by withdrawing their on-demand accommodation privileges. No more could Overend Gurney, or any other bill broker, raise cash at the Bank by presenting the accustomed collateral at a time of the broker's own choosing. The brokers might borrow only at the end of a calendar quarter, when the bunching of dividend payments ordinarily pressured the money market. The Bank so acted to induce the brokers, Overend Gurney in particular, to hold reserves against times of trouble. Overend Gurney, which had sought and received massive accommodation in the 1857 blow, preferred the old way of doing things, but the Bank, concerned that it was now underwriting recklessness, refused to reconsider. It did not sweeten relations between the two institutions when, at the end of March 1860, the bill discount rate popped up—an unusual decision, as the Bank was in the habit of holding its rate steady at quarter-end.

To Overend Gurney, the move was a declaration of war on the bill market in general and on itself, the preeminent bill broker, in particular. It was therefore necessary to organize a reprisal. In league with other discount houses, the Overend Gurney partners arranged for the sudden withdrawal of £1.4 million in Bank of England notes from the Bank's own vaults. Lombard Street, caught unawares, feared that the monetary exodus was a sign of trouble with the currency, or with the Bank. Overend Gurney—or someone pretending to act for Overend Gurney—followed up this probing action with an unsigned letter to the governor of the Bank threatening a still more damaging demonstration the next time.

But when the incident was brought to Parliament, the Bank stood firm, and Overend Gurney backed down, apologizing.

OVEREND, GURNEY AND CO. seemed almost to comprise two hermetically sealed divisions, one crooked and loss-making, the other upstanding and profitable. In 1864, Robert Birkbeck, a junior partner in the honest wing of the business, confronted Edwards about the mounting losses in the corrupt subsidiary. Edwards thereupon resigned, though not empty-handed. Having signed a five-year employment contract in 1863, he carried off a douceur of £20,000. There was nothing sentimental about this going-away gift. Edwards, as Chapman later acknowledged, "had become possessed of sufficient knowledge to have forced us to put up our shutters within 24 hours."[24]

By 1865, the great Overend Gurney firm was insolvent. Its assets footed to some £15 million, of which about £4 million's worth was impaired, doubtful, or desperate. The partners judged that, among these nonperforming loans and investments, £1 million's worth was eventually salvageable. Against an indicated loss of £3 million stood £1 million in partners' capital. The partners' personal estates were said to be more than adequate to cover the remaining troubled £2 million. Cash on hand totaled £120,000.

Confronting these facts, the sadder and wiser partners faced a momentous decision: wind up the business, or persevere. If the latter, they might carry on as they were, a private company, or become a public one. To quit would of course be devastating; quite apart from considerations of family and social standing, the old business had never ceased to be profitable. Over the ten years leading up to 1864, it had produced average gross earnings of £227,000 per year, before bad debts and income tax. For the first six of those ten years—before the full onset of the Edwards plague—the actual distribution of profits averaged £185,000 a year, net of write-offs on "ascertained" bad debts.

The partners resolved to continue, though not as the ancient, still estimable, private partnership of yore, but rather as the limited-liability joint-stock company of modern times. The firm was going public. There would be a pronounced reduction in social status, but the public, though it brought no luster, would contribute money, and with that money the chance to begin the business anew, sans Edwards. They would issue a prospectus and sell shares to any and all, and with the proceeds of the sale, the new Overend Gurney would purchase and recapitalize the old one. Four new directors would be recruited to join three of the old partners on the board of the new firm, lending their imprimatur to the still luminous Overend Gurney name.

In confidential communication with the prospective board members, the partners laid their cards on the table. They wanted to put their blunders behind them, and provided an overview of ten years' operating results and a description of the crippling "extraneous" business into which they had "unadvisedly entered." As later came out in court, the legacy partners provided the incoming directors with "the fullest disclosure of the state of the concern."

As far as the public was concerned, more was withheld than disclosed. The prospectus, only five paragraphs long, contained neither current financial information nor financial history. It enumerated no risk factors, and conspicuously failed to mention the £4 million deficiency. There was only one, indirect reference to the Edwards era: the firm would be sold with "the vendors guaranteeing the company against any loss on the assets and liabilities transferred." The meaning of "any" was left to the reader's imagination, as was the size of the pool of private wealth from which the partners of Overend Gurney could draw to make good their contingent liability.

Thus enlightened, the public was invited to purchase 100,000 shares at £50 each, of which £15 would be paid, with the remaining £35 callable in a future time of trouble.* "The directors," the document went on to say, "will give their zealous attention to the cultivation of business of a first-class character only, it being their conviction that they will thus most effectually promote the prosperity of the company and the permanent interests of the shareholders." Any in search of further detail—"the company's memorandum and articles of association, as well as the deed of covenant in relation to the transfer of the business"—were invited to visit the offices of the company's solicitors. "Such terms," stated the document, "in the opinion of the directors, cannot fail to insure a highly remunerative return to the shareholders."

---

* Actually, not quite 100,000 shares were on offer, as the selling partners consented to take half of the cash portion of the purchase money in the form of shares in the new company. The other half they accepted in the shape of a credit to an account in support of their guarantee. So, the selling partners received not one shilling of cash from the sale. The price of the business was determined to be £500,000—the sellers' reckoning of goodwill, or the value in excess of assets minus liabilities. It proved a generous reckoning.

When all was said and done, the new Overend Gurney took in £1.25 million.* The prospectus did hint that there was a deficiency on the balance sheet, but it hardly mattered; only thirty or forty curious people turned up at the solicitors' offices to examine the fine print. Complacent investors subscribed for more than twice as many shares as were offered for sale.[25]

Editorial reception of the IPO ranged from respectful to rapturous. *The Times* contented itself with a reference to the wealth and honor of the selling partners and to the acumen of the incoming directors ("it may be inferred that in that respect due judgment has been exercised"). The *Bankers' Magazine* treated the Overend Gurney conversion as the culminating triumph of the doctrine of limited liability. Once upon a time, it had been taken for granted that "public confidence could only be secured by establishments whose every shareholder stood in peril of the ruin," but with the transformation of Overend Gurney into a public company that fear was finally put to rest. Were the investors getting a fair valuation? Like *The Times*, *Bankers' Magazine* was content to accept the judgment of "the eminent gentlemen who constitute the new blood of the board." All would win by this transaction:

> The members of the firm, if they lose something in position, gain a good deal in pocket, and something also in ease of mind by the division of their responsibility, especially in times of financial difficulty. To depositors and discounters it is unquestionably an advantage to have the unpaid capital of a number of shareholders, as a practically inexhaustible reserve, to fall back upon. And to the political economist it is a source of gratification to see the mass of small capitalists admitted to a participation in the profits which result from great commercial undertakings.

---

* 100,000 shares times £15 minus the £250,000 worth of stock that the selling partners accepted in lieu of cash.

Yes, the magazine's editors admitted, there were "errors, failures and frauds," but human imperfection could not efface the vast net benefit of public ownership of profitable enterprise. The sun was setting on the age in which the rich got richer and the poor got poorer.

The *Money Market Review*, the *Economist*'s would-be rival, weighed in at the extreme side of rapture, seeming to pull its forelock to the third generation of Gurney bankers ("riper and richer in years as in wealth"), celebrating the triumph of the system of limited liability, credulously repeating a story about the partnership's historically unblemished credit experience, and concluding with a word of advice to its readers: "Upon the whole, we must say we know of few commercial undertakings of recent date which may be more strongly commended to the investing public."

Few were better qualified to pass judgment on this seminal transaction than the editor of the *Economist*. Bagehot and Stuckey's Banking Company had grown up together. Since his fumbling start with columns of figures that refused to add up, the assets of the firm had expanded to £3 million from £2.5 million, and the annual remuneration of the proprietors—Walter Bagehot among them—from £7 to £12 a share. Bagehot knew what a successful financial institution looked like.

Indeed, Stuckey's seemed crisis-proof. It sailed regally through the Panic of 1857, the American Civil War, and the occasional poor West Country harvest. And the 7 percent interest rates of 1864—the year of the "cotton famine," so devastating to the Lancashire textile industry—had served only to afford management wider opportunities for the profitable deployment of borrowed funds. In January 1865, the directors were able to report that "the commercial disasters which have reduced the profits of many banks have not visited either Somersetshire or Bristol, the result of the half year's operations are very satisfactory." There was a 10 percent bonus for long-serving clerks, but no such emolument for the stockholders, as "it would be inexpedient, out of temporary and extraordinary profits, still further to increase a dividend which has

been augmented so rapidly to so high an amount." Instead, the directors voted to carry forward £11,000 in earnings in order to fortify a balance sheet for which the partners of Overend Gurney would have given
their eye teeth, and, still deeming their position insufficiently strong,
the board presently resolved to raise more capital. What we today call a
"culture of risk management" was something that Bagehot might have
absorbed around the Langport dinner table.

Bagehot was, of course, more than a banker, even more than a bank
director; it was in his capacity of thinker, editor, and essayist that the
members of the Political Economy Club tapped him for membership
in May 1864. John Stuart Mill, the economist John E. Cairnes, Lord
Overstone, William E. Gladstone, and the parliamentarian Robert
Lowe were among the company that so honored him. Founded in 1821
by the likes of Thomas Tooke, David Ricardo, James Mill, and the
Rev. Thomas Robert Malthus, the club gathered for discussion on the
first Friday of the month, December to July (January omitted). Friday
was the night that the *Economist* went to press, but Bagehot did not
hang back on that account. He led his first discussion at the March 3,
1865 meeting with a question that suggested he had been talking to
Goschen, himself a newly elected member: "Are there circumstances
which should induce us to think that the average rate of interest in
this country has a tendency to rise as compared with the rate (say) ten
years back?"

What, then, did this more-than-journalist have to say about Overend Gurney?

To write about finance in a useful way is to take an unconventional view of the future (there's not much demand for what everybody
already knows). It is good to write well about dry subjects—a pleasing
style would suffice to support a financial paper if only the readers read
for pleasure, but then and now, they mainly read for profit.

Since the future does not exist, the useful financial writer must try
to imagine it. So imagining, he or she enters into the non-factual field

of speculation. Speculation can be highly lucrative, though it is rarely so for the mid-level journalistic employee. The journalistic proprietor is in a very different position. For him, speculative success pays the tangible dividend of a growing readership. Bagehot, who earned a share of the *Economist*'s profits and who was married to a stock-holding member of the founder's family, was a proprietor in fact if not in name; his financial interest in correct prognostication was direct and immediate.

The new Overend Gurney was three days old when the July 15 edition of the *Economist* hit the stands; Bagehot, unsigned as usual, reviewed the financing. He began with a remark on the wondrously changing times: "among those who are guided by their notions and their conduct rather by present facts than by past facts, the step which Messrs. Overend have taken is generally approved of."

Cast in the passive voice, the sentence committed the paper to no editorial judgment. Bagehot seemed to have his doubts about something. He quotes "a well known case" in which one of the Chapman brothers admitted to having lent "certain parties money upon 'some shells,'" a confession that had set tongues wagging. "All the country bankers in England began to ask, 'Is our money put out in shells or not'?" Overend Gurney had not done much of this unorthodox business, Bagehot asserted, but exactly how much would now come to light: "*Now* we shall know this. It will be incumbent on the new company to publish such an account as will tell the shareholders and the public the principal points of its business." The *Economist* wasn't the only curious party, he continued: "we have heard many people with *real* money say that they should like to know the proportion between the pure bill-broking business of Messrs. Overend, and the *extra* and accessory business which their large superfluous means had led them also to undertake."

The possibility that this "extra and accessory business" was large and rotten enough to threaten the solvency of the firm was a risk Bagehot seemed not to consider. As to the management of the new enterprise, he gave it a backhanded vote of confidence:

We will not say anything unfavorable of any one, but we only
speak the admitted conclusions of Lombard street when we
say that the continuing partners—the practical managers, as we
apprehend, of all the detail of the new concern—are men with
whom everyone would delight to do business. The name of Mr.
John Henry Gurney is a guarantee of solid wealth, and that of
the other continuing partners for sound and careful management,
when they are left to themselves and can act without disturbance
as they like.

Bagehot was similarly ambivalent about the valuation of the new Overend, Gurney & Co. Lombard Street thought that the price was reasonable, "but we have no means of really judging—we have not seen,
and the public has not seen, the interior." The law required no such
disclosure, nor did Bagehot propose that the law be revised to demand
it. Public investors must trust in the new directors.

The *Economist* then struck a bullish note: "Therefore, we entirely
approve of the step which this great firm have taken, and sincerely hope
that it will be the means of handing down to posterity the historical
name of 'Overend.' It is not without value to have hereditary names in
the money market as well as in politics. They are incentives to preser-
vative caution."

Bagehot went on like a man who has something to say but can't
quite come out with it. He entered some cautionary observations about
the legal nature of the old partners' guarantees, noted that risks are
inherent in the very nature of a discount company, and speculated
about the nature and size of Overend Gurney's deposits. Then, finally,
he said this:

Anyhow, Overend's must have much money left with them; and
doubtless all of it will remain under the new firm as under the
old. The house is not weakened but strengthened by what has

occurred. As to the management, there ought to be, and must be, great traditional knowledge and skill in a concern which has been so very profitable so very long, and where such vast sums have gradually been made.

He would soon rue it. The shares bounded to £25 from the £15 offering price, but flattened and faltered in the new year. Rumors were making the rounds that Overend Gurney partners were selling their estates to raise cash. It was later revealed that members of the Gurney family pitched in with £2,000 to persuade one of the partners, John Gurney, not to fire his servants, lest the discharged help spread worrying stories.

At the end of January, the Joint Stock Discount Company, one of the new limited liability flotations, announced that the expected dividend would go unpaid. Worse, the directors found it necessary to issue a capital call, the second of the firm's short public career.* The news seemed not to tarnish Overend Gurney, though the Joint Stock Discount Company bore more than a passing resemblance to the Corner House. An old-line partnership, the Joint Stock firm had issued limited-liability shares to the public in 1863. By and by, the old management, which had made a good living in the staid business of bill brokering, had taken up riskier lines of lending. It did so out of necessity, as its own cost of funds (for deposits at fourteen days' notice) was fully 7 percent.

"To finance" was a new verb on Lombard Street, the one-time noun now pressed into service to describe the new array of French-imported credit operations.[26] To earn a rate of return in excess of its elevated cost

---

* The Joint Stock Discount Company made its public debut in February 1863 with a nominal capitalization of £2 million; 80,000 shares were issued at a par value of £25, of which £5 was paid in. Early in 1865 came a call for another £5 per share on account of a temporary setback caused by the failure of the Leeds Banking Company, among other difficulties. "One of latest inventions of modern ingenuity," *The Times*, February 2, 1866.

of borrowing, the Joint Stock Discount Company had financed, among other speculative-grade businesses, the railroad contracting firm of Overend, Watson & Co. A known heavy borrower from the new cohort of finance companies and risk-tolerant bill brokers, Overend Watson was now bankrupt.

The *Economist* remained sanguine: such difficulties as these implied nothing adverse about the general state of affairs. "Ordinary credit is sound," the paper opined. "The revelations of the Joint Stock Discount Company and other such Companies are disastrous to those concerned, but they have no diffused effect. The public at large never heard of them; their momentary success was known only within a small circle, and their present disasters will spread dismay within that circle only."[27] Still, the market's suspicions were aroused. It did not escape public notice that the first name of the failed railroad contractor matched that of the storied bill broker (though there was no known direct connection between the two companies). Deposits began to leak from Overend, Gurney & Co.

On one hand, Overend Gurney's was hardly to blame for the threat of war between Prussia and Austria, falling share prices, falling commodity prices, the rash of business insolvencies, or the jump in the bank's bill deposit rate, all of which contributed to a loss of business confidence in the early months of 1866. On the other hand, only Overend Gurney was responsible for the blunder of lending £422,565 to the Millwall Ironworks Company, resulting in the ultimate loss of precisely £422,565.

Details of the goings-on at Overend Gurney were years in coming to light, but not so the criminal incompetence of the management of the Joint Stock Discount Company: it blazed forth in a March 16 shareholders' meeting. A new set of directors had inspected the books (such as they were), inventoried the assets and liabilities, and, out of their own pockets, stumped up the funds with which to pay up to £50,000 in immediately maturing debt. While the balance sheet showed assets of £4,851,000 with which to cover liabilities of £3,892,000, the quality of those assets was a mystery. The new directors readily supplied their qualitative assessment: in one case, the securities were not worth "the snap of a finger," and in another, more general case, on "a large amount of securities on which advances had been made it was found that, when the securities came to be examined, a considerable proportion were missing, and that others had been substituted which were worthless."[28]

The fall in share prices of limited-liability finance companies turned into a panic, though not a conventional one. Panics by their nature are undifferentiating, but this was a panic largely confined to financial and discount shares. Neither *The Times* nor the *Economist* had seen the likes of it before. Good luck to the burnt speculators in the formerly white-hot financial shares, the two journals agreed; they deserved everything that was coming to them.

No "competent person" was taken unawares, Bagehot wrote. "The wonder has been how it has been postponed so long." He had known it all along, he intimated, though "the feeling is not one which could find expression with propriety in print."[29] The *Economist* had been predicting a decline in interest rates, and it renewed that forecast in mid-April. It likewise repeated its conviction that no harm would come to "sound people" and that the authorities had the situation well in hand:

> The Bank of England now manage well, and they used to manage ill. The directors used to let the reserve run low, and at every period of consecutive failures there was then the probability of a panic. Now the Bank of England manage well, keep their till full, and the failure of fifty discount companies, and the depreciation of all manner of shares, produces no real effect on the world at large.

By the time the Overend Gurney directors met in the first week of May to consider a capital call, the situation was irretrievable. Their only recourse was to their former savior, and, subsequent to 1857, their nemesis, the Bank of England. Would the Old Lady extend a helping hand to the troublesome people at 65 Lombard Street? The Bank dispatched a three-man team to inspect the supplicant's books. The verdict was negative—the Corner House was insolvent—and the Bank declined to assist. The heretofore unimaginable occurred at 3:30 p.m. on Thursday, May 10. Overend Gurney closed its doors.

The ensuing panic exhausted the descriptive powers of the financial press. One observer likened the crisis to an earthquake: "It is impossible to describe the terror and anxiety which took possession of men's minds for the remainder of that and the whole of the succeeding day. No man felt safe."[30] There were exceptions, though: prospering bears who had sold short the overvalued shares of Overend Gurney and those of its major clients, some of whom had, in addition, hammered the shares of innocent financial institutions about which they had planted malicious rumors. In the best of times, not many banks and discount houses could have exchanged their liabilities for gold sovereigns if the depositors demanded their money at once. In the worst of times, such a transformative feat was impossible.

On Friday—Black Friday, and therefore, inconveniently for the *Economist*, a going-to-press day—Bagehot scribbled a live report to Chancellor William Gladstone:

> A complete collapse of credit in Lombard Street and a greater amount of anxiety that I have ever seen. . . . There is much foreign money in London invested in bills, many due in May; I fear this money will be withdrawn from a general apprehension that English credit is not to be relied on."[31]

Next he wrote for the waiting presses in the basement of 340 Strand. Nine months earlier, Bagehot had stamped the going-public transaction with his paper's seal of approval. He had not said "buy," and he had, indeed, dropped hints of concern, but the tone of the article was largely positive. It would likely have dissuaded no one from making a costly mistake.

But mea culpa was no part of the repertoire of Victorian financial commentators, including Bagehot. On the contrary, he acknowledged no error, and instead invited his readers to recall how right he had been. He had known, even if he had been unable to commit that knowledge to paper:

> It will be found that when that firm was converted into a private company we expressed ourselves most anxiously and guardedly as to the value of their shares. Of course we could not say what we then believed, and what was generally known, that the old firm had by most reckless management reduced one of the most profitable concerns in England to one of the most losing concerns. We can only say what we can *prove*, and though we thought this as much as we now think it, we could not say it in print without legal consequences. We expressed ourselves with guarded caution, and under the circumstances this is all which we could do.[32]

How vast, Bagehot continues, is the gulf in knowledge between outsiders and insiders. There can be no doubt on which side of the informational divide the editor is privileged to sit:

> We have often heard it said, and we ourselves believed that the failure of Overend, Gurney & Co. (Limited) (which we have thought possible any time this three months) would not produce at all the effect which would have been produced by the failure of the private firm some years since. But in fact, the failure of Overend's could hardly in their most reputable days have produced a greater effect. It has been signally shown how much an old name, which all really instructed people knew to have lost its virtue, still retains its magical potency over the multitude.[33]

If Bagehot had not foreseen the downfall of Overend, Gurney & Co., still he excelled at describing it. In the very fire of the panic, he produced a lengthy article on the nature of credit, the uses of bank notes in a financial system rapidly converting to checks, and the methods by which banks cleared their reciprocal debits and credits, methods that wonderfully economized on paper currency. The piece renews the *Economist*'s longstanding criticism of Peel's Act: there ought to be an opt-out clause in the law, he urges, by which the chancellor and the First Lord of the Treasury could themselves issue an order allowing the Bank of England to issue enough currency to quell a panic—for, in a panic, people clamored for legal tender, the Bank's own notes.

That being said, Bagehot concludes, the *Economist* was far from advocating "laxity," or "insolvency." It rather supported an improvement in the machinery by which the government and the Bank could spare the community unnecessary suffering. As things stood, days dragged by before the Bank and the government could combine to suspend the strictures of the 1844 Act. Each day seemed like an eternity. "We have," Bagehot reminds his readers,

> often before quoted a saying of Sir George Lewis. He said that Peel's Act did so much evil in the panic week that it made one doubt if, on the whole, it were not bad rather than good, notwithstanding all the good it did at other times. Yesterday was perhaps the worst day ever known in a week of that sort, and our proposal would save at least half the agony of such days as these. If the Act of 1844 is to stand at all, it can stand only by such an alteration as this.[34]

The magnificently talented Bagehot proved, at last, no more clairvoyant than are most of his journalistic descendants. With Overend Gurney, as with America's Civil War, he did his best work after the fact.

CHAPTER 10

"THE MUDDY SLIME OF BAGEHOT'S CROTCHETS AND HERESIES"

Thomson Hankey's scraggly sideburns drew only momentary attention from his bald head, weak chin, and inexpressive eyes. His clothes hung loosely on an unathletic frame. Unprepossessing though he may have been, Hankey was a man of substance. A one-time governor of the Bank of England, he provoked Bagehot into a monetary controversy that nudged the editor of the *Economist* in the fruitful direction of *Lombard Street*—that seminal description of the workings of Victorian finance which twenty-first-century central bankers would use to justify the doctrine that Hankey most abhorred, and that, in its extreme form, Bagehot himself might have condemned.

Born in 1805, the eldest of eight children, Hankey became the long-serving senior partner of his father's firm, Thomson Hankey & Co., plantation owners and West Indies merchants. (His father and he were recipients of government compensation for the slaves they owned in Grenada, under the Slave Emancipation Act of 1833.) Hankey became a director of the Bank in 1835, though not because he had ever worked in a bank; merchants and businessmen, as we have seen, predominated in the Court of Directors. London bankers were barred on the grounds that the Bank, in its commercial capacity, competed against them, and they against it—never mind that a banker knew something about banking.*

Hankey was elected governor in 1851, at the dawn of the golden '50s. In 1853, at the end of his two-year term, he entered Parliament as the Liberal member for Peterborough. In the wake of the Panic of 1857, he favored his constituents with a series of lectures on banking; a decade later, provoked by heretical doctrine, including Bagehot's, he turned those lectures into a book under the title *The Principles of Banking, Its Utility and Economy; with Remarks on the Working and Management of the Bank of England.* His stance on monetary policy boiled down to this: A good banker had no need of a central bank and a bad banker had no claim on a central bank.

There was nothing ornamental about Hankey's writing and speaking: the plain facts were his stock-in-trade, let those facts irk whom they might. When, for instance, the Bishop of London preached at St. George's Church, Hanover Square, London, and *The Times* reported that no collection had been taken, as if that fact deserved censure. Hankey wrote to rebuke the editors that the churchwardens, of whom he was one, chose not to pass the plate for perfectly sound reasons which they had thought out well before the service. Readers of *The Times* came to know Hankey's views on a variety of other topics, as well: the £20,000 estimated cost of repairing the Westminster clock was too high, he contended; the Metropolitan Visiting Association, with which he was associated, should not yield to more energetic charitable organizations; and the directors of the Great Eastern Railway Company incurred debt too casually.

If there was a theme to Hankey's public advocacy, it was to hold to account persons occupying offices of trust. He closed another letter

---

* "In politics, in cricket, in Threadneedle Street, the cult of the disinterested amateur was only just approaching its apogee," observes David Kynaston, historian of the Bank of England. David Kynaston, *Till Time's Last Sand: A History of the Bank of England 1694–2013* (London: Bloomsbury, 2017), 210.

concerning railway finance, this one in August 1866, with a reminder as to the moral obligations of the governing capitalists: "and above all do I hope that in future the directors of these great and most beneficial undertakings will avoid incurring responsibilities in the way of pecuniary arguments which they are clearly not able effectively to carry into question."

By this time, the shocking failure of Overend Gurney, three and a half months before, had become a dull, aching fact. Stockholders who had nursed the early hope that they would suffer no permanent loss were resigning themselves to a heavy assessment.* The emergency 10 percent Bank Rate, imposed on May 12 as a condition of the temporary suspension of the Act of 1844,† had only just been trimmed to 8 percent.[1]

In Parliament, there were calls for a Royal Commission to investigate the upheaval. Though Overend Gurney's failure approximately conformed to the decennial rhythm of nineteenth-century boom and bust, and though every crisis had as its underlying cause the overextension of credit, the 1866 affair exhibited a worrying new aspect: while the visible symptom of the 1847 panic had been railway speculation, and that of 1857 had been unsound American banking practices, Over-

---

* Viscount Cranborne, MP, later Lord Salisbury, the future Conservative prime minister, was one of these disappointed investors. "I have no reason to fear any ultimate loss," he wrote hopefully to his father on May 14 in seeking a loan of as much as £6,000 to tide him over a period of temporary illiquidity. On May 17, Cranborne again wrote to his father to acknowledge that his ultimate liability, if the entire unpaid portion of the capital were called, could be in excess of £18,000. Besides his exposure to Overend, Gurney & Co., Cranborne was evidently an investor in the Imperial Mercantile Credit Association, a financial flotation with roots in the unhappy family of companies promoted by associates of the aforementioned Albert Grant, MP. Cranborne, thirty-six, who had not yet come into his substantial inheritance, was making a living by contributing articles to the *Saturday Review.* W.T.C. King, *History of the London Discount Market* (London: Frank Cass, 1972), 232. Cranborne archives; Smith, "Lord Salisbury on Politics," 4.
† By which the Bank was allowed to issue notes uncollateralized by gold; in fact, no such increment of notes entered circulation.

end Gurney featured a home-grown credit disaster. The failure of a single limited-liability bill broker—albeit a most eminent one—had transformed the cool and calculating financiers of the City of London into a mob.

Sir Edward Watkin, a gruff, public-spirited railway promoter, rose in the House of Commons at the end of July to propose a commission of inquiry. He demanded to know why the Bank of England had done so little—really, "nothing"—to help to subdue the panic: "They have not given the accommodation which, under the circumstances, we had a right to expect would have been rendered."[2]

In referring to the Bank, Watkins called it "the Bank of Recourse," but John G. Hubbard, MP, a member of the Court of Directors, denied that it was any such thing. He likewise corrected Watkins's facts. Far from doing nothing, the Bank had provided massive infusions of cash: £12,225,000 in five days in advances and discounts on commercial bills, as Gladstone, the chancellor of the exchequer, subsequently informed Parliament. Not that such openhandedness was desirable; "in no case," Hubbard told the House, "should encouragement be given to the banking world to assume that, in any emergency, they had a right to ask the Government to supply them at any price with a reserve which they should in common prudence have secured for themselves."[3]

Hubbard and Watkins clashed on the fundamental question of the Bank's reason for being. Whose bank was it, the stockholders' or the public's? What duty, if any, did the Bank owe the public? Excessive borrowing was the downfall of many a troubled business. Might not the Bank, through a too-ready willingness to help, encourage the accumulation of excessive debt, thereby causing the panics it was then expected to quell?

Watkins's Bank of Recourse did exist on Threadneedle Street, in practice if not in law. The Old Lady, affirmed Sir Francis Baring, founder of the great merchant banking house of Baring Brothers & Co., had been the *"dernier ressort"* in a crisis as long ago as 1797.[4] To relieve the crisis of 1825, as Jeremiah Harman, longtime member of the Court of Directors, testified, "We lent it by every possible means and in modes that we never had adopted before. . . . and we were not upon some occasions over nice." The question, in 1866, was whether the Bank was precommitted—duty-bound—to lend. Was it, by obligation as well as by precedent, the lender of last resort?

The Bank's charter was no help; in its vagueness, it was as thoroughly English as the English Constitution. Joseph Pease, a northeast England manufacturer and mine operator and the first Quaker to sit in the House of Commons,[5] remarked on this problem to a parliamentary committee in 1848: "[The Bank] frequently appears to me to act as a private individual would act, and then at other times it appears to act as having certain national objects to sustain or difficulties to meet; so that a country tradesman, like myself, has no idea what the policy of the Bank is."[6]

In hearings that followed the 1847 maelstrom, neither of the Bank's two senior officers acknowledged that the institution they led owed the public so much as a penny. The public, testified another long-serving director, George Warde Norman, grandfather of the future governor Montagu Norman, must be disabused of the notion that an institution such as a Bank of Recourse existed or ought to exist.[7] On this critical question Norman was as one with Lord Overstone, the prophet who marked the Bank's unstinting assistance to Overend Gurney during the Panic of 1857 as the precursor to bigger troubles. The entitled recipient, he had predicted, would take still greater risks if the government deemed it too big to fail.[8]

Hankey was on Overstone's side, Bagehot on the other.

AS A RULE, the semiannual meetings of the stockholders of the Bank of England were dull and peremptory, but on September 13, 1866, governor Lancelot Holland, a linen manufacturer, enlivened the proceedings by recalling the stirring days of May. Not only "this house," he said, but also the rest of the London financial community, had acquitted themselves ably and honorably. "Banking is a very peculiar business," Holland went on,

> and it depends so much upon credit that the least blast of sus-
> picion is sufficient to sweep away, as it were, the harvest of a
> whole year.
>
> This house exerted itself to the utmost—and exerted itself
> most successfully—to meet the crisis. We did not flinch from our
> post. When the storm came upon us, on the morning on which
> it became known that the house of Overend Gurney and Co.
> had failed, we were in as sound and healthy a position as any
> banking establishment could hold; and on that day, and through-
> out the succeeding week we made advances which would hardly
> be credited.

Holland said he wasn't surprised that "a certain degree of alarm should have taken possession of the public mind"—a magnificent understatement—or that representatives of needy institutions should have besieged the chancellor to allow the temporary issuance of bank notes beyond the limit established by the 1844 Act. There was no time to wait for official clearance, the governor continued, because

> we had to act before we could receive any such power, and before
> the Chancellor of the Exchequer was perhaps out of his bed we
> had advanced one-half of our reserves, which were certainly thus
> reduced to an amount which we could not witness without regret.
> But we would not flinch from the duty which we conceived was
> imposed upon us of supporting the banking community, and I
> am not aware that any legitimate application for assistance to this
> house was refused.[9]

Bagehot seized on Holland's words; in the *Economist*, he almost audibly cheered (writing under the almost inaudible headline, "The Great Importance of the Late Meeting of the Proprietors of the Bank of England"). At long last the Bank had acknowledged its responsibility to hold the banking reserve of England.

The truth was, Bagehot went on, that the Bank did hold the greater part of that reserve. It was a fact. More important than even the fact was that the Bank had admitted it. "Now," wrote Bagehot,

> this is distinctly saying that the other banks of the country need not keep any such banking reserve—any such sum of actual cash—of real sovereigns and [B]ank notes, as will help them through a sudden panic. It acknowledges a "duty" on the part of the Bank of England to "support the banking community," to make the reserve of the Bank of England do for them as well as for itself.

Bagehot wrote with a depth of knowledge that few journalists have ever possessed. He also wrote as an interested party.* In 1865, Stuckey's returned no less than 48 percent on stockholders' equity, but it would earn a good deal less if the monetary rules required it to stockpile its share of non-interest-bearing cash that the Bank of England now husbanded for the banking community as a whole. Gold might have been the bedrock of English credit, but that did not mean that the banks wanted it taking up valuable space on their balance sheets.

So it was decided, Bagehot declared. The Bank would bear the cost

---

* The Stuckey's directors' minutes recorded shareholdings only intermittently. As of May 1, 1867, Bagehot owned 130 shares, 46 more than his father and 3.4 percent of the 3,830 shares issued and outstanding. If Bagehot had held that position in 1866, he would have earned £1,560 in dividend income alone, apart from his salary in the neighborhood of £400 a year. It appears that the *Economist* paid him on the order of £780 a year.

of prudence, and it would lend and discount in the hour of need: "[It] agrees in fact, if not in name, to make unlimited advances on proper security to anyone who applies for it. And the Bank do not say to the mercantile community or to the bankers, 'Do not come to us again. We helped you once. But do not look upon it as a precedent. We will not help you again.' On the contrary, the evident and intended implication is that under like circumstances the Bank would act again as it has now acted."

THE EDITOR OF THE *Economist* was either a fool or a knave. So Lord Overstone asserted to George Norman, who, besides his service as a Bank director, was a sometime contributor to the *Economist*, an acquaintance of Bagehot's, and a bosom friend of Overstone's. Long before Bagehot arrived at the *Economist*, James Wilson had led the journalistic attack on what became the Act of 1844. It could not have pleased Overstone, as the intellectual father of that key legislation, that Bagehot had perpetuated Wilson's editorial line. Even so, his animus toward Bagehot was extreme. "The muddy slime of Bagehot's crotchets and heresies" was one of the nobleman's harsher turns of phrase, though it was not his most damning. Overstone cut deeper in contending to Norman that Bagehot was only a country banker and the editor of a weekly paper "which must produce some exciting topic in each succeeding publication—and also a man of vanity and crotchets."[10]

Bagehot was neither fool nor knave, but he was, indeed, a country banker whose earnings were a tiny morsel of Overstone's 1866 income of £96,000.[11] And he was very much a weekly journalist whose first obligation was, in fact, to engage his readers and not to weary them. His playful turn of mind was more likely to puzzle than to bore. Such was the case with the *Economist*'s changeable editorial line on the critical matter of the stewardship of the English bank reserve: the paper's opinion seemed to shift before the readers' eyes.

The issue of the *Economist* just sampled—that of September 22, 1866—was clear enough in commending the Bank of England for coming around to admit its duty to keep the English treasure and serve as lender of last resort. But less than a month before, the same paper and the identical editor had made a persuasive case for a decentralized reserve. The system in which a privileged, monopolistic, government-chartered bank holds the gold for all the other banks—i.e., the system in place—was not one that any thoughtful person would have invented, Bagehot had written then. It was "not a natural, an expedient, or an universal system, or one which we should prescribe where a country has its banking system to choose, and is not controlled by an imperious history."[12]

Was there a contradiction? If so, it was up to the reader to resolve it. The clue was "imperious history." Habits were adamantine and unchangeable, and half of the bankers in England, Bagehot asserted, wouldn't know "what was meant by 'keeping their own reserve.' "[13] So English finance was unreformable; there was no turning away from the doctrine that Holland described and that Bagehot, in the September 22 *Economist*, so heartily endorsed.

As Bagehot delighted in paradox, it pleased him to stand with Holland in support of a system that he himself had just poked holes in. Thomson Hankey, an official personage—he was still a director of the Bank of England—took no such pleasure in intellectual gymnastics. Bagehot's September 22 essay offended him just as it did Overstone. Some weeks later Hankey's lecture series appeared between hard covers with a new preface that took aim at Bagehot's doctrine of the lender of last resort.

"The 'Economist' newspaper," Hankey charged,

> has put forth what, in my opinion, is the most mischievous doctrine ever broached in the monetary or banking world in this country; viz., that it is one of the proper functions of the Bank

of England to keep money available at all times to supply the
demands of bankers who have rendered their own assets unavail-
able. Until such a doctrine is repudiated by the banking interest,
the difficulty of pursuing any sound principle of banking in London will always be very great.[14]

It surprised him, Hankey went on, that a paper as respectable as
the *Economist* should fall for such nonsense. Did Bagehot really mean
that the Bank should ride to the rescue whenever bankers cried for
help? That it should forever stand ready to exchange commercial bills
for cash? That it should perform this benefaction because bankers were
uniquely deserving of it? Well, if bankers were deserving, so were railroad contractors, public works engineers, dock builders, shipbuilders
and house builders. Yet the Bank of England made them no gifts. It
was a rank injustice: "what is really asked for by the advocates of the
right of the holders of bills of exchange at all times discounted by the
Bank of England is, that one class in the country shall be benefited at
the expense of the rest of the community."[15]

Nor did Hankey accept that the banking industry, uniquely among
industries, needed special assistance. He quoted his famous relative,
C. Poulett Thomson, a member of Parliament and the first governor
general of Canada: "nothing was easier to conduct than the business of
a banker, if he would only learn the difference between a mortgage and
a bill of exchange."[16]

A mortgage was illiquid; that was its nature. A commercial bill was
liquid; that was *its* nature. A mortgage didn't turn itself into cash, as a
commercial bill did. The mortgagor—the borrower—had to refinance
it or sell the collateral. Real estate takes time to sell, and in a financial
panic there is no time.

Compare and contrast a short-dated bill of exchange. It was an asset
that almost transmuted itself. On the due date, money and merchandise
changed hands. Bills, though not cash, were first cousins to cash, while

mortgages bore no known familial relation to cash, or, as Hankey called it, "ready money."

Ready money was the nub of the matter. A tillful would suffice on most occasions, a vaultful on others, but vaults filled with gold contributed nothing to a banker's income, nor even, in boom times, to his well-being, when an excess of prudence is seen not as strength of character but as weakness of mind.

"[It] is a most valuable thing," Hankey observed of gold and the notes of the Bank of England, "and cannot from its very essence bear interest; everyone is therefore constantly endeavoring to make it profitable and at the same time to retain its use as ready money, which is simply impossible." The remote cause of every crisis was "the constant attempt to perform this miracle which leads to all sorts of confusion with respect to credit." To prosper through the business cycle, a banker must husband cash even when it seemed undesirable. There was no telling when it would become precious.[17]

THAT BAGEHOT'S IDEAS WOULD prove more durable than Hankey's was anything but obvious in the months following Black Friday. A flurry of pamphlets appeared in support of the ex-governor's position. In his 1866 *Inquiry into the Causes of Money Panics*, John Benjamin Smith, the first president of the Anti-Corn Law League and a lifetime adherent of liberal causes, staked out the position on the gold reserve that Bagehot himself had espoused, before espousing its opposite. John P. Gassiot, a founding member both of the Chemical Society and the London Electrical Society and a fellow of the Royal Society, approvingly quoted Hankey in his 1867 *Monetary Panics and their Remedy*. That same year, the Lombard Street banker William Fowler, who had been two years ahead of Bagehot at University College London, wrote in defense of the 1844 Act in *The Crisis of 1866*.

In the autumn of 1866, Bagehot's erstwhile West Country banking clients issued a "Memorial" to the chancellor of the day, Benjamin Disraeli. Over the signature of the Bristol Chamber of Commerce, the petitioners urged a line of monetary policy in keeping with Hankey's ideas. Bagehot was all for the unrestricted issue of bank notes in times of peril, but the men of Bristol rejected "[the] delusive belief that an unrestrained issue of notes by the Bank of England would restore the confidence lost through over-trading or injudicious lending." As for the supposed impossibility of charging each banker with the duty of maintaining his own reserve, the memorialists advocated exactly that—it was a far better thing, they held, than vesting their hopes in the Bank and on the "vague reliance of a permission" to break the law, i.e., the Act of 1844, in times of distress. To Bagehot's credit, the *Economist* printed this Hankeyesque document in its edition of October 20.

But that did not mean the editor had changed his mind. He led off a December 8 article—"A Bank Director On Banking And The Currency"—with a nod to his sparring partner: Hankey's book was the one to read to understand the inner workings of the Bank of England, Bagehot allowed. What it was not was a guide to wise policy. It was foolish to believe that the English banking community could, or would, line its vaults with gold; there was no idle cash for such a purpose. The Bank kept a reserve equivalent to 40 percent of its liabilities. A dead weight of that size in the world of private banking would collapse the dividend income on which the shareholders depended (or, perhaps, to which they felt entitled).

Lombard Street relied on the Bank for the single reserve and as the ultimate lender; it was the constitution of the money market. If Hankey wanted to amend that constitution, Bagehot taunted him, he should rise in Parliament—of which he was a member—to form a committee to propose a new way of doing things. The committee might examine the Bank directors, perhaps extracting from them a pledge to resettle the burden of holding a reserve on individual bankers. "But until that warning is given," Bagehot concluded, "the history of the recent past will be the inevitable guide of the future, and the doctrine Mr. Hankey thinks so mischievous—the doctrine of Mr. Norman—will be the ruling principle of Lombard Street."

In citing the views of George Norman in support of his argument, Bagehot erred, as Norman was, in fact, an out-and-out Hankey man. Bagehot's mistake inflamed Overstone, who prodded Norman, who duly wrote to correct the record.[18]

Norman's letter, which appeared on December 22, politely exposed the error while raising a useful question: concerning the maintenance of the single reserve, "How is it possible that the directors [of the Bank] should know at any given time, the aggregate demand that may be made upon their resources, and provide accordingly?" Norman next declared that the system in place—in which inadequate bankers' reserves supported "immense amounts" of callable deposits—was inherently unsafe. The danger was "obvious and inevitable, and I fully expect that younger men than myself will witness such a financial catastrophe as we have never yet seen nor can now imagine."

ON BOXING DAY, December 26, 1866, *The Times* paid Hankey the compliment of publishing a long essay on his book. The unsigned critic, evidently a member of the editorial staff of *The Times*, was erudite, and the essay began at the beginning. "What is money?" it asked—gold, or proper receipts for gold, is money, it replied—and "What is a banker?"—a dealer in borrowed money.

Hankey and *The Times*'s author were birds of a feather, though they did not agree on every point. For instance, the critic would not go so far as Hankey did in excluding any illiquid asset from a banker's investment portfolio. Some mortgage-like assets there may be—probably must be, inasmuch as they yield more than high-grade, short-dated bills,

and a banker must make a living. The acid test was not the purity of
the assets, as defined in Hankey's text, but a banker's ability to meet
his every obligation.

The critic was a man after the heart of old James Wilson, but though
he deprecated governmental interference with money and banking, he
was under no illusion about the nature of the human beings who exercise their right to lend and borrow. Some people would abuse it:

> A banker's profit arises from the difference between what he gets
> from those who borrow from him and what he pays to those from
> whom he borrows. He is therefore constantly tempted to lend
> to the uttermost verge of prudence, both as to the quality and
> amount of his loans. High interest tempts him to lend on bad
> security; the desire to lend as much as possible tempts him to
> abridge his reserve.

In a bull market, no one need be the wiser, but the upswing always
ends, punctuated by a bankruptcy. Perhaps the bankrupt is he who has
lent the most, or paid the highest deposit rates, in the just-concluded
boom. Few have ever matched the clarity of the *Times*'s anonymous
critic in the description of what inevitably follows:

> It is remembered that bankers have struggled as to which should
> be foremost in the race. They have vied with one another in
> offers to induce the owners of money to lend it to them; they
> have been compelled to adventure in all directions to keep their
> position. Under such circumstances the failure of one of their
> number begets a distrust of all. Men in general, and capitalists
> in particular, are very like sheep passing through alternate fits of
> unreasoning confidence and unreasoning suspicion. The depos-
> its made with bankers are withdrawn; the bankers, acting on
> the commonest dictates of prudence, attempt to diminish the

advances they have made and to lessen the demands made on them for loans by advancing the rate of interest. The merchants who have maintained themselves by the help of the loans they have been able to obtain succumb, the distrust increases and becomes a panic, and for a season commerce is paralyzed.

Even for a season, paralysis was undesirable, but was it unavoidable? The critic suggested that it was. Certainly, he contended, there were worse things than a slump, and relaxing the Act of 1844 in a time of panic was one of them. He doubted it was ever justified,

since it is certain that whenever it has taken place houses which were insolvent and ought to have fallen beneath the attacks of their distrustful creditors have been enabled to weather the storm only to fall at length in greater ruin. Had permission not been given to violate the Act in 1857 the great leather-houses which failed a few years later would certainly have succumbed, it is not improbable that Overend, Gurney & Co., who were to a large extent their creditors, would have had to suspend payments, and that Sir S. Morton Peto's firm would have been in the same condition. Can it be said that the country has benefited from keeping alive these houses? Is it not rather certain that if they had fallen in 1857 they would have been prevented from increasing, as they have done, the area of their mischief, and would have brought about far less misery by their failures.

The Times's writer did not name Bagehot, but seemed to be not far from his mind. The editor of the *Economist* had protested that bankers could not continue to pay their accustomed dividends if a change in the rules required them to hold vaults of sterile gold. Well, *The Times*'s man countered, so be it: A banker's first duty is solvency, not dividend disbursement. And as for the Bank of England, what is it except a joint-stock bank? How could it justify the policy of holding idle balances for the benefit of its London competitors? "Noblesse oblige is a motto at the Bank of England and the directors of that establishment think they should act the part of a paternal Government in banking," said the critic. But, he continued,

> Never was there a greater mistake. It is founded on a misconception of the position of the Bank, which differs in no essential particular from that of its neighbors. It tends to aggravate panics, since it encourages other banks to push their trade to the utmost, and so bring all the weight of the reaction upon the reserve of one establishment. The erroneous policy on the part of the Bank directors, which, though sanctioned by the language of the Governor at the last meeting, has perhaps never been distinctly conceived, should be at once repudiated; the directors of other banks should be warned that they must take care of their own solvency; and if such a lesson be learnt, the crisis of 1866 will not have happened in vain.

Strong and prescient words, but Bagehot's would ring down through the years. In *Lombard Street*, the quotable phrases of the *Economist*'s most famous editor would serve to lighten the burdens of the directors of the very largest banks. In a crisis, the solvency of the institutions they directed would at last become the public's business as much as their own. They would look not to their own reserve but to the central bank's.

Bankers are mortal, said Vincent Stuckey, Bagehot's astute uncle, but banks should live forever. No more than his famous nephew did Stuckey suspect that government succor would one day save from extinction the largest British bank, indeed the world's largest bank, the Royal Bank of Scotland Group. It would not, however, have surprised Hankey.

CHAPTER 11

THE GREAT SCRUM OF REFORM

The *Economist* went to press on Friday night, panic or no panic. On Black Friday, May 11, 1866, Bagehot put to bed twenty-eight pages of text, advertising, and statistical matter. Editorial coverage ranged from Overend Gurney to foreign affairs, the Irish land question to practical farming, including a lengthy how-to article which ran out under the plain-Jane headline "Horse-Breeding."

A good editor would have read all this copy and reviewed the crowded pages of statistics, those data being much improved and expanded by the contributions of the economist William Newmarch.* Bagehot was a superb editor. What he lacked in patience for detail, he more than made up for in verve, facility, and speed.

He was, of course, a writing editor. His stylistic watermark was obvious in the panic articles, which he must have composed on a hot deadline: "The State Of The City," which led the paper, and a follow-up analysis, "What A Panic Is And How It Might Be Mitigated." A third

---

* As to the statistics, a sampling: "Bank Returns and Money Market," "Corn Returns," "The Cotton Trade," "American Grain and Flour Markets," "London Markets," "Imports and Exports."

essay, likewise in his voice, commented on the Russell government's legislation to reform British elections ("The Distribution Of Seats Bill"). These three articles encompassed 6,128 words, the equivalent of twenty-four and a half double-spaced typewritten pages. Bagehot wrote fast and fluently—and with a steel pen. The Remington typewriter would not arrive in Britain for seven more years.[1]

But on that crowded Friday, the editor had more on his mind than the ticking journalistic clock—more, even, than the Stuckey's London operation, which was his to oversee. Walter Bagehot was going to become a politician.

The Bridgwater Liberals had recently approached him to stand for Parliament in the upcoming June election. The town, a seafaring and manufacturing center, was a dozen miles southeast of Langport; as it had a Stuckey's branch, Bagehot knew the monied residents. He was to meet a visiting Liberal delegation at his London home on Saturday afternoon. Thoughts of that imminent appointment might have distracted a banker–editor–commentator even in the midst of a financial panic on a press day.

Bagehot's credentials could hardly have been better. In a "speaking and writing age," as the candidate himself described the time in which he lived, who better to shine? Bagehot was forty years old, nice to look at, financially comfortable. He was a hunter and horseman, or at least had been as a younger man. He was the husband of the eldest daughter of the late, distinguished James Wilson. His connection to Stuckey's was similarly to his credit. And if his speaking voice lacked power, that was not so very important; it could hardly give out in the few short days allotted to electioneering.

Bagehot also knew well the significance of the ripe political moment. He had lived through many. The 1832 Reform Act almost doubled the size of the parliamentary electorate, while still leaving half the middle class and virtually the entire working class voteless. The 1846 repeal of the Corn Laws marked the dawn of free trade and the beginning of the end of rule by the landed aristocracy. British military reverses in the Crimean War in the mid-1850s provoked a public outcry against the incompetence of the aristocratic officer corps. A decade later, the American Civil War cleaved British ideological loyalties, the Lancashire cotton workers siding with the North and Lincoln, the rich and well-born supporting the South and Jefferson Davis.

The Union victory emboldened the rising democrats. "Slavery has measured itself against freedom, and slavery has perished in the struggle," John Bright, that relentless exponent of free trade and working-class suffrage, jotted in his private journal upon receipt of the happy news from Appomattox. "The friends of freedom everywhere should thank God and take courage—they may believe that the world is not forsaken by Him who made it and who rules it."[2]

For Bright and his Radical allies, the struggle for reason in public affairs had begun with the victory of free trade over protection in the matter of the Corn Laws. Perhaps the fight would never end, but it certainly could not end until the multitudes gained their political voice. In 1865, few Englishmen, and not one English woman, had the vote in a parliamentary election; a property qualification debarred the poor, virtually all agricultural laborers, and most of the working class. Long-outmoded electoral constituencies virtually disenfranchised many eligible voters who lived in the newly populous industrial cities. To the Radicals, it was galling and absurd that tiny Knaresborough, with 271 electors, or Thetford, with 223, should be as strongly represented in Parliament as the cities of Birmingham, Manchester, and Liverpool, thronged with striving, intelligent, skilled, politically mute workmen. Forty boroughs with a combined 200,000 people and 16,000 voters returned sixty-four members to the House of Commons; the county of Lanarkshire, with a population of 530,000, sent but one.[3] What was to be done? Much, the reformers cried, and now was the time to do it.

John Stuart Mill, the great philosopher, economist, author, and feminist, had accepted an invitation to stand as a Liberal candidate for the borough of Westminster, in central London, in the general election of July 1865. He did so on three conditions: he would incur no election expenses, conduct no campaign, and deliver two speeches only, one to the electors and the other to the disenfranchised.

The slim, sandy-haired man who faced the voteless citizens of Westminster on the night of Saturday, July 8, 1865, had never been to school, perhaps like some of them. Born in 1806, the eldest of nine children, Mill got his education at home. His formidable and irascible father, James Mill—radical reformer, economist, historian of British India, chief exponent of Jeremy Bentham's utilitarian philosophy, collaborator of David Ricardo, abettor of the 1832 Reform Act—set him to learning Greek at the age of three, reading Plato by eight, Virgil and Horace by twelve, political economy and Tacitus at thirteen. Young Mill wrote and read all day long, except, between the ages of four and nine, during a daily afternoon walk with his father, with whom he would discuss Gibbon's *The History of the Decline and Fall of the Roman Empire* and other such incidental reading. Arithmetic, as Mill recalled, "was the task of the evenings, and I well remember its disagreeableness." As for a university education, his father said it was out of the question—the boy already knew more than Cambridge could teach him. So John Stuart Mill, at the age of seventeen, followed James Mill into the Examiners Department of the East India Company, invariably beginning each day at his desk with a boiled egg, bread, butter, and tea, the only food that passed his lips until a simple dinner at 6 p.m.[4] Now a retired Chief Examiner—in this, too, he succeeded his father—Mill rose to address his non-voting public.

If he had had his way, they could surely have voted. He declared that he was standing to protest the "money power." It was wrong that the rich dominated Parliament, he said, even if those fortunate people performed commendable acts of charity toward the many who lacked the political means to help themselves. "[T]hey had," said Mill of this elite, "a kind of patronizing and protective sympathy for the poor, such as shepherds had for their flocks—[laughter and cheers]—only that was conditional upon the flock always behaving like sheep [renewed laughter, and 'Hear, hear.']" Mill arraigned the English upper classes for their affinity for the Confederate slave-drivers in the recently concluded Civil War.

Under questioning, the candidate admitted to having written the provoking words that the British working classes, "though differing from those of some other countries in being ashamed of lying, are yet generally liars."[5] Mill explained himself: "the passage applied to the natural state of those who were both uneducated and subjected. If they were educated and became free citizens, then he should not be afraid of them. Lying was the vice of slaves, and they would never find slaves who were not liars. It was not a reproach that they were what slavery had made them." At least, he told his admirers, the British "lower classes" were ashamed to lie. "[It] was more than he could venture to say of the same class in any other nation which he knew."[6]

All should be represented, one way or another, Mill went on. Suppose that a certain constituency had 5,000 electors, of whom 3,000 voted Tory and 2,000 Liberal. Quite properly, the majority should send their man to the House of Commons. What about the other 2,000? Well, said Mill, if they could find another 1,000 who agreed with them, they should band together to elect their own representative. Combining thus, all Englishmen—whether in the majority or minority in their own particular constituency—would enjoy direct parliamentary representation.[7]

IT WAS ONE THING to be cheered, as Mill was cheered in Westminster that evening. It was another to be adulated, as Giuseppe Garibaldi, the Italian nationalist and soldier, had been during his visit to Britain a year previously, in 1864. All classes, all parties, hailed the man who had liberated Sicily, marched on Rome in order to unify Italy, and fought for the cause of liberation in South America. Trade unionists, City bankers, members of the Reform Club, and ministers of state competed to do him honor. Garibaldi dined with Gladstone, sailed on the yacht of the Duke of Sutherland, received the freedom of the City of London, and earned the editorial blessing of *The Times*, which could find no similar republican virtue in Abraham Lincoln.

The *Economist*, at least, succeeded in maintaining its English reserve. Yes, Bagehot acknowledged, Garibaldi was "a great and true-hearted patriot," and faith he had to spare. "But unfortunately his faith is promiscuous and unsifting. He has faith in special providences, in wild schemes, in weak men and bad men. He is easily impressed, easily bamboozled, easily misled. He is, in fact, an intensely amiable, affectionate, believing, unsuspecting *child*."[8]

It was in the wake of his dinner with this supposed child that Gladstone uttered the politically prophetic words, "I venture to say that every man who is not presumably incapacitated by some consideration of personal unfitness or of political danger is morally entitled to come within the pale of the constitution." So saying, the chancellor presaged his own, failed reform bill in 1866, as well as Benjamin Disraeli's successful, incongruous retort, the Reform Act of 1867.[9]

BETWEEN THE TIME OF Garibaldi's visit and Mill's election—the philosopher won by 701 votes out of 12,883 cast—Bagehot began to apply his powers to a study of the body of law and custom known as the English Constitution. The first fruits of that work, an essay entitled "The Cabinet," appeared in the maiden issue of the *Fortnightly Review*, in May 1865. Bagehot's article was, in fact, the lead article in that first number, with essays by Anthony Trollope, F. T. Palgrave, and George Eliot filling out the magazine.*

---

* George Henry Lewes, the celebrated biographer of Goethe and a jack of all the London literary trades, was the journal's founding editor. He and Mary Ann Evans, otherwise known as the best-selling novelist George Eliot, were husband and wife except for the legalities.

Bagehot developed his constitutional thinking in subsequent issues of the *Fortnightly*. Somehow, between *Economist* deadlines, he found time to write the articles—later chapters—entitled "The Prerequisites of Cabinet Government, and the Peculiar Form which they have assumed in England"; "The Monarchy"; "The House of Lords"; and "The House of Commons," which would form slightly more than half of *The English Constitution*, published in 1867. Alongside his later works *Physics and Politics* and *Lombard Street*, *The English Constitution* forms the bedrock of Bagehot's reputation as the keenest political, social, and financial observer of his day.[*]

The visiting emissaries from Bridgwater therefore need not have wondered which political and constitutional principles Bagehot would carry with him to the House of Commons, as the author–candidate was literally an open book. He was, of course, a Liberal, meaning one who believed in progress, religious liberty, limited government, clean elections, non-entanglement in foreign wars, free trade, and, at least in Bagehot's case, free banking, meaning the right of an individual to found a bank with minimum state interference. Staking out the political middle ground, he was as impatient with the mystic Burkean conservatism of the Tories as he was with the leveling democratic ideals of the Radicals. Society was bound to change—in a time of capitalist innovation, it could hardly be otherwise—and as it changed, so must the composition and distribution of the electorate. Let some of the workers have their vote, Bagehot and the *Economist* therefore concluded. But universal manhood suffrage? Woe betide Britain if the lower orders ever gained the whip hand.

At University College, Bagehot had been all for laissez-faire, but had gradually come to believe that it was the government's business to rationalize—even to nationalize—competing railway lines, to educate

---

[*] At least, the foremost such observer among the many who wrote nonfiction; to George Eliot may go the observational laurels in the wider category of any who wrote.

the poor, and to sweeten the public health.* He insisted that the Bank of England should hold the nation's bullion reserve (relieving banks of that costly necessity) and serve as lender of last resort. "I often ventured to say to him," recalled John Morley, successor to George Lewes as editor of the *Fortnightly*, of Bagehot, "'You have only one defect; you do not feel the inherent power and glory of the principle of Liberty.'"[10]

The Liberal Party was large enough, inclusive enough, and fractious enough to contain Mill, a kind of democrat who, by the time of the publication of the third edition of *Principles of Political Economy*, was espousing some sympathy for socialism; Robert Lowe, a kind of aristocrat, a pure anti-democrat and free-market-adhering capitalist; and Bagehot, whose political watchwords were "animated moderation." The party made room even for Bright, a free-trader whose affinities toward the ballot were perhaps to the left of Mill's. Gladstone led the unruly bedfellows in Parliament.

IN HIS WORKADAY JOB, Bagehot wrote for money, but outside the offices of the *Economist*, he sometimes wrote to answer an intellectual adversary. In the case of *Lombard Street*, that provoking agent would be Thomson Hankey. But first, for *The English Constitution*, the goad was John Stuart Mill.

Of the not-yet-named job description of "public intellectual," Bagehot and Mill were fellow practitioners. While on the payroll of the East India Company, Mill found that he could finish his day's work in three hours,[11] leaving plenty of time for the production of such volumes as *A System of Logic Ratiocinative and Inductive* in 1843, *Essays on Some Unsettled Questions of Political Economy* in 1844, and *Principles of Political Economy*

---

* Though as late as 1866, in his fortieth year, he could still write, "whatever is unnecessary in government is pernicious. Human life makes so much complexity necessary that an artificial addition is sure to do harm; you cannot tell where the needless bit of machinery will catch and clog the hundred needful wheels. . . ." Norman St John-Stevas, ed., *The Collected Works of Walter Bagehot*, vol. 5 (London: the Economist, 1974), 273.

in 1848, as well as such works as "Guizot's Essays and Lectures on History" in 1845 and "M. de Tocqueville on Democracy in America" in 1849.

Bagehot made no secret of his admiration for the man whom Gladstone called "the Saint of Rationalism."[12] In fact, *The English Constitution* begins with a quotation from Mill: "'On all great subjects,' says Mr. Mill, 'much remains to be said,' and of none is this more true than of the English Constitution." And when Mill announced his intention to stand for Parliament, the *Economist* remarked that the philosopher would improve the caliber of debate in the House of Commons simply by representing himself, never mind his constituents. Nor did it matter which line of argument Mill might choose to pursue—the free play of his mind would constitute a public benefaction. How good it would be for the country if other boroughs, taking Westminster's cue, returned the kind of men "who would contribute something to the general stock of Parliamentary ideas, rather than minutely represent the electors' views."

Still, Bagehot took exception to Mill's *Representative Government*. In it, the new member for Westminster ascribed the smooth functioning of the British government to the checks and balances of the English Constitution. The Commons counterbalanced the Lords, while, together, the two legislative houses protected against the overreach of the monarchy. Bagehot denied that it was so. It was rather the unity of the legislative and executive functions that animated the English state: "The efficient secret of the English Constitution may be described as the close union, the nearly complete fusion, of the executive and legislative powers. The connecting link is the cabinet," i.e., a committee of legislators chosen to head the various major governmental bureaucracies.*

In America, cabinet officers served the president alone; they had no

---

* They were: First Lord of the Treasury, Lord Chancellor, Lord President, Lord Privy Seal, Home Secretary, Foreign Secretary, Colonial Secretary, War Secretary, Indian Secretary, Chancellor of the Exchequer, First Lord of the Admiralty, President of the Board of Trade, President of the Poor Law Board, First Commissioner of Works, Chief Secretary for Ireland. Robert Blake, *Disraeli* (London: Prion Books, 1998), 447.

legislative role. In England, the ministers, as members of Parliament, discharged duties both executive and legislative. It was the "union, the nearly complete fusion," of the two roles for which Englishmen should give thanks. The conjoining of powers was key, "all the books" to the contrary, Bagehot grandly asserted, notwithstanding.[13]

The politicos from Bridgwater, practical men determined to put their candidate in a place where he might do them some good, may or may not have noticed the serialized unveiling of the still-untitled *English Constitution*. What might they have thought of it, if they chanced to read it? We can only know that they would have been able to understand it: Bagehot's arguments were as plain as day. He wrote like the journalistic observer he was, brilliant, irreverent, and aphoristic. As *Lombard Street* was a description of the money market, in the words of its subtitle, so *The English Constitution* was a description of British politics, as living politicians actually practiced them.

Paradox is the recurrent theme in *The English Constitution*, as it is in so many of Bagehot's writings. What you thought about the Constitution isn't so, the author taunts the reader. What is so, you had always overlooked or, happening to see it, had put out of mind because it seems so implausible.

Bagehot's fundamental observation is that the English government takes two basic forms, the efficient and the theatrical. The efficient segment—cabinet, administrative departments, working committees of Parliament—does the work. "The Crown is, according to the saying, the 'fountain of honor,'" he writes, "but the treasury is the spring of business."[14]

The theatrical segment, meanwhile—the royals, the nobility, the scenic rich—inspires the deference which keeps the lower orders in line. How much better is this arrangement for England than the one across the Atlantic, Bagehot reflects: "royalty is a government in which the attention of the nation is concentrated on one person doing interesting actions. A republic is a government in which that attention is divided between many, who are all doing uninteresting actions. Accordingly, so long as the human heart is strong and the human reason weak, royalty will be strong because it appeals to diffused feeling, and republics weak because they appeal to the understanding."[15]

The secrecy, aloofness, and mystery of the sovereign, which is seemingly of no importance to English public life, is in fact essential to good order: "The existence of this secret power is, according to abstract theory, a defect in our constitutional polity, but it is a defect incident to a civilization such as ours, where august and therefore unknown powers are needed, as well as known and serviceable powers."[16]

A good thing it is, Bagehot goes on, that the poorest can't vote. Lucky, too, that the qualified electors vote with no great conviction and that the members they do elect willingly yield to party discipline. It is this show of human weakness that throws the management of the affairs of state on to the wise old heads in the cabinet.

Better, surely, the cabinet than the House of Commons, when it comes to drafting legislation. Imagine the House, convened in plenum, as a Committee of the Whole, Bagehot invites his readers; imagine it trying to write a "bill of many clauses which eager enemies are trying to spoil, and various friends are trying to mend. An Act of Parliament is at least as complex as a marriage settlement; and it is made much as a settlement would be if it were left to the vote and settled by the major part of persons concerned, including the unborn children."[17]

As for the Lords, you may have thought that that noble branch passes wise and disinterested judgment on the sometimes impetuous Commons, but the fact is that Lords rarely do so. "On free trade, for example," writes Bagehot, instancing the founding cause of the family newspaper, "no one can doubt that the Lords—in opinion, in what they wished to do, and would have done, if they had acted on their own minds—were utterly wrong. Commerce is like war; its result is patent. Do you make money or do you not make it? There is as little appeal from figures as from battle."[18]

Grant the Lords, though, or at least some lords, the virtue of intimidating the rustics: "An old lord will get infinite respect. His very existence is so far useful that it awakens the sensation of obedience to a sort of mind in the coarse, contracted multitude, who could neither appreciate nor perceive any other."[19]

Once upon a time, a belief was prevalent that universal education and rising incomes could erase the differences between individuals and classes, as all would converge at the same level. "But now," Bagehot argues,

> when we see by the painful history of mankind at what point we began, by what slow toil, what favorable circumstances, what accumulated achievements, civilized man has become at all worthy in any degree so to call himself . . . our perceptions are sharpened as to the relative steps of our long and gradual progress. We have in a great community like England crowds of people scarcely more civilized than the majority of two thousand years ago; we have others, even more numerous, such as the best people were a thousand years since. The lower orders, the middle orders, are still, when tried by what is the standard of the educated "ten thousand," narrow-minded, unintelligent, incurious. It is useless to pile up abstract words.[20]

Do you doubt the inferiority of the lower orders, he challenges. Just try to strike up a conversation with the servants in the kitchen. "The dullest platitude" will stump them.* "Great communities are like great mountains—they have in them the primary, secondary and ter-

---

* Perhaps the servants lacked the time and energy for banter. The diary of Hannah Culwick, a fourteen-year-old servant, describes the work she did in 1847 for the salary of £6 a year. There were eight children to look after, "all their boots to clean and the large nurseries on my hands and knees and a long passage and stairs, all their meals to get and our own [the other servants] . . . the water to carry up and down for their baths, and coal for the fire, put all the children to bed, and wash and dress of a morning by 8 o'clock." Liza Picard, *Victorian London: The Life of a City 1840–1870* (New York: St. Martin's Press, 2005), 121.

tiary strata of human progress; the characteristics of the lower regions resemble the life of old times rather than the present life of the higher regions. And a philosophy which does not ceaselessly remember, which does not continually obtrude, the palpable differences of the various parts, will be a theory radically false, because it has omitted a capital reality—will be a theory essentially misleading, because it will lead men to expect what does not exist, and not to anticipate that which they will find."[21]

The schoolboy who had called his classmates "the mob" had grown up to become a supercilious man. Bagehot scorned the "vacant many," including the rather less numerous noble owners of vast tracts of land who "generally cannot speak, and often cannot think." To twenty-first-century sensibilities, this contempt for his fellow man—especially the "little people,"[22] as Bagehot was wont to call the underlings—is jarring. It discomfited some of his contemporaries, too, including the unsigned author of the *Spectator*'s review of *The English Constitution*, which came out shortly after the work appeared between covers in 1867.* But even the democrats of Bagehot's day stopped short at extending a universal invitation to join the body politic to the working multitudes. John Bright, when it came to it, would exclude the lowest rung of society, "the residuum," the wretched poor, and Mill, a proponent of almost universal suffrage, women as well as men, would administer a literary and numeracy test to establish fitness for the vote. Disqualified would be any on parish relief and those who paid no taxes.[23] Nor was Mill prepared to accept the American notion that "one man ('with a white skin') is as good as any other"; the official propagation of such a canard,

---

* "This is probably the ablest, the most amusing, and the most thoughtful, though in a certain sense the most scornful book, that has ever been written on The English Constitution," the review led off. It was a knowing critic who remarked on Bagehot's "alloy" of "the peculiar intellectual superciliousness of great talent." If Richard Holt Hutton, Bagehot's close friend and editor of the *Spectator*, did not write those words, he at least did not choose to take a blue pencil to them.

said the philosopher, was about as "detrimental to moral and intellectual excellence [as] any effect which most forms of government can
produce."[24]

As for the merits of Bagehot's book, the judgment of the constitutional scholar A. V. Dicey, a long-lived contemporary of Bagehot's,
seems valid even today: "His *English Constitution* is so full of brightness,
originality, and wit, that few students notice how full it is also of knowledge, of wisdom, and of insight."[25]

IN MARCH 1866, William Gladstone brought forward the government's
bill to draw more British subjects within the pale of the Constitution.
The proposed reform would extend the franchise by reducing the property qualification to vote, and would redistribute seats, taking from the
old, stable constituencies and giving to the new, growing ones.

The English sorted electoral districts as "county," meaning rural, or
"borough," meaning city or town. They likewise sorted people. Birth,
income, and occupation defined one's class, with working, middle,
upper, and aristocratic being the principal delineations. The working
classes were subdivided, in ascending order of respectability, into laborers, working men, and artisans.

One hundred pounds sterling a year was a commonly perceived
threshold of middle income, though exceptions to this rule of thumb
abounded. An expert coach maker, earning as much as £250 a year,
belonged to the working class, while a postal clerk, making £90, saw
himself—dressed as he was in black suit and top hat—as a member in
good standing of the middle class.[26]

The amount of rent you paid decided your eligibility to vote in
parliamentary elections. In the boroughs, £10 per annum was the minimum. In the counties, £50 gained you a vote, though qualifications for
voting in local or municipal elections were set within easier reach. But

since 1832, the year of the Great Reform Act, Britain had become less agricultural and more populous, and it was past time for change, Gladstone told the Commons.*

In its simplest form, Gladstone's bill would confer the franchise on male town-dwellers who paid a yearly rent of at least £7, rather than £10, and on county renters at £14 rather than £50. By such provision, said the chancellor, 144,000 new working-class voters would be brought into the electoral fold, a 14 percent increase to the 126,000 already on the rolls. And if, as he expected, another 60,000 of their brethren would presently be enfranchised, the prospective grand total of 330,000 working-class electors would constitute a cohort not much smaller than the 362,000 middle-class-and-higher voters in Britain, out of an overall British male population of five and a half million.[27]

Gladstone faced stiff resistance from the Conservative Party and not a little from his own party. Robert Lowe led the insubordinate Liberals. Lowe's position was not, exactly, that "the lower orders" were unfit to vote, though he did not scruple to say that many would fail the test; he rather took his stand on the principle that voting was not an end in itself but a means to the end of good government. To dilute the quality of the franchise was to devalue the caliber of the House of Commons and thus of Great Britain. Better that the would-be electors raise themselves to meet the standard than that the standard be lowered to flatter them. John Bright, no hearty friend of a bill that, as he contended, failed to go far enough, likened the opponents of reform to

---

* It was testament to the stability of British prices under the gold standard that the purchasing power of £10 in 1866 was essentially unchanged from the £10 of 1832. Lowe, for one, argued that the influx of gold in the 1850s had inflated wages and rents by more than enough to infuse the electorate with satisfactory working-class representation, but the claim was controversial. It certainly did not satisfy the economist Mill. "Bracket creep," as the inflationary escalator of taxable incomes is known to the readers of these pages, did not yet exist.

the disaffected Israelites in the Book of Samuel who gathered to plot and sulk in the cave of Adullam.

Lowe, the leader of these Adullamites, was an albino. One eye was blind, the other dim.

His handsome head was the purest white. Born in 1811, the son of an athletic, well-read Nottingham vicar and prebendary, young Bobby excelled at Winchester school, tormented though he was for his shortsightedness and curious appearance. He compensated for these defects by distinguishing himself in classics, then as later the heart of the public school curriculum. Hard work at length raised him to a position in the schoolboy hierarchy at which he could return his tormentors' favors. "No one knew what a bully was till he knew *him*," attested James D'Israeli, one of Lowe's schoolboy underlings, according to James's illustrious brother, Benjamin, who had little more use for Lowe than Lowe had for him.[28]

At University College, Oxford, which he entered in 1829, Lowe earned a first in classics but a second in mathematics. Like the young Bagehot arguing with the results of double-entry bookkeeping, Lowe, as he told the story, held that there was more opinion than fact in the answers that he couldn't seem to solve for (or, indeed, see clearly on the page).

Failing to win a hoped-for academic appointment, Lowe tutored in classics, read law, was called to the bar, and emigrated to Australia, his doctors having astoundingly misinformed him that the glaring antipodean sunshine was just what his weak eyes needed to stave off otherwise-certain blindness. In Sydney the newcomer built a lucrative law practice and made a name for himself in the New South Wales legislative council as an espouser of controversial causes. He returned to London in 1850 determined to enter British politics. He joined the editorial page of *The Times* in 1851 and was returned as MP for Kidderminster in the general election of 1852. Not infrequently,

Lowe the leader-writer commended the political agenda of Lowe the parliamentarian.

The Times and its knowing editorialist did not underestimate Lowe's parliamentary achievements. In a succession of subministerial offices under Viscount Palmerston, Lowe performed the essential work that was, as he put it, "too hard or too dangerous for aristocratic hands."[29] As vice president of the Board of Trade, he put through what proved to be his signal legislative success, the Joint Stock Companies Act of 1856, which, along with the amendments of 1857 and 1858, permitted the creation of businesses whose investors risked their equity capital alone and not, as before, a pro rata share of the debts which their firm incurred. It was an incautious entrepreneur who took a chance in founding a business when the cost of failure could make him a personal (in addition to corporate) bankrupt. Correctly, Lowe viewed limited liability as a force for democracy in capitalism and for equality of opportunity between the rich and the aspiring rich.

In 1859, once more disappointed at being bypassed for high office, Lowe settled for the management of the departments of health and education in the second Palmerston government. For the sake of the cause of compulsory immunization against smallpox, he put aside his libertarian principles, and he held them in abeyance in waging the fights for pure water, the healthful disposal of urban waste, and the regulation of poisons, each reform entailing a measure of state coercion. In education, he strove to introduce accountability into subsidized elementary education: teachers should be paid according to the results their pupils achieved on standardized tests, he asserted. To make the point, he mischievously introduced a bill to cast Eton, Harrow, and the rest into the web of mandatory testing, legislation certain to go nowhere in Houses of Parliament packed with so-called public school alumni. His point made, he withdrew the legislation, while sure that, at least in the case of his own alma mater, the students would flunk. Endowed schools were the worst offenders against the common-sense stricture that teachers must teach so that students might learn. With those privileged institutions, said Lowe, it was "all salaries and no work, all teachers and no taught."[30]

Lowe, later to be created Viscount Sherbrooke, had always had a noble bearing. Gladstone judged that, in the parliamentary debate of 1866, he was "at the very top of the tree." His jeremiads against democracy, laced with wit and classical allusions, won the admiration of both sides of the House. Like Bagehot, with whom he rubbed elbows socially—he was among the guests whom James Wilson assembled in 1859 to toast Bagehot on the publication of his pamphlet on electoral reform—the member for Kidderminster believed in progress uninhibited by tradition. He marveled at the working of the free market: unguided by government, he elegiacally wrote, the interplay of prices performs its function of "correction and compensating errors—one extreme invariably producing another—dearness producing cheapness, and cheapness dearness; and thus the great machine of society is constantly left oscillating to its center."[31] Seemingly inoculated against nostalgia, Lowe looked ahead to an England in which scientific education pushed aside the classics—an odd, even a philistine, view for a classics tutor, some said—and merit supplanted aristocratic privilege.

Excellence, most of all, was what Lowe stood for, and he did not always find it in the constituency that sent him to Parliament. Returning to Kidderminster in 1857 to stand for reelection in the general election of that year, Lowe loudly announced that he would pay no bribes, nor buy the town a beer, nor stoop to "mob oratory"—he would leave all that to his Tory opponent. Situated 16 miles southeast of Birmingham, in the county of Worcestershire, Kidderminster was famous for its carpet makers. To the many currently unemployed carpet weavers, the town was notorious for Lord Ward's steam looms, just then displacing human labor. Would the Liberal candidate support policies to relieve local unemployment? In reply, Lowe suggested emigration, perhaps to Australia.[32] He himself had made his fortune Down Under, and no less a humanitarian reformer than the Earl of Shaftesbury supported that plan for self-betterment.[33] It did not charm the townspeople.

Politically, the candidate risked little with such provoking speech: Kidderminster was a Liberal riding, and Lowe was sure to win. The trouble started after the results came in. Among the unemployed, unbribed, and thirsty people in and around Kidderminster, there were those who wanted to kill him, and thousands of hostile men and women were happy to lend moral support to these assailants ("Kill the bastard; kill the pink-eye"). Retiring on foot from the ceremony that closed the balloting, Lowe and his party, locking arms behind a small police escort, passed through a hailstorm of rocks and bricks. Men fell under the barrage, including the brave Constable Jukes, who later died of his wounds. Except for the courage of the headmaster of a local grammar school, who dragged the wounded candidate into the safety of his house, Lowe might have died, too. As it was, the Liberal victor suffered a broken skull. Blood streamed down his alabaster face.

LOWE HAD MADE A memorable anticipatory contribution to the reform dialogue in 1865. The franchise was already open to tens of thousands of voteless working men, he insisted. It was theirs for the taking. According to government figures, the average Englishman consumed 240 quarts of beer a year, representing an outlay of £4.[34] Any who wanted to meet the customary £10 standard had only to stop drinking. Many would rather have boarded a boat for Australia.

In 1866, on the second night of debate on the reform measure, Lowe speculated on what it might mean if the working class did, indeed, gain electoral control. He was now the member for Calne, having decided not to face his homicidal constituents in Kidderminster again. "Look at what that implies," he warned the House on March 13:

> I shall speak very frankly on this subject, for having lost my character by saying that the working man could get the franchise for himself, which has been proved to be true, and for saying which he and his friends will not hate me one bit the less, I shall say exactly what I think. Let any Gentleman consider—I have had such unhappy experiences, and many of us have—let any Gentleman consider the constituencies he has had the honor to be concerned with. If you want venality,—if you want ignorance, if you want drunkenness, and facility for being intimidated; or if, on the other hand, you want impulsive, unreflecting and violent people, where do you look for them in the constituencies? Do you go to the top or to the bottom?

Gladstone said that Lowe wrote on rock with a steel pen, and certainly, those words of his had staying power. They would be quoted against the man who spoke them for years to come. If the bill were to pass, Lowe went on, it would be

> in mere deference to numbers at the expense of property and intelligence, in deference to a love of symmetry and equality— at least that is the name under which the democratic passion of envy generally disguises itself, and which will only be satisfied by symmetry and equality—I feel convinced that when you have given all the right hon. Gentleman [Gladstone] asks you will still leave plenty of inequalities, enough to stir up this passion anew. The grievance being theoretical and not practical will survive as long as practice does not conform to theory; and practice will never conform to theory until you have got to universal suffrage and equal election districts.

A government with everyone having a voice in it, said the author of the 1856 limited liability law, was like a joint-stock company "in which everyone is a director."

Bagehot, writing in the *Economist*, judged that some electoral reform was overdue, and he applauded the proposed reduction in the qualification for the borough, or urban, franchise. The big landowners wielded too much power, and this was a way to redistribute the surplus. But like Lowe, who had charged the working classes with "venality," Bagehot warned that the most certain effect of the bill would be to increase the already shocking level of electoral bribery. "All over England," he predicted, "this Bill will enfranchise a very large number of persons who will consider their votes, and whose wives will consider their votes, as so much saleable property." You didn't need a parliamentary commission to know that; everyone knew it.[35]

"IT IS REALLY CURIOUS how things drop into your hands when you want them," Bright remarked drily as he answered Lowe on the floor of the House. What had so conveniently surfaced on Bright's desk was an 1859 newspaper article that quoted Lowe, then Palmerston's vice president of the Committee of Council on Education, on the necessity of a new, moderate reform bill. Well, Bright demanded, what was the bill now in front of the House except that very measure? Bright urged the naysayers to recall the French Revolution and the less tumultuous European disturbances of 1848. Accidents do happen, he said, particularly when unwise statesmen carelessly put in place the conditions to cause them.

"I ask hon. Gentlemen," Bright went on,

> whether it is not better to accept a measure so moderate, and if
> you like, as may be said by many in the country, so inadequate,
> but still to some extent, so good? Is it not better to accept this

measure, and show your confidence in the people, than to take the advice of the right hon. Member for Calne—the most revolutionary advice that was ever given in this House—and shut your doors against five millions of people, and tell them that unless they can scramble over this £10 barrier none of them shall ever find a direct representation in this House?

Mill, speaking a month later, on April 13, 1866, also took aim at Lowe, while generously conceding the good that his opponent had done for English schoolchildren. The former minister for education had contended that the reform bill would deliver no practical benefit, but he could not really know that any more than the statesmen of 1832 could have known what, in the train of their enlightened legislation, would come of the abolition of the Corn Laws, the abolition of the Navigation Laws, and the granting of "free trade to all foreigners without reciprocity." Yet much good had blessedly come to pass.

To persuade the mighty to relinquish some of their power, Mill went on, do not tell them that they have been abusing it—"which, if it were true, they could not be expected to be aware of"—but instead remind them "of what they are aware of—their own fallibility." He continued, "we all of us know that we hold many erroneous opinions, but we do not know which of our opinions these are, for if we did they would not be our opinions. Therefore, reflecting men take precautions beforehand against their own errors."

The precaution that the members should take was to admit a new class of expert into their midst. As it was, merchants, lawyers, bankers, farmers, and landowners occupied the benches of the House, and they did not hold back from espousing the claims of their respective occupations and classes. Wanted were authorities on apprenticeships, wages, hours of work, child labor, occupational health and safety. "Is there, I wonder," asked Mill, "a single Member of this House who thoroughly knows the working men's view of trades unions, or of strikes, and could bring it before the House in a manner satisfactory to working men?" No one was asking that the working class be given the keys to the kingdom, Mill went on, but rather, "What is asked is a sufficient representation to ensure that their opinions are fairly placed before the House, and are met by real arguments, addressed to their own reason, by people who can enter into their way of looking at the subjects in which they are concerned."

The final and eighth night of debate, on Friday, April 27, was a contest of physical endurance almost as much as political strength and oratorical skill: by the time Disraeli got to his feet, to raucous cheers, it was after 10 p.m. The Tory leader denied that the Conservatives were afraid of the working classes. The real question was whether the government's bill would improve the English Constitution—and it would do no such thing, but rather lead to the importation of American-style democracy, a good thing for America, a fatal thing for England. Disraeli taunted Gladstone for his opposition to the Reform Act of 1832—though it was an opposition, as Gladstone would presently remind him, that he had voiced as a student in an Oxford Union debate in 1831[36]—and warned against a debasement of the character of the House should the working classes gain a disproportionate representation in it.

"You may talk of the rudeness of Monarchical Government," said Disraeli, quoting Sir George Cornewall Lewis, James Wilson's old friend, "but I defy you to point out anything in Monarchy so irrational as counting votes, instead of weighing them, as making a decision depend not on the knowledge, ability, experience, or fitness of the judges, but upon their number."

Gladstone had looked "careworn and pale" when he arrived at the House in an open carriage, in the opinion of a *Times* reporter. When he rose to follow Disraeli and close the debate, it was 1 a.m. The bill was in trouble, and the chancellor spoke to save it as well as the government that had brought it forward. He praised Lowe's extraordinary eloquence—a pity that the member from Calne had squandered his gifts on the wrong cause. Now addressing the chief Adullamite, Gladstone continued,

> Will my right hon. Friend permit me to apply to him the story which is told of the mother of the regent Duke of Orleans, Elizabeth the Princess Palatine of Bavaria. She said of her son, what I will venture to apply to my right. hon. Friend. Her story was, that at his birth the fairies were invited to attend. Each came, and each brought the infant the gift of a talent. But in sending the invitations one fairy had unhappily been forgotten. She came unasked, and said for her revenge, "Yes, he shall have all the talents except one, that of knowing how and for what end to apply them."[37]

Lowe had asserted that the House knew nothing about the kinds of people it was asked to enfranchise. Gladstone retorted that a single word of description would suffice. "Lancashire" was that word, the city being synonymous with the suffering of the English textile operatives during America's Civil War. "They knew," said Gladstone of the pro-Union working men, "that the source of their distress lay in the war, yet they never uttered or entertained the wish that any effort should be made to put an end to it, as they held it to be a war of justice, and for freedom"—a handsome tribute from a man who had bought Confederate cotton bonds.

"Sir," Gladstone went on, as the hands of the clock approached 3 a.m., "the hour has arrived when this protracted debate must come to an end [Cheers]." Reform had been the stumbling block of the House in the thirty-four years since the Act of 1832. Four previous attempts to broaden the franchise and redefine constituencies had gone down in failure, nor was this one assured of success. And if it did fail, said Gladstone, quoting the prime minister, Lord Russell, so would the government. Gladstone conceded the possibility. Addressing Disraeli and his Tory opposition, he concluded,

> You may drive us from our seats. You may bury the Bill that we have introduced, but we will write upon its gravestone for an epitaph this line, with certain confidence in its fulfillment— "Exoriare aliquis nostris ex ossibus ultor."[38] You cannot fight against the future. Time is on our side. The great social forces which move onwards in their might and majesty, and which the tumult of our debates does not for a moment impede or disturb— those great social forces are against you; they are marshalled on our side; and the banner which we now carry in this fight, though perhaps at some point it may droop over our sinking heads, yet it soon again will float in the eye of heaven, and it will be borne by the firm hands of the united people of the three kingdoms, perhaps not to an easy, but to a certain and to a not distant victory.[39]

When, two hours after he rose, Gladstone slumped back into his seat to immense cheering, he looked as if he were ready to faint. Presently, the Speaker announced the division: "Ayes to the right, noes to the left." The results were as Gladstone had feared: the government prevailed by a mere five votes, fifty-five shy of the estimated potential Liberal majority in the House.[40] It was a virtual defeat—and an absolute victory for Lowe, who, his face as ruddy as Gladstone's was pallid, "took off his hat, waved it in wide and triumphant circles over the heads of the very men who had just gone into the lobby against him."[41]

This momentous political occasion called forth a commensurate journalistic effort, *The Times* sending relays of messengers from the House of Commons to Printing House Square at five-minute intervals. The final parliamentary dispatch was handed to the printers at 4:10 a.m.

on Saturday, just in time to be loaded on to the waiting mail trains for national distribution.*

A week later, in the *Economist*, Bagehot appealed to "the moderate and thinking section of both parties" to come together to produce legislation to throw a suitable measure of political power to the mass of the English people. It would take good will and compromise to produce a suitable bill: "all must be ready to make sacrifices—to abandon secret hopes and cherished ideas—to submit to what is commonplace—to support what they can prove to be but second rate—to tolerate small evils that they may keep out great evils."[42] If, as Bismarck would say, "Politics is the art of the possible, the attainable—the art of the next best," the prospective Liberal member for Bridgwater showed promising signs of a statesmanlike temper.

---

* Saturday's paper included a leading article extolling the wisdom and eloquence of Robert Lowe. Perhaps the parliamentarian–editorialist who had thus incurred *The Times*'s favor had entrusted authorship of this comment to someone who was not then seated in the House of Commons.

CHAPTER 12

A LOSER BY SEVEN BOUGHT VOTES

B ridgwater was not the first constituency to recruit Walter Bagehot to stand for Parliament: Liberals in the northern manufacturing city of Manchester had asked about his availability on the
eve of the general election of 1865. The incumbent Liberal MP, James
Aspinall Turner, sixty-eight years old, cotton manufacturer and amateur
entomologist, had decided not to seek reelection, and when no strong
local successor presented himself, party leaders cast around for a suitable import. Manchester was famously hospitable to the doctrine of free
trade. Would the editor of the *Economist* be willing to stand?

Bagehot was certainly eager, and others were eager on his behalf.
Gladstone wrote him a fulsome letter of introduction, and William
Rathbone Greg, *Economist* contributor, and husband of the daughter
of a Manchester physician, seconded Gladstone. On July 3, Bagehot
presented himself at Manchester Town Hall. Four hundred people—
Liberals, Conservatives, and Radicals, working men, trade unionists,
textile makers—were on hand to appraise the candidates.[1]

The chairman of the meeting, R. W. Wood, announced that Bagehot had come up from London on the train to say a few words, if the
people would care to hear him. Were the people amenable? Partisan

voices cried, "Hear, hear!" or "No! No!" A man called out: was this Bagehot not the son-in-law of the late James Wilson, founder of the *Economist* and a political ally of John Bright, famed champion of free trade and one-time member of Parliament for Manchester? And if he were that eminence—though all that the people really knew about him was that the *Manchester Guardian* had printed his name—why was he not already in Parliament serving a constituency that "rejoiced in his presence," say, the City of London? Laughter rippled through the hall. The voice continued: "If all that they knew of him was that he was called Bagehot or Baggott, might they not, as regarded Manchester, look on him as the *Manchester Guardian*'s 'bagged fox'?"[2] The crowd laughed and cheered.

Bagehot had come cold into the room. A Manchester political audience was notoriously boisterous.[3] Bagehot was a famous talker in small groups, and had wowed the audiences who heard him debate at University College, but this audience was different.

Bagehot said that, if they would have him, he would be happy to represent the "moderate Liberal interest for Manchester." He had heard in London that this particular wing of the Liberal Party was dead. He could see for himself that it wasn't. ("Not yet, lad," someone yelled.) "[L]iving beings actuated by real life and energy"—what he saw in front of him—contradicted what he had read in the *Saturday Review* and what he had heard in the south of England, Bagehot continued.

The crowd needed no persuading that the London snobs were against them, and something in the speaker's manner, or in his invocation of the high-toned, Tory *Saturday Review*, turned the crowd against him. People now started to laugh, not with Bagehot but at him. They hissed him and whistled. Wood called for order. "Send him back to London," someone cried. But

order had been restored, Mr. Bagehot continued. He said that after what he had heard he fancied that some people were there

who were not moderate; who had extravagant sentiments and fla-
grant ideas, or they would not hiss. —["Oh."] He was explaining
that in the South of England and in London people had an idea
that there was no moderate party in Manchester. That its political
element was entirely composed of an extreme section, that the
most democratic sentiments were the most popular, and that nothing would go down except an abolition of everything that exists.
—["Oh," and laughter. "Turn him out."] He maintained from all
that he had seen that was completely false. —[Ironical applause.]
He maintained that there was a very large section which would
support moderate views, and it was with that view that he wished
to present himself. —[Laughter.][4]

Now Bagehot came to the contentious issue of the franchise. Just
how far should it be expanded? If you continued to lower the electoral
bar, as the Radicals demanded, you would presently arrive at universal
franchise, he said. Bagehot asked the crowd if that would be a good
thing or a bad thing. "A bad," someone called. Yes, agreed Bagehot, a
bad, even a fatal thing.

"Mr. Bright some years ago had put it in a very attractive form," the
candidate went on, "which if adopted would lead to the agricultural and
manufacturing classes banding together in classes. ['Send him back to
London,' and laughter.] Bagehot chafed at the derision. He asked if "any
working man who might be present" would care to debate the point
with him. This was met with a voice calling out, "We are all working
men." Bagehot retorted, "So am I," which elicited more laughter and
a voice saying, "Nay, Lord Dundreary."* Bagehot rushed to clarify. He
meant, was there a factory hand present "who would care to argue out
the question with him whether the laboring class should have the com-

---

* Dundreary, a character in *Our American Cousin*, an 1858 English stage production,
was the epitome of the dimwitted English aristocrat.

plete power in this country." The audience laughed at the absurdity of the challenge. Undaunted, Bagehot continued, "Having a numerical majority, they would get an absolute supremacy. He would like to hear if that was right. He maintained that no one class ought to have supreme power. [Hear, hear.] Parliament should be the impartial tribunal of all."

It was not an unreasonable proposition. Still, voices bellowed, "Shut up!" After the noise abated, Wood relayed a question from the audience: Would Bagehot care to give his opinion on some other timely political topic? The crowd answered before the candidate could: "The question was drowned with cries of 'No,' and the meeting declined to hear Mr. Bagehot any further."[5]

"Badly received," Eliza jotted in her diary.

THE THIRTY-NINE-YEAR-OLD Bagehot had ruminated on the difficulties of entering politics in the *Economist* only three weeks before he presented himself to the electors of Manchester. An aspirant must be young, he judged: "Statesmanship—political business—is a profession which a man must learn while young, and to which he must serve a practical apprenticeship; and in England, the House of Commons is the only school for acquiring the necessary skill, aptitude and knowledge."

Not quite one year later, on the afternoon of Saturday, May 14, 1866, three emissaries from Bridgwater came knocking at the door of his home in Upper Belgrave Street.[6] They proceeded to brief him on the local state of play.

He was not the Liberals' first choice: they had previously tapped Sir John Villiers Shelley, whom the Conservative Henry Westropp and his money had defeated in 1865. Shelley was of the fourth generation of a line of Sussex baronets to sit successively in the House of Commons; he had earlier represented the constituency of Westminster. Years before, Shelley had astounded the reforming elements with his matter-of-fact defense of rotten boroughs: they were, he stoutly maintained, the only constituencies in which a statesman could speak his mind for the simple reason that he had no voters to answer to. As the years passed, Shelley changed his views. He was now for reform and electoral purity.

In 1865, Shelley had paid no bribes to the vendible Bridgwater electorate. That none should be paid on his behalf was the condition he set for standing. This iron stipulation was known only to a few at the top of the local Liberal Party, and caused considerable grumbling when word seeped out on election day. Against Westropp's gold, Shelley's sound Liberal principles and amiable character stood not a remote chance. So Sir John declined the invitation to stand again in 1866, though 200 Bridgwater voters had signed a petition urging him to return. He "could not succeed against the corruption practiced by the Tories," he told them.[7]

Westropp himself would not be around to corrupt the 1866 election; the very crimes against which Shelley protested had led to his expulsion from Parliament. The editor of the *Economist* knew enough about the situation to extract from his visitors a kind of purity pledge. He assumed, he told them, that the election would be conducted on the straight and narrow. "Oh, yes," they replied.

Bagehot asked no questions about the likely expense of the race—a curious omission, the Liberal scouts thought. He did agree to contribute £600 to the cost of legal action after the election if the Conservatives were found to be up to their old tricks. Asked to submit a letter to the Bridgwater voters setting out his views on the issues of the day, the literary candidate wrote one, then a second and a third, each dated May 8.

ELECTION BRIBERY WAS A hardy English perennial, and had prospered in spite of more than a century's worth of legislation intended to stamp it out. The Treating Act of 1696 forbade the kind of hospitality that led a voter to cast a grateful ballot for the man who bought him a drink. The Bribery Act of 1726 prescribed a £500 fine for any who would sell a vote. There were additional clean-election laws in 1841 and 1842, and a Corrupt Practices Act in 1854.

It is beyond knowing how debauched English politics might have been in the absence of these attempts to eradicate corruption; as it was, according to twentieth-century estimates, bribery was endemic in one-third to one-half of all English constituencies at about the time that Bagehot committed to stand as member for Bridgwater.[8] In the estimation of John Stuart Mill, in 1864, corruption threatened "the vitality of representative government."

The issue was front and center in Parliament. On May 1, 1866, the House of Commons heard findings that in the borough of Totnes, votes were "quoted like a share-list on the Stock Exchange" and in Great Yarmouth, the rising price of a vote resembled the bull market in oysters in London. Before the 1832 Reform Act, two guineas had secured a Great Yarmouth ballot, but after that landmark legislation, the price jumped to £3. It pushed to £10 in 1852, between £13 and £16 in 1860, and as much as £30 in 1864. The expense was considerable even when the voters patronized only one bribing agent; it doubled when enterprising citizens tickled money from the pockets of both sides.

In some precincts, voters regarded the taking of a bribe as a venial sin, like robbing an orchard.[9] In others, they looked upon it as a kind of right. In Reigate, where £5 per ballot was the market rate, a voter went to court in 1864 to secure the payment that he said had been promised but never paid. "When the case came on in the County Court," the MPs heard, "forty other voters cherishing a similar grievance were present in court, fully resolved to follow his example if he were successful, but of course he was not."[10]

Bagehot knew all about these goings-on. In 1864, the *Economist* had apprised its readers of a new kind of bribery: rather than buying votes on election day, a monied candidate would shower a community with philanthropy in the months or years leading up to the vote. The aspiring parliamentarian, perhaps one of the new millionaires that Britain's industrial prosperity was so freely minting, would found a school or restore a cathedral. The grateful community would dispatch its patron to Parliament. To the description of this form of seduction, Bagehot added, "we have known the cases we quote."

On the eve of the 1866 election, the *Economist* remonstrated against bribery in an article headed "The Way To Reduce Electoral Corruption." The writer of the unsigned piece sounded a great deal like the Liberal candidate for Bridgwater. The way to stamp out corruption was to throw the book at bribe-takers, the paper argued; fine them the equivalent of the bribe they had accepted and deny them a vote for life. As for the statesman himself, the man ultimately behind the bribe, remove him from Parliament and bar him from the civil service. Inasmuch as bribe givers enter politics to raise their social status, the threat of stigma should keep them on the straight and narrow.[11]

IT WAS THUS AS an apostle of electoral purity that Bagehot presented himself to the people of Bridgwater on the eve of the balloting. His audience received him like the neighbor he virtually was—no cutting witticisms, no hissing and mockery this time around. "I need say no more to you on the state of the nation," Bagehot told the cheering Liberals,

> but I want to say one word on the state of the borough. We know that for a long time the Liberal party has been triumphant here, and we know that at the last election that party suffered a temporary but disastrous eclipse, and we know by what foul means that eclipse was produced [hear, hear.] I do not mean to touch the details, but I have a practical remark to make about it. There is a remarkable class of people whose position in the matter I do not understand. I understand Mr. Westropp's, and I do not want to be hard on him; after all, he has suffered a great penalty in being

excluded from Parliament. He was very ambitious of his seat, and therefore, had great temptation.

Bagehot could make allowances for poor voters who took a bribe. But the rich and respectable ones? "They are like a man who stole stinking fish. They commit a crime and they get no benefit." The people laughed from the belly. Bagehot closed with an appeal to the Liberals to form themselves "into one great vigilance committee" to force the Tories to toe the ethical mark.

Bagehot's opponent was a Scottish lawyer, George Patton, sixty-three years old—old enough to be Bagehot's father—who had studied at the University of Edinburgh and Trinity College, Cambridge. He was a railroad lawyer by profession—"Railway Patton," they called him—and a former solicitor general of Scotland. Like Bagehot, he was married and childless. Unlike Bagehot, he could claim no extraordinary intellectual gifts.

If corruption was the Tories' stratagem against Bagehot, Patton made an improbable bribe-giver. He had money to spend—his brother Thomas, a rich Glasgow merchant, had more than enough, even for crooked Bridgwater—but was without an ounce of guile; some rolled their eyes at this characterization of an old and seasoned lawyer, but Patton's friends swore to it. Then, too, as a Scotsman, the candidate lacked practical vote-buying experience, elections in Scotland being comparatively pure.

A stranger to Bridgwater and its ways—Patton, for instance—might not have supposed that an election that was specially called to choose a successor to an unseated bribe-giver could itself be corrupt. But to any who really knew the borough, it was the prospect of an honest election that beggared the imagination. Corruption had been the way of Bridgwater politics since at least the turn of the nineteenth century— the existence of books dating from 1807, in which were recorded the names of voters whom the Liberals had bribed, seemed to prove as much.[12] The Tories may or may not have been so indiscreet. However, the parties were equally seducible—honest Sir John Shelley was the rarest of exceptions—and the rich and the poor alike stuck out their hands. Ten pounds, the standard bribing rate, would pay a year's rent on a respectable dwelling place, which is why it had stood since 1832 as the criterion for electoral eligibility in towns and cities. Bribe-givers judged that two-thirds of the town's 600 eligible voters were for sale.

Money, liquor, and special effects made Bridgwater election days festive. Liberals fired off cannons, Conservatives rang church bells, and election agents handed out sovereigns. To receive a bribe, you might—for instance—take the gold-laden hand of a man who had hidden himself behind the door of a pub.[13] It fell to the candidates' agents to buy the optimum number of votes at minimum expense and with maximum discretion at just the right time.

Drinking, like balloting, started early in the morning. It began with beer and progressed to ginger brandy, which the revelers nipped from communal jugs. Sometimes election agents rounded up amenable voters, herded them into a party-affiliated public house, turned on the liquor, and locked the door. At length, the drunks would be led to the polling place where, under supervision, they would cast the appropriate ballot.

"WE HAVE KNOWN THE cases we quote," Bagehot had boasted in the *Economist* about the philanthropic techniques of corruption, perhaps thinking of the unseated Bridgwater Conservative. Henry Westropp had ingratiated himself with the electorate not only by buying votes, but also by contributing to municipal good works; over six years, 1859–65, he had sprinkled £2,250 into the right causes. Still and all, when election day came, the Conservative philanthropist had found it necessary to supplement the newer techniques of ingratiation with the time-tested methods.

Bagehot, a servant in tow, had arrived in town and checked into a hotel before the June 7 balloting, and on election day he walked the streets of Bridgwater with his handlers. More than once he fielded a question that sounded curiously like a proposition. "I won't vote for gentlefolks unless they do something for I," one man addressed him.[14] Bagehot kept on walking.

His agents took a more professional view of the opportunity. Unbeknownst to the candidate, they had brought with them £500 in gold, which they began to distribute as the polling got under way. It seemed almost too easy when Bagehot took an early lead. "I am getting nervous about this," one Liberal agent remarked to his confrere. "I do not think they are spending any money on the other side. This is a trap."[15]

The Conservatives, experienced in election-day commerce, gasped at the hypocrisy when they got wind of the early distribution of Liberal gold. Having so mightily protested against Westropp's bribe-giving, the Liberals were buying votes right and left.[16]

Like Bagehot, Patton had delegated election-day tactics to his agents. Deftly calculating the number of votes required to overcome the Liberal lead, the Tories requisitioned £300 to supplement the £750 they had already spent. The extra gold—"tin" was the slang of the political operatives—procured thirty new votes, which brought them nearly even with the Liberals. Too late did Bagehot's handlers wake up to the Tory surge. With few voters still uncommitted, the price of a loose vote went soaring. Early in the afternoon, one of the Liberal operatives, Reed, buttonholed an uncommitted townsman, Chedsey.

Had he voted? Reed inquired.

Chedsey had not, nor did he intend to.

"Would £50 be of any service?" Reed asked. It would not, answered Chedsey, an honest man.[17]

When the votes were counted, it was Patton 301, Bagehot 294. The Liberal agents were heartsick. Outgeneraled, they had ended the day with unspent gold in their pockets. They had missed their market.

Bagehot caught the eye of one of his agents after the returns were in. "Mr. Barham," said the candidate, "I am very much afraid from some things I have seen and observed today that some corrupt practices have been resorted to."

"Sir," replied Barham, "I am sorry to tell you that such is the case."

"I am very, very sorry for it," said Bagehot, and nothing more.

By the official record, neither candidate had spent a great deal. Patton admitted to £216 19s, Bagehot to £193 10s 2d. Actual outlays were, of course, much higher. Patton's side was out £3,500, Bagehot's more than £1,500. As Bagehot could console himself, there was no call for the £600 he had pledged to contribute to a legal challenge against the Conservatives for dirty dealing. It was obvious that his side's hands were no cleaner than the other's.

Patton had only a month to savor his victory before he was obliged to stump for still another election—named to ministerial office, he was bound under the prevailing rules to present himself to the voters again. The Liberals asked Bagehot if he was game for another contest. He was not, Bagehot replied, in the first place because he thought it was bad form to contest the election of a man in Patton's position and, in the second place, because he was disgusted by the corrupt methods of the first election. The Liberals continued their search. In Philip Vanderby, physician turned merchant, they found a candidate who was prepared to outbribe and outspend the Tories, which he did. In this second election, on July 12, 1866, Patton lost, 312 to 276. The Liberals, admitting to an outlay of less than £200, actually spent £4,000; Patton, admitting to legitimate expenses of less than £160, spent more than £2,500. The two elections had cost the temporary Conservative member of Parliament for the borough of Bridgwater the grand total of £6,150.[18]

"I HOPE THAT YOU won't leave us in the lurch," were the parting words of the Liberal agents to Bagehot as the defeated candidate returned home to London to lick his wounds. They were referring to more than £1,000 in bribes they had paid without the candidate's knowledge and in contravention of their assurances to him—and his assurances to the people—that no such methods would be employed. The custom of corruption held that a candidate should reimburse the money that was spent in his name, legitimately or otherwise. Would Bagehot play the game?

The election agents wanted £500 immediately, another £500 "as soon as possible." They told Bagehot's lawyer, George Upton Robins—the candidate himself wanted no part of the negotiations—that a refusal to pay would ruin Bagehot's reputation. His name would "stink," they said; anywhere he went, people would call him mean. They kept up the pressure, repeatedly calling and writing.

Robins reluctantly decided that Bagehot should pay, and so advised his client. Bagehot assented. He could afford it, though he was far from being the "man of large property" that some in Bridgwater had imagined him to be. A final payment of £240 for "professional fees" and "sundries" closed the matter, or so Bagehot and Robins assumed.[19]

The matter was not closed. Bridgwater's name turned out to be the one in bad odor, the fumes wafting all the way to the House of Commons. In 1869 Parliament mounted a full-scale investigation into the stories of the borough's corruption, calling and interviewing hundreds of witnesses reaching back as far as the election of 1831. Bagehot was on the list to testify, as was Bagehot's opponent, now the Right Honourable George Patton, Lord Justice Clerk of Scotland.

Papers relating to the Bridgwater corruption inquiry reached Patton in Scotland on the morning of Sunday, September 19, 1869; he seems to have read them before leaving home to attend Presbyterian services with his wife, Margaret. At church, Patton was unable to compose himself. He moved from seat to seat "as if in search of something, and kept turning over the leaves of the books lying in his pew."[20] On Monday morning, he vanished from his estate at Glenalmond, near the central Scottish district of Perth and Kinross, leaving behind only a straight-edged razor and black necktie, both blood-streaked. One week later, his body was discovered in the bed of the river Almond, his throat cut. The death was ruled a suicide.

In testimony before the bribery commission, George Thompson, a friend of Patton's, said that he had found the jurist in a "very great state of excitement" shortly before his death. Thompson said he had expected that the shame of the revelations about Bridgwater would cause Patton to resign his place on the bench. What he did not expect was that they would lead him to kill himself.[21]

Bagehot was sworn to testify three weeks after Patton's suicide. He did not speak about Patton, nor was he asked about him. He told the story of how he himself had come to stand for election, how his agents had bribed voters behind his back, and how their crimes had disgusted him. At the behest of the commissioners, he read aloud his rousing anti-corruption address, and he described his experiences on election day, including a direct proposition from a citizen for money in exchange for a vote.*

At length, the witness came under the questioning of commissioner Thomas Chisholm Anstey, former member of Parliament and ardent champion of the rights of Catholics in England and Ireland. Anstey was a man of fiery radical causes, universal suffrage among them, and could not have been more different than the calm and cool Bagehot. Anstey asked about the money Bagehot had paid to make good his agents' outlays for bribery. "Did not it occur to you," he demanded, "that it was retrospective bribery they were asking you to commit?"

"No," Bagehot replied, "I never heard there was such a thing. I

---

* Bagehot quoted the man in West Country dialect. The soliciting citizen had been standing in a doorway, sideways, Bagehot added, "as these rustics do."

never knew it until reading the Beverley Commission* the other day. I am not alleging this as an excuse, but I never knew there was any such crime. I never knew the paying money under such circumstances when bribery had taken place was a criminal offense at all, until the other day."

Anstey insisted: "Did it not strike you to be, whatever the law was, as complete an offense against the moral code as if you had previously authorized it?"

"I do not say it was right," Bagehot answered, "that is quite another thing, but I thought you were asking me as to the law."

Anstey: "Did you not think it a violation of that pledge which you gave so admirably in the words you have read in your speech?"

Bagehot: "I do not think I did. I know I did not want to pay the money then. It was very reluctantly I ever consented to it."

A second commissioner, Edwin Plumer Price, took over the interrogation. "Was great pressure put upon you to pay this money?" he asked.

Bagehot did not directly answer. He said that what caused him to pay was the fear of being branded a sore loser: "so far from making a good moral impression," he said, "I should only have made the impression that I was a mean person. A successful candidate, at any rate, can clear himself of that by giving up his seat, but a defeated candidate is left to be virtuous at other people's expense. That was the feeling in my mind. I am not by any means defending it."

In a subsequent exchange with Price, Bagehot went so far as to admit that his decision to pay was a "very questionable thing." The

---

* Beverley, in the East Riding of Yorkshire, was a notoriously corrupt constituency that Parliament disenfranchised in 1869. In the final election before it was stricken from the rolls, in 1868, the novelist Anthony Trollope traveled to Beverley to stand as a Liberal candidate for Parliament. He testified before the Bribery Commission that he spent £400, none of it for the purpose of buying votes or treating the electors to beer, for he had exacted an oral pledge from his managers beforehand. "How did you stand on the poll?" the author of *Phineas Finn* was asked. "At the bottom," Trollope replied.

commissioners probed further. They judged that Bagehot was "privy and assenting to some of the corrupt practices extensively prevailing" in the June 1866 by-election, as was the deceased George Patton. Sir John Villiers Shelley—who, like Patton, had died before he could testify—was found to be innocent. Which is to say, "not privy or assenting to any of the corrupt practices so prevailing."[22]

No legal charges were brought against Bagehot—the political principals in these cases were rarely charged. Neither were journalistic charges leveled, though the *Economist* might have had plenty to say against the candidate who turned a blind eye to bribery if that party did not happen to occupy the editor's chair. Nor did his uncomfortable experience before the Bridgwater commission cause Bagehot to refuse a later opportunity to stand for Parliament—this time as the member for his alma mater, University College London.

CHAPTER 13

BY "INFLUENCE AND CORRUPTION"

alter Bagehot loathed Benjamin Disraeli. Like most Liberal Victorian intellectuals, he charged the great Conservative leader with flippancy, effrontery, flamboyance, cynicism, and
recklessness. He was likely not amused—even if Victoria herself had
been—at the novelist–statesman's supposed quip to Her Majesty, "I
am the blank page between the Old and the New Testament." Nor
would he probably have approved of Disraeli impiously comparing the
1847 suspension of the Bank Charter Act to the miracle of the lique-
faction of St. Januarius's blood—"the remedy is equally efficient and
equally a hoax."[1]

Disraeli was born in London in 1804, the eldest son and second
child of Isaac Disraeli, whose private means allowed him to lead a life
of non-income-producing contemplation in the Reading Room of the
British Library. Born a Jew, Benjamin was baptized in the Church of
England at the age of twelve on the strength of a family friend's argument that the established church, whether or not it could open social
and professional doors for a man called Disraeli, at least wouldn't slam
them shut. Benjamin was also born a Romantic: pushed to the law (after
a course of schooling whose principal classroom was his father's library),

the twenty-something Disraeli rebelled. As he had one of his characters say in his novel *Vivian Grey*, "To be a great lawyer, I must give up my chance of being a great man."

Instead, young Disraeli determined to strike it rich, and joined a speculative pool in the waning months of the great financial levitation of the mid-1820s. The partners first bet on the short, or bearish side of the market, correctly judging that the bubble would burst. Incorrectly, they gambled that the bursting would occur on their own timetable—a necessarily foreshortened one, as they operated with borrowed money. When, instead, the market made one final upside lurch, they closed out what would prove to be their winning positions. Reversing course, they bought the very shares they had previously sold—South American mining equities, the darlings of the market—hoping to ride them higher. Instead, prices headed lower. Late in 1824, the speculators were out of pocket by £400. By mid-June 1825, they had lost £7,000. At such junctures, one can cut one's losses or dig in one's heels. Choosing the latter course, Disraeli produced a series of pamphlets describing the wondrous opportunities on offer in the shares that he and his partners precariously held and attacking the bears, including members of Parliament, who presumed to warn the public against the evident dangers. "It is impossible to say how far Disraeli believed in the correctness of his own statements in these pamphlets," according to Disraeli's biographer, Robert Blake, but "What is certain is that the companies which he puffed were worthless concerns based on fraud or at best folly. For one destined to become a master of the art of fiction, this literary debut was perhaps not inappropriate, but it was an odd beginning for a future Chancellor of the Exchequer."[2]

Disraeli had had little enough money at the start of this formative investment experience; by the time it was over, he was left with debts that dogged him for decades, and which formed an integral part of a reputation unlikely to win the admiration of a frugal West Country banker.

Impassive by nature, Disraeli bore this crushing obligation with no outward sign of distress. He dressed as exotically as if he were headed to a Byron-themed costume party, and traveled for months on end—in the company of, among others, Lord Byron's former servant, Tita[3]— indulging his senses in Turkey, Greece, Egypt, and Spain. Upon returning to England in 1831, he was treated for venereal disease.[4]

"Miserable" was how Disraeli recalled his aimless twenties,[5] but he was not entirely without a plan: he set out to win a seat in Parliament. While members of Parliament received no pay, they enjoyed something that Disraeli had particular reason to value—immunity from imprisonment for debt.*

He stood for Parliament in 1832 as a Radical and lost. Three more attempts ended in defeat, but he was finally handed a safe seat—he was by now a Conservative—and at last entered Parliament in 1837, where he fell in with the Young England reaction against utilitarianism, reform, and the budding art of economic analysis. A protectionist, he favored the landed aristocracy against the theories of the Anti-Corn Law League, and when the Tory prime minister Robert Peel, an avowed protectionist, turned his coat to support free trade, it was Disraeli's pyrotechnical invective that people remembered. Disraeli spoke like the gifted writer he was. His *Sybil, or The Two Nations* drew popular attention to the horrific conditions of Britain's working poor.†

When the Conservative Party won the general election of 1852 and the Tory prime minister, Lord Derby, found himself in need of a suitable chancellor of the exchequer, he fixed on the party's rising star. Against the insolvent Disraeli's protests that he knew demonstrably little about finance, Derby reassured him, "You know as much as Mr.

---

* His 1839 marriage to Mary Anne Lewis, a delightful flibbertigibbet with a widow's income of £5,000 a year (half the amount that Bagehot defined as the threshold of being rich) was a blessing in many respects. Financially, it helped only a little. Jonathan Parry, "Disraeli, Benjamin, earl of Beaconsfield (1804-1881)," Oxford Dictionary of National Biography.

† It was published in 1845, midway through the Hungry Forties, the same year as Friedrich Engels's *The Condition of the Working Class in England in 1844.*

Canning did. They give you the figures." The new chancellor served with flair in a government that lasted only ten months.*

Disraeli returned as Derby's chancellor in a second government that was formed in 1858. Reducing and redefining the property qualifications for voting ("Reform!") was at the top of the legislative agenda, and it fell to Disraeli to steer the government's bill through the House of Commons. When that reform legislation failed, so did the government— again. Yet the *Economist* begrudged the chancellor a word of praise: It was Disraeli, and only Disraeli, who had kept the wheels on the Derby omnibus, Bagehot said. Since his less auspicious showing in 1852, he had learned "to lead with dignity and fail with dignity."[6]

Not that Disraeli entirely measured up to Bagehot's standards: This most original figure lacked originality, according to the editor.† He had no political philosophy, no "political faith—he probably does not know what it means"; his speeches were no more substantive than his novels. The redeeming features of his parliamentary performances were the jibes he deployed in debate—a case of "turning his literary plough- shares and pruning hooks into swords and spears."[7]

It would not have been the safest bet in British politics that the prin- cipal Tory opponent of Gladstone's 1866 reform would himself, the very next year, drive through a Conservative reform measure more radical

---

* In 1853, his wax likeness took its place in Madame Tussaud's famous museum, a full seventeen years before the representation of his archrival, Gladstone.

† An inexplicable misjudgment, the very opposite of the truth. "Bagehot was fond of paradoxes, and this is one of his most foolish," observed Arthur Anthony Bau- mann, a near contemporary of Bagehot and Disraeli, in his book of reminiscences, *The Last Victorians.* "The education of our public schools and universities has indis- putable merits, but it has the fault of turning out its pupils in a conventional mold. Disraeli had not learned to speak at 'Pop' [the Eton debating society] or the Union [the Oxford &/or Cambridge counterpart]; he taught himself on the hustings and rehearsed in his father's library. It was his detachment from the vulgar prejudices of the upper and middle classes, his isolated and purely literary upbringing, that gave freshness and force to his speculations on politics." Arthur Anthony Baumann, *The Last Victorians* (Philadelphia: J.B. Lippincott, 1927), 46.

than the one he himself had decried in the wee hours of April 27, 1866,*
though Bagehot himself could not have been surprised. Philosophical
flexibility was, after all, Dizzy's creed. Following Gladstone's failure—
or, equally, Lowe's victory—in 1866, the Queen had pressed for a new
reform bill; in the wake of Black Friday, Reform League demonstrations
drew tens of thousands to Trafalgar Square and Hyde Park to bear witness to the iniquity of the English franchise. Derby and Disraeli, succeeding Russell and Gladstone, resolved to sponsor reform legislation
that would one-up the Liberals—or, in Derby's immortal phrase, "dish
the Whigs" ("Whigs," in this case, being synonymous with the party of
Gladstone). When, at length, the Tories did just that, Bagehot stood at
his desk to render the *Economist*'s verdict.

"It *is* Mr. Disraeli's bill," Bagehot judged. "For this end, [Disraeli]
induced his party to surrender their creed and their policy; he altered
what his followers had to say, even more than the Constitution under
which they are going to live. How then did he attain such a singular success?

"It is usual," he went on, "to say that he attained it by fraud and
deceit. And we certainly are not about to defend his morality. On the
contrary, we have attacked it often, and, if need were, would attack it
now." But fraud alone could not explain it—it is "too ugly and coarse."
There must be something else. What could that something be? Not—to
be sure—Disraeli's power of abstract reasoning, for of this he had none.

---

* The Representation of the People Act of 1867 virtually doubled the number of eligible electors to two million, out of seven million adult males in England and Wales.
In urban and suburban constituencies, i.e., the boroughs, it extended the franchise
to all householders as well as to any lodger paying the annual rent of £10 or more, the
threshold in place since 1832. In the counties, it gave the vote to agricultural landowners. Wikipedia contributors, "Reform Act 1867," *Wikipedia, The Free Encyclopedia*, https://en.wikipedia.org/w/index/php?title=Reform_Act_1867&oldid=82136628
(accessed February 8, 2018).

"You never know what he is talking about, or whether it means much or little."

Nor could you tell what he was thinking. Not even his wife, Mary Anne, knew. Among the treasures in the Disraeli papers is a comparison of his personal traits to those of his wife—his to the left, hers to the right, penned in her hand—including:

Very calm	Very effervescent
Manners grave and almost sad	Gay and happy looking when speaking
Never irritable	Very irritable
Often says what he does not think.	Never says anything she does not think.
It is impossible to find out who he likes or dislikes from his manner. He does not show his feelings	Her manner is quite different, and to those she likes she shows her feelings.[8]

Everyone was struck by Disraeli's impassivity; his face was a mask to friend and foe alike. To the quickness of "a keen man," Bagehot perceived, "he joins, by some freak of nature, the imperturbability of an apathetic man. Whether he is quite as impassive as he seems may, indeed, be doubted. Very near observers are said to be able to detect shades of wincing. But very impassible he must be; and it is a sort of 'double first' in skirmishing to be so quick to hit, and so hard to be hit."

A stick-and-move welterweight, then, was the *Economist*'s estimation of the fighting Disraeli. Yes, he possessed "the most ingenious and manipulating intellect of his generation" and, yes, he led one of the two principal political parties of the world's greatest empire. But his party was a party of dunces: "The grade of gentry who fill the country seats, and mostly compose the Conservative party in the Commons, are perhaps the least able and valuable part of English society."[9]

Bagehot did have a point with respect to abstract political theorizing: it was not Dizzy's strong suit, though the Conservative leader was capable of spinning a theory of the English Constitution that passed muster with the master and wardens of the Merchant Taylors' Company. "My lords and gentlemen," Disraeli began in an 1868 address to that ancient City guild,

> the Constitution of England is not a paper Constitution. [Hear.] It is an aggregation of institutions, many of them founded merely upon prescription, some of them fortified by muniments, but all of them the fruit and experience of an ancient and illustrious people. [Cheers.] And the consequence of this peculiar Constitution has been this—one experienced by no other European nation—that in England, society has always been more powerful than the State [hear].[10]

The Church of England and the landed interest formed the beating heart of what Disraeli called the "territorial constitution," and it was the happy alliance of church and state that nurtured the historically rare coexistence of liberty and order. "[I]n the age in which we live," said Disraeli, "the duties of Government each year become more social than political. I am at a loss to know how these duties can be fulfilled if the State be not in intimate relation with an order of men set apart, who, by their piety, their learning and their social devotion, not only guide and control, but soften and assuage the asperities of conflicting creeds. [Cheers]."

Disraeli was no deeper a theologian than he was a constitutional theorist, and when he talked about God—playing his "religious trombone," as the Tory chronicler Arthur Baumann called it—even some of his admirers covered their ears. However, Disraeli's social and literary gifts were of a different order. His speech and bearing had a magical effect on many who heard him in parliamentary action, and Baumann was among the affectionate observers who sat in the House of Lords when Disraeli rose to speak on the Treaty of Berlin, by which the Great Powers put their stamp on the recently concluded Russo-Turkish War of 1877–78. "He divided his speech into two parts," Baumann recalled,

> the first dealing with Europe, the second treating of the Eastern possessions of the Sultan. After dismissing the absurd pretentions of Greece with a counsel of patience, he stopped and put his hand into the inner breast-pocket of his frock coat. He pulled out a tiny silver flask, deliberately unscrewed the top, took a pull at its contents, as deliberately replaced it, and turning to a grave and silent House said, "And now, my lords, I will ask you to accompany me into Asia." A well-bred ripple ran along the scarlet benches.[11]

On May 20, 1867, John Stuart Mill made what he came to regard as "the only really important public service I performed in the capacity of a member of Parliament": he proposed substituting "person" for "man" in Disraeli's suffrage bill, the nascent 1867 Reform Act. Hoots of male derision met the suggestion that women, of all creatures, should be given the vote. "It is thought, perhaps," said Mill, "that those who are principally charged with the moral education of the future generations of men, cannot be fit to form an opinion about the moral and educational interests of a people; and that those whose chief daily business is the judicious laying-out of money, so as to produce the greatest results with the smallest means, cannot possibly give any lessons to the right. hon. Gentlemen on the other side of the house, or on this, who contrive to produce such singularly small results with such vast means."

Disraeli, who, as chancellor, had everything to do with the production of those singularly small results, chose not to enter the debate, nor did he vote on the motion, which failed 196–73. According to Robert Blake, "Disraeli was by no means unfriendly to the idea, anyway in principle. Indeed, few people would have gained more than he by votes for women. But he did not regard the proposal as practical politics."[12]

It was at about this time that Emily Davies, the suffragist and educational reformer, was recruiting distinguished men and women to support her work to found a women's college of Oxbridge caliber. Tennyson, Browning, Ruskin, several members of Parliament, and the economist William Newmarch were among the 175 who consented to sign the memorial or to serve on an organizing committee. The editor of the *Economist*, too, was asked to participate. Bagehot replied as follows:

> I assure you I am not an enemy of women, I am very favorable to their employment as *laborers* or in other *menial* capacity. I have, however, doubts as to the likelihood of their succeeding in business as capitalists. I am sure the nerves of most women would break down under the anxiety, and that most of them are utterly destitute of the disciplined reticence, necessary to every sort of cooperation. Two thousand years hence you may have changed it all, but the present women will only flirt with men, and quarrel with each other.[13]

Possibly, Bagehot was being facetious (though, if so, where was the fun?), or blowing off steam in response to some unknown provocation, though it can't be denied that he had a misogynistic side. A tone of overbearing masculine superiority hung heavily over even an 1874 article throwing the *Economist*'s weight behind the decision to allow women to enroll in degree-granting course work at the University of London.*[14]

What was Bagehot's true position on the Woman Question? The connective tissue between his private communication to Emily Davies—who would go on to found Girton College, later absorbed into Cambridge University—and his 1874 article was a scorn for those he considered lesser beings. Neither Disraeli nor Mill was given to sneering at the weak or the ignorant. Bagehot sneered habitually.

In the political negotiations for reform, Disraeli consented to the granting of a new parliamentary constituency for the University of London. As Oxford and Cambridge had their seat, so, now, would Bagehot's alma mater.

And as UCL gained, so did Robert Lowe lose; Calne, the pocket borough he represented in Parliament—the trousers of that pocket belonging to Lord Landsdowne—was being reformed out of existence. Where else might the nation's foremost opponent of the enfranchisement of the working classes turn for electoral support? Not to those first-time working-class voters, nor still to the Liberal Party leadership, who would not soon forget Lowe's signal contribution to the defeat of the Russell–Gladstone ministry in 1866 and the reciprocal rise of the Derby–Disraeli government in 1867. There was one flicker of hope, however. Lowe's work in the cause of public health had won him the gratitude of the medical profession, including the many physician–alumni of UCL. And though Lowe was an Oxford man, he had served

---

* "We believe that no [educated] women are so little likely to be forward and presumptuous as those who have received an education above their fellows. Instead of encouraging them to pass into conflicts for which they are not fitted, it will, we believe, tend to a very remarkable degree to put a drag on that excitable and dangerous feminine enthusiasm which is so marked a feature of our time, not because the leaders are educated, but because they are uneducated." Norman St John-Stevas, ed., *The Collected Works of Walter Bagehot*, vol. 7 (London: the Economist, 1974), 414.

UCL as a member of its senate and in the House of Commons, which had blocked a plan that would have split the honor of a new parliamentary seat between UCL and Durham. Thanks to Lowe, UCL alone gained its parliamentary voice.

Richard Holt Hutton, still a close friend of Bagehot's, was not alone in thinking that UCL should send one of its own to Parliament, rather than go crawling to Oxford or Cambridge for political talent. Bagehot was of the same view. Hutton and he likewise agreed that the editor of the *Economist* should be that favorite son.

Hutton, taking charge of his friend's campaign, presented Bagehot to the electors first as a distinguished man of letters, second as the author of *The English Constitution*, third as a banker and economist, and only fourth as the editor of the *Economist*. As to character and convictions, Hutton noted Bagehot's "cordial adhesion to those principles of religious liberty of which our University may fairly be considered the embodiment, and his personal attachment to the Liberal cause."[15]

Bagehot attracted strong early support: the banker and politician George Goschen, the economist Stanley Jevons, and the author and jurist Fitzjames Stephen signed on for him. The very conservative Lord Stanley said that, naturally, he would prefer a good Tory, but Bagehot would otherwise nicely do.

John Lubbock, a thirty-four-year-old London private banker, naturalist, mathematician, and intellectual ally of his Kent neighbor, Charles Darwin, also signaled his support—until deciding to stand himself.*

---

* Lubbock, who knew Bagehot as a fellow banker, wanted no intra-Liberal row. He cautioned a supporter, "I have a great personal regard for him, and think moreover that an attack on his peculiar manner would be regarded by many as going a step too far and defeat its own object." At the time, "peculiar" signified "singular," not necessarily strange, and Bagehot's writing certainly made him singular. His conduct at the Manchester Town Hall, in which he challenged the working men in the audience to debate, or in Bridgwater, when he was a silent partner in vote-buying, reveal another dimension of peculiarity with Bagehot: a striking lack of self-awareness. *The Collected Works of Walter Bagehot*, 13:624.

Edwin Chadwick, sixty-eight years old, revered fighter for public health, was another contender for the UCL seat. All, like Lowe, were Liberals.

Bagehot, as he addressed the UCL electors late in June 1867 in the form of a letter to Hutton, said he would waste no breath decrying the Tories' "leap in the dark," as Derby famously styled their great reform. "The sudden extension of the franchise is one of those 'facts of the first magnitude' which are never long resisted." In the wake of the first reform, in 1832, the call went forth to mobilize the new electors; "Register! Register! Register!" the victorious progressives cried. Now, said Bagehot, the cry must be, "Educate! Educate! Educate!" To this end, the government would have to "intervene far more widely than is as yet thought ere the problem of wide education in a mixed society is solved."

Some would oppose this breach of the tenets of limited government, Bagehot went on, perhaps recalling his own libertarian convictions. They should not:

> The English State is but another name for the English people, and to be afraid of it, is to be alarmed at ourselves. From countless causes the age of great cities requires a strong government. The due extension of the functions of the State is superintending the health and in lessening the vice and misery of our large towns must receive speedy attention from a Parliament in which most of the inhabitants of those towns are for the first time directly represented.[16]

The would-be member for UCL would, if elected, work to sweep away the remaining pocket boroughs, stewpots of electoral corruption. The status of the established Irish Protestant Church, the English flower long ago transplanted into Catholic soil but never taking root, was another hotly contested issue of the day; Bagehot pledged to disestablish it.

Bagehot closed his message with an appeal to restore Gladstone to power, a harmless enough rousing of the Liberal faithful. Anything but anodyne was what followed: "Mr. Disraeli . . . believes that by influence and corruption the mass of the new voters may be made to aid him. But I do not believe that a Government based on influence and corruption is possible in England."[17] To hint at Disraeli's "deceit," as Bagehot had done anonymously in an *Economist* article was one thing. To level a charge of personal corruption against him in a signed election document was something very different. Bagehot's pen, Baumann observed, "had run away with him," and now UCL's Tory rump was mobilized against Bagehot even as the Liberal vote was split four ways.

Or it would have been so split, had not contestants serially withdrawn from the race. Bagehot quit in July 1868, leaving Lowe as the only serious contender remaining on the ballot. The member for the doomed constituency of Calne had, by then, patched things up with Gladstone, who was said to be considering Lowe for a ministerial post in the next administration. Of Lowe, Bagehot wrote graciously (and truly) in his resignation message, "He has one merit, which, with me at least, weighs much. In an age when the fear to offend and the wish to be thought safe tend to cloak the thoughts of public men in a uniform coating of common-place phrases, Mr. Lowe always expresses marked thoughts in characteristic words; at every conjuncture he is at least himself, and in this age that is a rare merit."

Lowe won the seat in an uncontested election in November 1868. Nationally, the Liberals stormed back into power with Gladstone in the vanguard. Lowe, possessor of every talent but the one governing the wise use of all other talents, became Gladstone's chancellor of the exchequer.

As for Bagehot, he resolved never again to seek parliamentary office, and he was as good as his word, though his friends implored him to try. The depth of his disappointment at failing to reach the House of Commons was only revealed years later.

Bagehot was a member of the Metaphysical Society, a kind of reconstitution of the Cambridge Apostles for brainy gentlemen at the height of their post-collegiate careers. In 1870, Bagehot read a paper to the members concerning his experience at Bridgwater. Curiously, he said, he was still overcome with the strongest sensation that he should be the member for Bridgwater, almost four years after he fell seven votes short. It made no difference that he couldn't possibly hold the position now; as punishment for its corruption, the borough had recently been disenfranchised. If he let his mind wander back to the day he was formally nominated, "with all the people's hands outstretched, and all their excited faces," the "old feeling almost comes back upon me, and for a moment I believe that I shall be member for Bridgwater."[18]

CHAPTER 14

"IN THE FIRST RANK"

There was nothing of the mass market about Walter Bagehot. The *Fortnightly Review*, which serially published *The English Constitution* and *Physics and Politics*, claimed only 2,500 subscribers at its peak circulation in 1872. A year later, the *Economist* achieved a grand total of 3,690 paid subscribers—and that, too, was a high-water mark. It was an elite and intimate circle in which Bagehot made his reputation.

Writing in the *Economist*, he addressed the bankers and merchants in James Wilson's no-frills, business-style prose, but he was under no such stylistic stricture with the readers of the *Fortnightly*. If, for them, he quoted a passage in French or Greek, that passage would likely go untranslated—the learned subscribers needed no crutch. And when he mentioned domestic servants, as he occasionally did in order to mark their intellectual or moral inferiority, he used the inclusive phrase "our servants."

Bagehot was a part of what the radical John Bright derisively termed "Clubland": he belonged to the Windham*[1] and to the Whiggish and

---

* Defunct since 1946. According to a *Short Account of the Windham Club from its Formation in 1828*, Bagehot "suffered from indifferent health, especially in the matter of digestion, and was heard on one occasion to say that, although he belonged to another well-known club, nothing would induce him to dine elsewhere than at the

aristocratic Brooks's, both on St James's Street. He would one day be received into the Athenaeum, the inner sanctum of the English intelligentsia.

No aristocrat, at least not by birth, Bagehot nevertheless moved comfortably among the well-born, including his sponsors for Brooks's: Charles Villiers, MP, and George Leveson-Gower, the second Earl Granville. Villiers was a hero of the Anti-Corn Law League, a campaigner for poor-law reform, and a fixture of London society—"ill-dressed but witty, informed, civilized, at times mischievous."[2] Granville, a great Whig magnate, the son of a British ambassador in Paris (where the young Granville had learned to speak French with "the accent of the ancien regime"), led the Liberal Party in the House of Lords. In 1869, the year of Bagehot's admission to Brooks's, Granville was Gladstone's colonial secretary. Fellow members of the Brooks's class of 1869 included the brewer Michael Bass, a Royal Navy captain, three MPs, and an earl.

Bagehot was a banker before he was an editor, but he was neither a long-established London private banker nor a moneybags London joint-stock banker. Stuckey's was, for a country bank, big and profitable, but it was still a country bank. Its London representative enjoyed no particular stature in Lombard Street.

Still less did the descriptor "journalist" lend distinction. Then, as now, a newsman was a supplicant; such access to power as he enjoyed was that which someone chose to grant him. The gift was rarely an expression of pure friendship, and the wise journalist, if he hoped to receive additional favors, took care to give something in return. Information in exchange for publicity—publicity either given or withheld, as one's source preferred—was and remains the basic journalistic transaction. Bagehot transacted deftly, though he was no collector of people.

Windham." Norman St John-Stevas, ed., *The Collected Works of Walter Bagehot*, vol. 13 (London: the Economist, 1896), 632.

"It is inconceivable to me," he remarked, "to like to see many people and even to speak to them. Every new person you know is an intellectual burden because you may see them again, and must be able to recognize and willing to converse with them."[3] It was not the attitude that typically advances a journalistic career.

Notorious though he was within the Wilson sisterhood for ducking out from balls or for ignoring the chatty "pillars of crinoline" who flanked him at dinner parties, Bagehot shone in conversation when others returned the favor. James Bryce, the Victorian jurist, historian, chronicler of America, diplomat, amateur botanist, world traveler, mountain climber, and Liberal politician, once fell into conversation with Bagehot at a party at George Eliot's home. Of that and similar invigorating encounters, Bryce recalled, "one seemed to gain more profit as well as pleasure from a talk with [Bagehot] than with almost anyone else, all the more so because, however much one felt his superiority, it always remained conversation, and not, as so often with great talkers, a lecture or a declamation."[4]

Among his self-limited circle of friends and acquaintances, Bagehot made room for Tories as well as Liberals. He formed a deep attachment to Lord Carnarvon, the Conservative colonial secretary who resigned his ministerial post to protest the 1867 Reform Act. Carnarvon was "one of my sort," as Bagehot told his parents in a note describing a weekend party at the earl's country house among "the fast people":

> The women wore wonderful dresses, and we played cards rather high, always in the evening and sometimes in the morning—at least some people played in the morning.—I kept my character for wisdom and did not. Lady Carnarvon is very clever and literary—at least with *snaps* of Literature. They will be *people* for some years to come, for they are both clever, very ambitious and have a beautiful place near London to entertain in.[5]

The economist William Stanley Jevons, the jurist Henry Sumner Maine, the poet and theologian John Henry Newman, and Gladstone were among his correspondents. The poet Matthew Arnold was a frequent dinner guest and visited Bagehot when he fell ill.[6] George Eliot and he talked shop at one of her Sunday afternoon parties, she complaining about "the pain of composition." If Bagehot expressed sympathy, it was likely out of fellow-feeling rather than any personal experience with writer's block: his pen fairly flew across the page.[7]

Few journalists have ever enjoyed the kind of rapport with politicians that Bagehot enjoyed with Gladstone. If it was a transactional union, it was also a meeting of minds and spirits. And if Bagehot, sixteen years younger, was, of necessity, the junior partner, he was still that bookish politician's intellectual peer.

In 1865, Gladstone had thrown his weight behind the nascent Bagehot-for-Parliament campaign in Manchester. "If," said Gladstone's testimonial, which he addressed to Bagehot for circulation to the appropriate political powers, "thorough acquaintance with economic science, extensive and accurate knowledge, ready and practical habits of business and a conciliatory disposition, go to fit a man for the representation of these great national interests, it certainly appears to me that your fitness must stand without dispute in the first rank."[8] Bagehot did possess each of the qualities Gladstone named, even if he lacked the common touch. He might have made a political career if he, like certain lucky ungregarious politicians—Sir George Lewis, or the Conservative leader and future prime minister Lord Stanley were examples—could have procured a parliamentary seat without having had to stand in a contested election.

On Black Friday, May 11, 1866, the day of the Overend Gurney panic, Bagehot made time to brief Gladstone, then the chancellor, on just how bad things were in the City. They met twice more the following week. Evidently, the chancellor was planning to revive his plan to regulate the country-bank issues, since Bagehot, on May 21, wrote to advise against it. The private circulation of the country banks was yesteryear's problem, Bagehot counseled—as indeed it was.[9] Gladstone took his advice.

In the course of making his unsuccessful run to become the first member of Parliament for University College London one year later, Bagehot attested of Gladstone, "In amplitude of knowledge, intensity of labor, in a flexible eloquence suited either to the highest discussions or to the meanest details of public business, he has no living equal." Certainly, there was no comparing the Liberal statesman with the corrupt Tory Disraeli.

Bagehot became a confidant not only of Gladstone, but also his inner circle. On October 11, 1870, in the opening months of the Franco-Prussian War, the Earl of Granville, by now Gladstone's foreign secretary, addressed a confidential letter to the editor of the *Economist*, whom he'd recommended to Brooks's a year before. It closed with an unusual request:

> May I ask you in anything you say, which always comes with so much weight both from the high character of your paper and the great ability of the articles, not to write anything which will give the thoughtful Germans reason to believe that they have just cause of complaint against us. You will believe me when I say the request is exclusively on public grounds.[10]

In the October 15 *Economist*, under the headline "Count Bernstorff's Rejoinder to Lord Granville on Neutrality," there duly appeared an article noting that, while England had indeed sent munitions to France, she had likewise shipped field blankets to Prussia, thereby favoring neither side and violating no rule of neutrality.[11]

John Thadeus Delane of *The Times* and Edward Levy-Lawson, proprietor of the *Daily Telegraph*, were arguably the most influential journalists in London: they alone were accorded the privilege of standing at the bar of the House of Lords, along with members of the House of Commons. Yet while Delane's name turns up in Gladstone's diary 58 times and Levy-Lawson's 53, Bagehot rated 125 mentions, 17 of which occur after his death, denoting that Gladstone had either been reading Bagehot's writing or corresponding with his widow. During their courtship, Bagehot confessed to Eliza that his ambition was to write in such a way as to wield some influence "over people's wills, faculties and conduct," and in that he succeeded.

BAGEHOT'S HEALTH BEGAN TO FAIL around Christmas, 1867. Returning from midnight church services, he "caught a chill which developed into a severe case of internal inflammation," which left him too weak even to read. The malady persisted, and Eliza's diary increasingly came to feature such entries as "Walter poorly," "Walter not well," "Walter in bed." In 1868, he hired Robert Giffen, the economist whom Alfred Marshall would later call the "Prince of Statisticians," to help him do the things he had previously done on his own.[12] He suffered an attack in August 1869 that left him bedridden for a month.

News of the death of Bagehot's mother arrived by telegram on February 21, 1870, after Bagehot had left the house for a day at the office. Emilie Barrington, a Bagehot biographer and the youngest Wilson daughter, dispatched her husband to intercept him, and the brothers-in-law met on the platform of Cannon Street station—by which time Bagehot had already found out. "He looked scared," Emilie recalled her husband telling her, "and his eyes wild. He exclaimed briefly, as if astonished at the sound of his own words—'My mother is dead.'"[13]

Bagehot loved his mother tenderly, treated her with the respect she often did not receive from others, and flew to her side whenever she lost control. After her funeral, he told Emilie how shocked he was to be consoled by well-intentioned people who felt her death was all for the best, as she had suffered so.

Operating at less than full capacity, Bagehot nonetheless managed to produce some of his best writing in the aftermath of his mother's death. *Physics and Politics* appeared serially in the *Fortnightly Review* beginning in 1867. The toll that lingering ill health took on Bagehot was evident in the uncharacteristically slow tempo of its publication; the finished book did not appear until 1872. The title was a misnomer— "Biology and Politics" would have been more descriptive.

Physics and Politics owes its inspiration in part to Sir Henry Maine and his ideas about the evolution of society from status to contract, in part to Herbert Spencer and Thomas Malthus and their notions about the struggle for existence, and—in trace amounts—to Charles Darwin and the broadly defined theory of evolution. Though the publisher, Henry S. King, packaged the slim, 224-page volume as part of its International Scientific Series, *Physics and Politics* is a production not of science, but of imagination and supposition. It is anthropology without the fieldwork, science without the laboratory, and scholarship without the footnotes. It is the daring and ambitious speculation of an educated Victorian amateur on a branch of knowledge about which he admits he knows little.[14]

Progress is rare and stagnation common in human society, Bagehot observes. He sets himself the task of explaining why some nations advance and others stand still. "National character," the source of which is the "innate tendency of the human mind to like what is around it," explains a great deal. All this began in a time before nations, at the beginning of human society.

First came the pre-economic, or "preliminary," age, then the "age of fighting," then the "age of discussion." Darwin and his acolytes had put God on the defensive. Anticipating his critics, Bagehot announces that he has no quarrel with religion; "Providence" finds a place in his worldview.[15] Bagehot describes the dawn of civilization with the authority of a man who was there to see it:

Man, being the strongest of all animals, differs from the rest; he was obliged to be his own domesticator; he had to tame himself.

And the way in which it happened was, that the most obedient, the tamest tribes are, at the first stage in the real struggle of life, the strongest and the conquerors. All are very wild then; the animal vigor, the savage virtue of the race has died out in none, and all have enough of it. But what makes one tribe—one incipient tribe, one bit of a tribe—to differ from another is their relative faculty of coherence. The slightest symptom of legal development, the least indication of a military bond, is then enough to turn the scale. The compact tribes win, and the compact tribes are the tamest. Civilization begins, because the beginning of civilization is a military advantage.[16]

Change—variation, adaptation, originality—is the key to progress. And rare are the conditions that obtain it. It is "only possible in those happy cases where the force of legality has gone far enough to bind the nation together, but not far enough to kill out all varieties and destroy man's perpetual tendency to change."[17]

In this clinical way, Bagehot deals with the unlovely human institutions of slavery and warfare. He deems the first a kind of blessing in early days, when slaves afforded leisure to those who would otherwise have had no time to think.[18] War, too, served its purpose, conquest being "the missionary of valor, and the hard impact of military virtues beats meanness out of the world."* Nor, he goes on, should one "be surprised at the

---

* In "From Luther to Hitler," a history of Fascist and Nazi thought published in 1941, William Montgomery McGovern, a professor of political science at Northwestern University, contended that Bagehot's writings, especially *Physics and Politics*, served to inspire Adolf Hitler. If so, the Führer overlooked Bagehot's expressed preference for discussion over battle and his plea, contained in his 1870 article "The Late Lord Clarendon," for nonintervention in foreign conflicts. Thus, "We wish that foreign nations should, as far as may be, solve their own problems; we wish them to gain all the good they can by their own exertions, and to remove all the evil. But we do not wish to take part in their struggles." David Clinton, "'Dash and Doubt,' Walter Bagehot and International Restraint," *Review of Politics* 65(1):107.

prominence given to war. We are dealing with early ages; nation-making is the occupation of man in these ages, and it is war that makes nations."[19]

He then reflects on the well-known homogeneity of the savage tribes—all the civilized travelers, he notes, have remarked on it. What accounts for the undifferentiated quality of primitive peoples is their "extreme propensity to imitation." They are afraid to break the "cake of custom." So it is that "When you have seen one Fuegian, you have seen all Fuegians—one Tasmanian, all Tasmanians." The "higher savages," like the Maori, may appear less homogeneous yet "much of the same monotonous nature clings to them, too. A savage tribe resembles a herd of gregarious beasts; where the leader goes they go too; they copy blindly his habits, and thus soon become that which he already is."[20] To the student of financial anthropology, Bagehot's "herd of gregarious beasts," blindly following the leader, resembles nothing so much as the stampede to sell by presumably civilized, certainly white, shareholders when the bottom falls out of the stock market. It's an analogy that Bagehot chooses not to draw.

What of morality? It was formerly held that all men had an equal measure of conscience, says Bagehot, but nobody believes that any more:

> if men differ in anything they differ in the fineness and the delicacy of their moral intuitions, however we may suppose those feelings to have been acquired. We need not go as far as savages to learn that lesson; we need only talk to the English poor or to our own servants, and we shall be taught it very completely. The lower classes in civilized countries, like all classes in uncivilized countries, are clearly wanting in the nicer part of those feelings which, taken together, we call the *sense* of morality.[21]

Bagehot divides the world in two. In the east, civilizations are old and stationary. In the West, civilizations are new and changeable. The "yoke of fixed custom" is what the newer, more dynamic civilizations have succeeded in throwing off. They have done it through the agency of "government by discussion." "The age of discussion" is the age in which his enlightened readers are privileged to live.

Among the savages, there is nothing to discuss. Everything is settled, either by custom or superstition. Evolved civilizations, by the mere act of inviting discussion, acknowledge that "there is no sacred authority—no one transcendent and divinely appointed man whom in that matter the community is bound to obey."[22]

Discussion teaches tolerance—and history shows that nothing else does:

> In all customary societies bigotry is the ruling principle. In rude places to this day any one who says anything new is looked on with suspicion, and is persecuted by opinion if not injured by penalty. One of the greatest pains to human nature is the pain of a new idea. It is, as common people say, so 'upsetting'; it makes you think that, after all, your favorite notions may be wrong . . . Naturally, therefore, common men hate a new idea, and are disposed more or less to ill-treat the original man who brings it.[23]

While antiquity belonged to men of action, modernity rewards the contemplative. Helmuth von Moltke, the learned and deliberate Prussian general—who could be "silent in seven languages"—is Bagehot's model of the nineteenth-century warrior, a player of "a restrained and considerate game of chess with his enemy." If only, Bagehot digresses, "the art of benefitting men had kept pace with the art of destroying them; for though war has become slow, philanthropy has remained hasty." In charitable work, the impulse to action—the call to "do something," anything—results in not only great good but also great harm.

Even business is harmed by the disposition to heedless action. The source of every speculative mania, besides corruptingly low interest rates, is the drive to do too much with too little. Investing one's own capital may occupy four hours a day. Trying to fill the other four, and to operate on a grander scale, restless people incur debt; it ruins them. "If they could only have sat idle the other four hours," Bagehot reflects of this still-recognizable speculative type, "they would have been rich men."[24]

Latching on to that paradox, Bagehot proposes a remedy: if you want to not do something, open the floor to discussion. Invite all sides to weigh in. To a degree, England was doing just that—regrettably so, according to Bagehot's contemporary Thomas Carlyle, the historian of heroes and heroism, who bemoaned the "national palaver." Bagehot countered that he wished there were more of it. If the "hereditary, barbaric impulse is decaying and dying out," credit should go to government by discussion, "which has fostered a general intellectual tone, a diffused disposition to weigh evidence, a conviction that much may be said on every side of everything, which the elder and more fanatic ages of the world wanted."[25]

There was a final benefit to government by discussion that Bagehot could not bring himself to address directly. It had to do with overpopulation, the reproductive urge, and "the great sin of great cities," as Bagehot's friend, William Rathbone Greg, termed the blight of prostitution. Roundaboutly but unmistakably, Bagehot is saying that there was too much sex.

In ages past, human numbers decided the competitive advantage between tribes and nations. The greater the numbers, the greater the success. While mere numbers no longer counted as they once did, the vestigial impulse to create those numbers persisted. Inching closer to the subject he was driving at, Bagehot argues that there remains "a desire far in excess of what is needed."[26]

In the civilized world, the progress of production could not keep pace with the growth in population: "How painful is the conclusion that it is dubious whether all the machines and inventions of mankind 'have yet lightened the day's labor of a human being.' They have enabled more people to exist, but these people work just as hard and are just as mean and miserable as the elder and the fewer."[27]

And how might government by discussion contain this Malthusian evil? Bagehot, invoking the authority of Herbert Spencer, argues that the energy required to lead a life of the mind—a life of political discussion—leaves less energy for reproduction:

> The perpetual atmosphere of intellectual inquiry acts powerfully, as every one may see by looking about him in London, upon the constitution both of men and women. There is only a certain quantum of power in each of our race; if it goes in one way it is spent, and cannot go in another. The intellectual atmosphere abstracts strength to intellectual matters; it tends to divert that strength which the circumstances of early society directed to the multiplication of numbers; and as a polity of discussion tends, above all things, to produce an intellectual atmosphere, the two things which seemed so far off have been shown to be near, and free government has, in a second case, been shown to tend to cure an inherited excess of human nature.[28]

What this interesting quotation might imply about the state of things chez Bagehot, one may only wonder.

Physics and Politics met a warm reception in Boston ("charming . . . rich in original thought"—*The Atlantic*) as well as in London ("a first and most successful attempt to invest re-historic researches with political interest"—*Pall Mall Gazette*). Today, its merit lies less in what Bagehot said than in the zestful way he said it. "A brilliant piece of dilletantism," the twentieth-century judgment of Joseph Schumpeter, still stands in the twenty-first.[29]

CHAPTER 15

NEVER A BULLISH WORD

In 1875, a select committee of the House of Commons, chaired by Robert Lowe, produced a history of eight years of English financial misadventure in faraway places. Central and South American governments had been borrowing money in London without repaying it—in some cases, without the means even to keep up the appearance of repaying it. "Semi-civilized," was Bagehot's characteristically unsentimental designation for the needy debtors.* Certainly, those governments were put upon, and some were insolvent. The parliamentary postmortem was a chronicle of rapacity and cupidity on the parts of the bankers, brokers, and loan managers, of venal ineptitude by the investors and borrowers. With one minor exception, none of the debtor governments had repaid "any portion of its indebtedness in respect of these loans, except from the proceeds of the loans themselves." Thus did the City of London and its foreign clients anticipate the methods of Charles Ponzi.

---

* "Third world," "lesser developed countries," "developing countries," and (most recently and optimistically) "emerging markets" are the successor labels of the late twentieth and early twenty-first centuries.

Censurable though it was, the MPs concluded, the malfeasance of the bankers, brokers, and loan contractors did not by itself clinch the case for remedial legislation. "Your Committee," concluded the report of the Select Committee on Loans to Foreign States, "feel that it is not their duty to apportion the blame to the different actors in these transactions." In support of this stance of moral neutrality, the committee quoted a comment attributed to the secretary of the London legation of the government of Honduras, in the wake of his country's default: "the fault of the failure falls with equal force upon all who have interests, rights, claims, complaints, or any participation whatever in these matters. It is a kind of *original sin*, which reaches the most innocent who have anything to do with this undertaking."[1]

Perhaps one man was without sin. If Walter Bagehot ever wrote a bullish word on the public securities of Honduras, Spain, Costa Rica, the city state of Santo Domingo, Peru, Bolivia, Egypt, or the Empire of Turkey, there is no record of it. Bagehot was bearish because the governments were unfit, and besides, the interest rates they paid—or at least contracted to pay—failed to compensate English lenders for the catastrophic risks they bore. A "margin of security" was what every investor required, Bagehot counseled his readers, which Honduras, Costa Rica, Santo Domingo, and the rest were unable to provide. So saying, the editor of the *Economist* anticipated the twentieth-century American value investor Benjamin Graham, who would build a philosophy of investment on the imperative need for a "margin of safety."

Demand for the high-yielding bonds of faraway states has waxed and waned for two centuries. It waxed in the boom of the 1820s and waned in the years succeeding the bust. Investors filtered back into the market arrived in force in the aftermath of the failure of Overend Gurney in 1866. In the dull, post-panic British economy, savers strained to earn more than the 3.25 percent available on perpetual British government bonds.

The straining was where the trouble started. Bagehot had warned about the perils of low interest rates since at least the early 1850s. "John Bull," as he advised the readers of the *Inquirer*, quoting but not naming himself, "can stand a great deal, but he cannot stand 2 percent." He pressed on: "People won't take 2 percent; they won't bear a loss of income. Instead of that dreadful event, they invest their careful savings in something impossible—a canal to Kamchatka, a railway to Watchet, a plan for animating the Dead Sea, a corporation for shipping skates to the Torrid Zone."[2] In 1867, with the Bank of England's discount rate quoted at 2 percent on the button, savers invested their careful savings across the seas. Bagehot anticipated the consequences of the coming bond bubble almost before it began to inflate.

Egypt, then a semi-autonomous province of the Ottoman Empire, was one such seeker of funds, and the *Economist* singled it out for special mention. "Many persons have not a distinct perception of the risk of lending to a country in a wholly different state of civilization," the editor advised his readers in November 1867. It was the very month in which the first installment of *Physics and Politics* hit the stands; Bagehot, for one, had been giving the nature of primitive societies close and concentrated thought. "They can hardly imagine the difficulties with which such a country struggles, and the dangers to which it is exposed. They forget that national good faith is a rare and recent thing."[3]

Before modern financial disclosure, corporate insiders generally had the information that the public lacked, but in the case of Egypt, not even the Egyptian government had the figures. It would later come to light that the Egyptian state—its finances casually commingled with those of the spendthrift autocrat Ismail—owed £30 million of debt on less than £6 million of annual revenue.[4] Neither did Bagehot have the Egyptian facts, though he intuited the essentials. "[O]ur notion of continuous political morality is very modern, and hardly penetrates to oriental despotisms," he observed, before closing with the kind of words that typically resonate more in the rueful aftermath of a crash than in the carefree boom that precedes it: "We lend to countries whose condition we do not know, and whose want of civilization we do not consider, and, therefore, we lose our money."[5] Still and all, a new Egyptian loan that year was priced to deliver a current yield of 10 percent.[6]

Admonitions were a staple of the *Economist*'s coverage of sovereign bond issuance in this era. Not quite three years later Bagehot wrote:

> in reality men of business have a great defect as investors of spare money. They are accustomed to a high rate of profit in their business, and they cannot but look with contempt on 5 per cent., 4½ per cent., and all such rates. They think that "any old woman could make those figures," but that they, with their long experience of business matters, ought to make something much better. But if the years after panics (and not less but more than any other, the last year since 1866) were examined it would be found that such men of business did not make more but less.[7]

Bagehot had pulled his punches in the critical months leading up to the Overend Gurney collapse—the legal risk made plain speech inadvisable, he claimed after the damage was done. There was no such holding back with respect to the risks of lending to improvident foreign governments. Here, Bagehot was forthright, unwavering, indefatigable, and seemingly indifferent to the City interests, both to their hostility and their blandishments.*

In exposing the dangers inherent in overseas bond investing, the

---

* Ismail, the Khedive of Egypt, spent lavishly on the journalists he hoped to influence, including the gift of an all-expense-paid junket to attend the opening of the Suez Canal in 1869. It appears that Bagehot did not avail himself of this hospitality. It is impossible to prove it, but the strongest circumstantial evidence suggests that neither he nor the *Economist* was ever for sale. J. Carlile McCoan, *Egypt Under Ismail: A Romance of History* (London: Chapman and Hall, 1889), 104.

Economist performed a public service unmatched by any other leading newspaper in England or Scotland.[8] And in urging the British government to forbear from intervening on behalf of English investors when foreign governments defaulted, Bagehot stood up for the ideal of personal responsibility in financial dealings. His literary, political, and biographical contributions to one side, the body of work he produced during the foreign-government bond craze of the late 1860s to the mid-1870s stands as his signal journalistic achievement.

No such glory covered the financial facilitators of the City. An 1869 loan to the Republic of Santo Domingo set the investment tone for the 1870s. The issuing government received proceeds of only £38,000 out of the many hundreds of thousands of pounds raised through bond sales in its name. As for the investors, they received neither interest on their investment nor the return of their principal. News that the Santo Domingo senate repudiated the loan in July 1870 somehow failed to cross the Atlantic until September 1872. Practically speaking, the loan was a hoax, the involvement of J. S. Morgan & Co.—the firm headed by Junius Spencer Morgan, successful and well-reputed father of J. P. Morgan—notwithstanding. Not all of the proceeds were unaccounted for. Some £93,000 came into the possession of the consul general for the Republic of Santo Domingo in London, Edward Herzberg Hartmont. These funds Hartmont retained for himself, as the committee dryly reported, "and invested in his business, 'partly good investments and partly bad investments.'" Certainly, in the case of Santo Domingo, original sin was front and center.

Peru was a heavy and frequent borrower, though the former Spanish colony was no pillar of political stability. In the first quarter century of its existence as an independent republic, the Pacific-facing nation had had "50 changes of government, five constitutions, countless internal rebellions and five foreign wars, including wars with each of its neighbors except Brazil."[9] That took Peruvian history to 1845. In the interval from 1845 to 1876, there had been sixteen more presidents, of whom "ten accessed power through violent means, usually after a major rebellion or civil war."[10]

The government of Peru had borrowed and defaulted in the mid-1820s; not until 1849 did it patch things up with its foreign creditors. This unpromising start to Peruvian sovereign finance made no indelible mark on the English investors of Bagehot's day. Like many investors in most days, they had no head for history.

Governments and wars came and went, but if the demand for capital was likewise perennial—there were armaments to buy and railroads to build—so, too, was the income afforded by guano exports.

English investors were content to trust in the seabirds whose droppings built the nitrogen-rich deposits on the Chincha Islands, 13 miles off the southwest coast of Peru. It was this ostensibly inexhaustible fertilizer revenue that paid the interest on the government's debt, whoever happened to occupy the office of president. Guano sales topped £2 million annually between the late 1850s and early 1870s. As British farmers furnished much of that revenue with their pounds and shillings, and since those funds were earmarked in London for paying the British holders of Peruvian debt, the brokers and bankers could say that the high-yielding bonds were absolutely safe.

Bagehot knew better. In 1870, he warned his readers against a pending £12 million Peruvian bond sale, observing that a drop in guano sales would ruin the government's finances. Without such revenue, there would be no means to service the debt already incurred, never mind the pending £12 million. The new loan, Bagehot pointed out,

> is for ten times the annual revenue of the State, exclusive of guano; if England were to borrow £600,000,000, it would only be borrowing in proportion. As soon as there is no more guano there will certainly be an enormous deficit, and the creditor will either have to be sacrificed, or his claims met out of new loans, a process which could not be of long continuance.

Then, too, receipts from the sale of guano weren't "revenue" at all—it was a misnomer. They rather represented the liquidation of the national capital stock, "an exactly equivalent process to incurring debt; and the financial consequences of both borrowing, and selling its property, do not require to be stated." One might ask, the banker-cum-journalist posed, why the government was borrowing at all. It must be that "the guano is not immediately available, that the Treasury is empty, and that is why Peru wants the money."[11]

Bagehot and the *Economist* were certainly correct, though it can't be said that their prescience altered the course of events. In that time, as in others, investors demanded income. And no more in their time than in ours did the recitation of the facts slake that thirst for high rates of interest when only low rates were quoted on safe investments. John Bull was falling into the recurrent cyclical trap.

Honduras, still another money pit, had raised £1 million in 1868 on the promise of a 10 percent yield, and was back again in June 1870 with another £2.5 million of bonds, also at 10 percent. On those £3.5 million of combined borrowings, the annual interest charge, £350,000, would amount to twice the government's evident annual revenue—three times as much when allowing for payments into a sinking fund. Here, in the *Economist*'s words, was a "half-civilized" government borrowing more than it could possibly repay. If Honduras could pass for a solvent nation, anything could.[12]

Bagehot was right about the market: it refused to listen. And he was right about the desperation of the Peruvian fiscal position. By 1872, the government in Lima was back to raise an additional £15 million. "If guano . . . does not yield at least £3,000,000," Bagehot predicted, "the creditors will not be paid."[13] It subsequently came to light that guano exports yielded only £2 million a year.[14] The creditors went unpaid.

Peru did sell its £15 million of bonds, though at a heavy discount from par. The price had already dropped to 71½ from 77½ in October 1872 when Bagehot returned to the then familiar subject under a headline which left no room for misinterpretation: "A Warning To Investors In Foreign Government Securities."

"At certain times," Bagehot resignedly led off, "it seems very useless to warn people about the risks of some foreign investments." And this was one of those times, as

almost any community that calls itself a State may obtain large sums from people who certainly make very little inquiry. They are tempted by the name of a State, the high rate of interest, the fact that everybody does the same, and other such irrelevant reasons, assisted too often, it is to be feared, by an artificial premium on the issues which the promoters contrive to maintain on the Stock Exchange.[15]

A sweet reward to the prescient financial journalist is the pleasure of self-quotation (as prescience is intermittent, so is the pleasure sporadic). Tastefully, Bagehot let a statistical table sing his praises, for circumstances in the foreign loan market indeed provided him wide scope for self-commendation. The figures compared the prices of loans at the date of issue with the marked-down prices prevailing at the *Economist*'s press time. Honduras showed especially well: a collapse from an issue price of 80 in 1870 to 36 in 1872. The Santo Domingo bonds of 1869 had declined from 70 to 50. Bolivian, Costa Rican, and Paraguayan securities had likewise depreciated.

"We doubt," Bagehot wrote,

if so great a disaster has for a long time befallen the investment of so considerable an amount of capital in Stock Exchange securities. The depreciation is almost on the scale which occurs when there is a great collapse of bubble companies, though the victims here are fortunately spared the worse aggravation of "calls" [the obligation on the part of the stockholder to stump up more money in the event of the insolvency of the enterprise in which he owns a fractional interest]. It is at least on a far larger scale than what takes place temporarily in an ordinary Stock Exchange "panic"—with this difference, that it has occurred in a quiet time, and from some inherent vice in the things themselves apart from the condition of the market.[16]

The times were quiet but the savers were frenzied. Low interest rates had tempted them into heedless action—the very kind Bagehot had decried in *Physics and Politics*.

THE YEAR 1873 IS notorious for the American financial panic that, while largely sparing London, disarranged commerce and finance on both sides of the Atlantic long after the first shock waves subsided. It was an autumn crisis, and Bagehot gave no warning of the coming storm that summer when he again took up the subject of Egypt. What he did foresee was the looming Egyptian bankruptcy—indeed, there was no need to foresee it. With some essential figures on Cairo's financial position at last placed on the public record, he could see it with his own eyes.

The nation that owed its creditors £30 million in 1867 was now on the hook for £63 million. Debt service alone exceeded £6 million a year, on annual revenue of perhaps £7.3 million. The difference left scant room for the tributes, bribes, wars, palace-building, harem maintenance, fetes, and public works that absorbed so much of the government's income. The Suez Canal, the greatest of these public works, was Egypt's to pay for and Europe's to profit by. The costs of the festival to celebrate its opening in 1869 were locally reckoned at £1.3 million. The cost of construction was as much as £17 million, by Egypt's telling, and £10 million according to the French builder, Ferdinand de Lesseps. The cost in human life borne by the hapless peasants—*fellaheen*—many of whom were conscripted into the murderous pick-and-shovel work, is estimated in thousands.

As for that £7.3 million in budgeted yearly revenue, Bagehot observed,

> according to our experience of foreign budgets, we should be inclined to doubt whether the actual revenue does not fall so far short of the estimate that the interest on the debt would absorb the whole of it. In other words, Egypt must be on the brink of insolvency, and entirely depends for paying its way on the funding or renewal of the immense mass of floating obligations at 12 percent interest.[17]

Egypt was an example of the new face of the sovereign bond market. Creditworthy countries rarely borrowed in times of peace—they had too high a regard for their financial reputation to run up debts for no essential purpose. The striking feature in the contemporary London market was the presence of governments that borrowed to service their previously incurred debts.

Spain was no newcomer to the concert of nations, but its government was one of these profligates. Spanish credit had fallen under suspicion when the cost of debt service came to absorb one-half of Spain's public revenue. Turkey and Egypt had strayed well beyond that red line by allocating between two-thirds and three-quarters of governmental receipts to keeping creditors at bay. For Spain, there was no way out except, in 1873, default (in the wake of which, the desperate government was reduced to paying rates of interest of 30 percent and up—way up, according to *The Times*, which, in 1876, cited one Spanish loan "which brought the lender 109 percent"). "Turkey and Egypt possess, no more than Spain did, immunity from the rules of financial arithmetic," the *Economist* warned, "and we cannot but believe that the same inexorable necessity will very soon arise."

It was in a style more didactic than Bagehot's, though with a sentiment identical to his, that the article concluded: "People who lend to States like Spain and Turkey and Egypt deserve to lose their money, and the clever people who think they will go in for a little time and get out before the crisis comes are among the most likely to lose."[18]

The clever people seemed unconvinced: preparations were soon under way for a mammoth new Egyptian loan. In 1868 the Khedive had pledged to issue no new bonds for five years, though he continued his heavy borrowing through other channels. On the dot of the fifth year, Egypt and its bankers returned to the City of London.

With the new Egyptian debt prospectus lying open before it, the *Economist* passed critical judgment. The country was still "semi-barbarous," the Khedive was his unregenerate self, and his illiterate people were still borne down by taxes. As for the merits of the pending bond issue, "incessant borrowings have been necessary for many years to pay the interest on an always augmenting debt; the revenue is now so deeply pledged that the debt charge can only be paid with more borrowings." The *Economist* was pleased by reports that the public was giving the bonds a wide berth.

Those securities proved, indeed, a hard sell, though they were immensely lucrative to the promoters, who presented old, heavily discounted Egyptian securities—available in the market at a price of 63—as scrip with which to buy quantities of new bonds, accepted at a value of 93. The dealers resold at a handsome profit to whatever remnant of clever people remained in the game. So it was that the Egyptian government realized a net cash receipt of only £11,750,000* on the sale of securities that bore a face value of £32 million. "The annals of State loans probably record no operation so ruinous for the borrower, or so profitable for the lenders and their friends as this," was the judgment

---

* Estimates varied widely, even within the same source; page 208 of McCoan's book states that Egypt realized £17 million out of the £32 million nominal value. In either case, the adjectives "ruinous" and "profitable" would seem to be well chosen.

of one eyewitness to the disaster, J. Carlile McCoan, author of *Egypt Under Ismail.*

SUPPOSEDLY BANKRUPT FOREIGN GOVERNMENTS would find the means to pay if the British lion would only growl at them. So contended an element of unhappy English creditors. In 1868, the *Economist* commended George Goschen for urging the British government not to become an international debt collector. Goschen, then thirty-seven, a rising Liberal MP for the City of London and a former director of the Bank of England, was addressing what would prove to be the nucleus of a contemplated Corporation of Foreign Bondholders. The founders envisioned an organization to prod sovereign states to honor their commitments to English investors. The role of the British government in this useful work was the question on Goschen's mind; there would be no harm in Whitehall using its good offices to advocate fair dealing, he said. Government-to-government coercion was another matter. "We should be damaged by the result of the meeting held today," Goschen told the investors,

> if it went forth that the meeting have endorsed the view that it is the duty of the English Government to compel foreign Governments to pay the debts incurred to English subjects. If the Government were to go to war for such a purpose with Venezuela, they would involve themselves in this position—that if larger Powers should act in the same way, they should also go to war with them. I think it is dangerous to have the idea go forth that when an Englishman lends money to a foreign Government he is creating a national obligation, guaranteed by the full weight of the English Government. The Englishman lends his money to a foreign Government, and gets a high rate of interest, because he incurs a risk.

Amen, said the *Economist*, adding the point that no one would know what a bond was really worth if the navy of the bondholder's government was forever on call to settle contractual disputes.

By 1876, the Corporation of Foreign Bondholders, now in its third year, was able to count seventeen defaulting borrowers. Among them were the ones on which the *Economist* had so presciently harped—Honduras, Santo Domingo, Peru, Paraguay, Bolivia, Turkey. The last-named was far and away the greatest of these truants, owing £197.3 million. Its default, formally acknowledged on October 7, 1875—it had been paying 18 percent to borrow the funds with which to keep current on interest to its foreign creditors—roiled the overseas loan market, especially the Egyptian branch.

Later in October, English holders of Turkish debt, under the Corporation's aegis, gathered to sound off and to chart a negotiating strategy with the authorities in Constantinople. Someone asked if the British government should not press the Turks to honor their engagements, "for was it not something that the interests of thousands of families should be imperiled?" The question drew cheers. Others, echoing the demand for official British intervention, recalled England's sacrifices on behalf of Turkey during the Crimean War, or invoked long-ago testimonials to Turkish financial solidity by Lord Palmerston and Lord Russell. And when J. Carlile McCoan, a self-described eighteen-year resident of Turkey—and, probably, the author of *Egypt under Ismail*—rose to berate the Turkish government for its corruption and insolvency and to marvel at the ignorance of the British press in its coverage of Turkish affairs,* he was shouted down. "He's a bear," the bondholders cried.

---

* The *Economist* and the *Money Market Review* each published a comment on prospects for Turkey's debt in issues dated September 19, 1874. Those prospects, according to the *Review*, were bright and brightening, as the Turkish government was shifting responsibility for administering state revenue to the Ottoman Bank. Alluding to a rally in Turkish bond prices from the lows of 1873, the paper made bold to declare, "It should be borne in mind that the tendency of Turkish Securities is unmistakably upward." The *Economist*, while conceding that the reform was

Bagehot was at least as bearish as McCoan. Commenting on the default ("The event will not surprise our readers"),[19] the *Economist* batted away the notion that the government owed a duty to the gullible bondholders:

> We cannot as a nation undertake to make foreign Governments perform their contracts to individuals; and the promise to pay particular persons first out of particular funds is but one of such contracts. If we once begin to interfere in such matters, the loan dealers of Europe will soon manufacture enough *first* mortgages to give us incessant employment.[20]

The Turkish default marked the end of an era in the English overseas loan market as well as a milestone for the *Economist*. Bagehot had carried the bearish torch for years, and collapsing prices for Central and South American debt had repeatedly proven him right. Now his vindication was nearly complete. One thing still puzzled him, however: "we still find it difficult to explain how the Turkish collapse did not come long ago."[21]

AT ABOUT THE TIME that Turkey admitted its inability to pay its creditors all that was due them, the Egyptian treasury was struggling to meet its December 1875 interest payments; not even a proffered 20 percent interest rate could bring forth the necessary funds.[22] Competing consortia of bankers in Paris and Alexandria proposed various exorbitant terms for a kind of margin loan: the Khedive would borrow £3 million to £4 million on the security of the government's holdings of shares in the Suez Canal Company (Egypt owned some 177,000 shares out of a

---

better than nothing, concluded that Turkish and Egyptian securities remained the speculative playthings they had always been. An advertisement for a new issue of Turkish debt appeared in the September 19 issue of the *Review*. There was no such ad in the *Economist*.

total of 400,000). The Khedive blew hot and cold on the terms, as he did on the French bankers. The conditions were punitive, but his need was great.

It was not Bagehot but another English journalist, Frederick Greenwood, editor of the *Pall Mall Gazette*, who, on November 15, alerted the British Foreign Office to the state of things in Egypt. Here was the chance to secure Britain's sea lane to India, Greenwood urged the foreign secretary, Lord Stanley, 15th Earl of Derby.* The available shares would confer no outright control but would at least deny that strategic advantage to the French. Benjamin Disraeli, by now prime minister—he had defeated Gladstone in the general election of 1874—was of the same mind.

It took just ten days from Greenwood's call to action for the cabinet to approve the purchase. On November 24, Disraeli wired his bid to the Khedive: £4 million for the outright purchase of 177,000 shares (or, as the figures finally fell out, £3,976,583 for 176,602 shares). The deal was done, though the government had nothing like £4 million in the bank. Disraeli dispatched his private secretary, Montagu Corry, to call on the banker Baron Lionel de Rothschild.

"Rothschild," as Corry reminisced, "picked up a muscatel grape, ate it, threw away the skin, and said deliberately, 'What is your security.' 'The British Government.' 'You shall have it.'" Whatever the literal truth of this story, shares and money changed hands, and Parliament—which was not sitting when Disraeli leapt into action—voted to ratify the transaction.

"It is just settled," Disraeli wrote to Queen Victoria:

you have it, Madam. The French Government has been out-generaled. They tried too much, offering loans at an usurious

---

* The 15th Earl of Derby and son of Edward Smith-Stanley, the 14th Earl of Derby, in whose three governments in the 1850s and 1860s Disraeli had served as chancellor.

rate, and with conditions which would have virtually given them the government of Egypt. The Khedive, in despair and disgust, offered your Majesty's Government to purchase his shares outright.

Four millions sterling! and almost immediately. There was only one firm that could do it—Rothschilds. They behaved admirably; advanced the money at a low rate, and the entire interest of the Khedive is now yours, Madam.

Announcement of the purchase secured for Disraeli more than the approval of his countrymen: it also won him the intense, if momentary, gratitude of the suffering holders of Egyptian debt, not least that of the French Crédit Foncier, a state-chartered mortgage bank shockingly caught out holding £6.7 million of Egyptian treasury bills against stockholders' equity of £1.8 million. The Turkish default had opened a trapdoor under the prices of the Khedive's bonds. Britain's investment in the Suez Canal Company shares could be read not only as a shrewd investment, which it proved to be, but also as a wedge for Western influence in Egyptian financial affairs, which it likewise became.

But these constructive influences—constructive, at least, from the Western vantage point—would play out over the course of years. At that moment, the Khedive and his government continued to careen toward default. The first, partial suspension of interest payments came on April 6, 1876.

The *Economist* had opposed Britain's purchase of the Canal Company shares on the grounds that it would lead to entanglements neither Disraeli nor his government could anticipate—and so it did. By and by, France and Britain dispatched, respectively, M. Joubert and George Goschen to Egypt to draw up a plan for financial reform. (The Goschen family investment bank, Fruhling and Goschen, had marketed at least one of the Egyptian issues in London.) Their recommendations gave rise to European control of Egyptian fiscal affairs, European mil-

itary and naval intervention—including, in 1882, the bombardment of
Alexandria by a flotilla of Royal Navy ironclads to beat back an Egyptian nationalist uprising against the then incumbent Khedive and his
friends, the foreign bankers—and, at length, long after Bagehot's death,
the temporary British occupation that, under Evelyn Baring, 1st Earl of
Cromer, became a thinly veiled British protectorate.

Reflecting on the glittery appeal of Egyptian investments in 1876,
the *Economist* posited what might fairly be termed "Bagehot's law of
15 percent":

> the human mind likes 15 percent; it likes things which promise
> much, which seem to bring large gains very close, which some-
> how excite sentiment and interest the imagination. The manu-
> facturers of "financial schemes" know this, and live by it. A long
> and painful experience is necessary to teach men that "15 per-
> cent" is dangerous; that new and showy schemes are to be dis-
> trusted; that the popular instinct on them is essentially fallible,
> and tends to prefer the brilliant policy above the sound—that
> which promises much and pays nothing, above that which, prom-
> ising but little, pays that little.

As the John Bull of Bagehot's day could not stand 2 percent, neither could he seize the chimera of 15 percent. Nor can his modern
descendants.

CHAPTER 16

GOVERNMENT BEARS THE COST

In 1865 the financial thinker and doer George W. Norman took the trouble to commit to paper the monetary views of the editor of the *Economist* and to contrast those opinions with his own. It was a mark of respect for Bagehot, as Norman was one of the grand old men of English monetary matters. A long-serving director of the Bank of England, he had joined the Court of Directors in 1821 at the age of twenty-eight. His nonpecuniary interests ranged from cricket to the language and literature of Norway, which he had studied while making his fortune in the family timber business, to Saxon archeology and the English poor laws. Bagehot and he likely exchanged ideas at the Political Economy Club, of which Norman was a founding member. They no doubt conferred on the topics that Norman addressed in his occasional contributions to the *Economist*. Still, two of England's most formidable monetary thinkers could not seem to agree on what money was.

According to Norman, Bagehot believed that nothing was money but gold and silver. Was not paper money also money? Bagehot denied it, absolutely. Norman just as insistently affirmed it, fixing on an etymological proof: the "universality" of the words "paper money." The phrase could be found in "all languages."

If gold and silver alone were money, it followed that bank notes, even the notes of the Bank of England, must be something other than money. To Bagehot, they were only credit instruments—promises to pay money, like personal checks or bills of exchange. He likewise held that "as a necessary consequence . . . any interference on the part of the state with the issue of bank notes as pernicious, and would leave every individual and corporation free to issue, and make use of such instruments as they might deem most conducive to their own interest."

So, in Bagehot's view, the doors to the banking business should be flung wide open; let anybody try his hand at taking deposits, issuing notes, and extending credit. It amazed Norman that someone so smart could be so wrong. Because bank notes *were* money, the older man was quite certain, not just anybody should be allowed to circulate them, certainly not any hole-in-the-wall country banker. Money was the government's business, or the business of the government's central bank. The value of notes in circulation should vary as "the metallic money which would be required to supply their place might vary." In the best of all worlds, there would be just one bank of issue, the Bank of England. Alas, that was politically impossible; the note-issuing English country bankers would never stand for it. So England must make do with the second-best solution, which had, indeed, become the law in 1844. The Bank Charter Act capped the size of the country circulation and denied the right of issuance to newly formed banks, to banks that had ever failed to redeem their notes in gold, and to banks of issue that had entered into a merger.

Bagehot's ideal was one of numerous competing banks of issue, all well managed and amply capitalized, "each keeping its own reserves and able to meet at any time the claims of note holders as well as its other liabilities." It was a pipe dream, Norman said. England had had its innumerable country issuers, and a quarter of them had gone to the wall in 1825. America still had its myriad currency-emitting banks, which

competed to print, issue, and, inevitably, overissue their own functionally inconvertible scrip.

Norman and Bagehot naturally found themselves on opposite sides
of the perpetually contentious question of the Act of 1844. It seemed
not to matter to Norman that he was writing a memo to himself; he
defended the law with all the vehemence of one who shared its intellectual paternity. The act was successful, Norman averred, because it
achieved its authors' intention—his and Lord Overstone's—of remov-
ing any doubt that the pound was convertible into gold at the fixed and
inviolable rate of £3 17s 9d to the ounce.

Norman made no attempt to deny that the English banking system
was still subject to breakdown, Sir Robert Peel's law notwithstanding.
In 1847, the railroad bubble had burst. In 1857, the American banks had
stopped payment. And yes, in response to those crises, chancellors of
the exchequer had overridden the 1844 Act to allow for an extralegal
emission of Bank of England notes. Only after the panic subsided was
the law reinstated.

These perhaps regrettable interventions were chargeable not to the
act, but to human nature, Norman wrote to himself: "no conceivable
arrangements as to the supply and arrangements of the currency can
obviate all or indeed many of the evils which arise from the cupidity,
the folly and the ignorance of mankind." Ricardo, too, had concluded
that legislation was powerless against a panic.

Could Parliament not craft a kind of escape clause to render Peel's
Act more humane? A way to allow the Bank to issue currency beyond
the limits prescribed by the act before a period of stringency turned
into a run on the banks? And to take such action without having to
waste the time involved in appealing to the chancellor? It was on this
question that the differences in worldview between Norman and Bagehot were most marked. "Such power of relaxation appears fraught with
evil," Norman jotted on his paper. "The exception would infallibly

become the rule—Nobody would regard the salutary provisions of the original law as final, and its objects would be gradually lost sight of, and finally disappear altogether."

Better to let the law stand, then, said Norman, "at all hazards." He granted that, in the recurrent episodes of financial disorder, some solvent businesses might be unable to borrow and that such deprivation could force some into bankruptcy. Well, if so, it was their own fault for sailing too close to the wind. In any case, crises soon passed. "The solvent would swim—the insolvent sink—and the public at large would learn a valuable lesson."[1]

A YEAR AFTER NORMAN wrote his memo to himself, the Overend Gurney failure of 1866 pushed Bagehot to express his own views in his own paper. They were just as Norman had rendered them: The Bank of England owed a duty to the nation, not just to its stockholders, and must collect and husband the nation's monetary gold. In a crisis, it must lend boldly at a high rate of interest. As for Norman's silver-lining theory of financial calamities, Bagehot wanted no part of it. A more flexible monetary approach would perhaps foreclose the need of perpetually relearning—or, at least, reteaching—the hard lessons of 1825, 1839, 1847, 1857, and 1866. The *Economist* had heaped praise on the governor of the Bank of England, Lancelot Holland, for seeming to embrace these Bagehotian principles in the aftermath of the collapse of Gurney's, but it was the praise of an editor who had reason to believe that his counsel had found its mark.

Was the matter then settled? It was not settled. In 1869, Robert Lowe, as Gladstone's chancellor of the exchequer, took the position that the government was under no obligation to assist the Bank of England to smooth the seasonal bumps in the money market. If, said Lowe, the exigencies of his tax policy caused the Treasury to deposit less than usual at the Bank in some months and more than usual in other months, so be it.

It was no duty of the chancellor to deposit funds in the Bank of England, either to help the Old Lady's shareholders or "to assist traders, or to set up storm signals announcing the coming of panics," he continued. "There is no monarch set up by any other department of business to warn those engaged in it of dangers to come; they must look out for themselves, and I don't see that Government should go out of its way merely to strengthen a great institution like the Bank of England."[2]

The money market, then, could take care of itself.

The money market could not take care of itself, insisted Bagehot. The chancellor must give it a helping hand, if only because he might have to borrow in it. Besides, the government created the market by creating the Bank. It was not by chance that the Bank of England was the government's sole depository or that, until the enactment of recent limited-liability legislation—another Robert Lowe creation—it was the only bank in England whose stockholders were not personally at risk for the solvency of the firm in which they owned a stake. The government had conferred those gifts and others on the Bank at its 1694 founding. With the passage of years had come reciprocal duties, whether or not the directors chose to acknowledge them. To hold the kingdom's principal banking reserve was the first; to lend when others withdrew from lending was the second.

The chancellor could neither rewrite the founding law nor repeal the consequences of that law—as those consequences had unfolded over 175 years. He could not arbitrarily decide to become a borrower in November, rather than, as was customary in that month, a lender. The autumn was a time of seasonal stress in the money market. The government's deposits, seasonally strong, strengthened the Bank when it most needed strengthening. The withdrawal of those funds would enfeeble the Bank and destabilize a vulnerable market. Said Bagehot: "When

one 'organization of credit,' as the French call it, has grown up, the difficulty of changing it is very great. 'Credit' is the historical element in
commerce; it rests on tradition and prestige; you cannot reshape it and
reform it as you like."[3]

Bagehot did not pause to explain what made the market vulnerable, nor why such prosperous London joint-stock banks as the London
& Westminster did not themselves take steps to make it safer. Perhaps
everyone knew why: a profit-seeking bank had stockholders to answer
to.* It had no constituency for the cause of promoting a safer money
market. A public-spirited policy of adding to one's gold reserve, if such
a thing could be imagined, would come at the cost of lower dividends,
shiny ingots having displaced interest-bearing securities. The stockholders of the Bank of England were well aware of the tradeoff. The
Old Lady owned plenty of gold and had, in comparison to the London & Westminster and its ilk, lower returns and smaller dividends
to show for it. A private bank would assuredly add to its stock of non-
yielding cash if by so doing it could enhance the value of its banking
franchise; the trouble was that the Bank of England, in assuming the
role of the steward of the nation's gold—even if it did not speak the
words to acknowledge it—had removed the incentive to private action.
The fact, if not the policy, of the single gold reserve, and of the associated understanding that the Bank would lend in a season of crisis, was a
kind of prototypical deposit insurance. If an archeological seeker of the
origins of the socialization of risk in high finance wants to find clues, let
him or her begin with an excavation of Lombard Street.

---

* Stuckey's remained liquid and immensely profitable. In 1868, profits weighed in
at £79,000, representing a 2.14 percent return on assets and a 29.6 percent return on
book equity. Capital of £266,708 represented 7.2 percent of assets of £3,675,274, of
which more than 40 percent comprised government securities, India bonds, railroad
debentures, short-term loans in London on bills and other securities, and cash on
deposit at banks. Such assets were either marketable or, in the case of short-dated
commercial bills, liquid by their nature; barring fraud or commercial catastrophe,
they would automatically turn into cash on their maturity date.

That the British gold reserve was centralized in the vaults of the Bank of England was a fact, as Bagehot had correctly observed. It fell to Thomson Hankey, Bagehot's old adversary, to analyze the consequences of that fact. Hankey did so in the language of what is today called moral hazard.

In letters to *The Times* in November 1872, Hankey, still a Bank director, denied that the Bank of England was encumbered by any such civic duty as Bagehot would saddle it with. In particular, the Bank was under no warrant to hold the reserves of gold that each bank should properly secure for itself. To maintain a comfortable cash reserve was simply sound banking practice, which the Bank did in its own interest, not the nation's. Certainly, the Bank held no gold for the purpose of meeting a potential foreign drain. The gold dealers—for there were many such people in London, the world's biggest gold market—would themselves contrive to find the bullion that might be required the next time foreigners lost confidence in British credit; Hankey estimated that there could be as much as £20 million worth of gold in the City available for export.[4]

Hankey's prose was the sensible-shoe kind. Bagehot's, in reply, fairly crackled—even, for once, in the headline: "The Dangerous Opinions Of A Bank Director."

"Mr. Thomson Hankey," the *Economist* responded, "—one of the most assiduous and influential of the Bank directors—has written a letter to the Times, of which the opinions seem to us to be so dangerous, that they call for careful comment. If we could believe that they represented the guiding policy of the Bank of England, we should expect a panic immediately."

An experienced reader of the *Economist* would have guessed why. English credit (promises to pay money) was large and growing—in fact too large, and growing too fast, in relation to England's gold. If the Bank, as Hankey rashly insisted, were to renounce responsibility for providing gold in times of monetary pressure, thoughtful people would take steps to protect themselves beforehand; they would sell securities and remove deposits from every bank but the Bank of England. Perhaps they would exchange credit instruments for gold. And since gold was scarce in relation to credit, the preemptive vanguard would prove the instigators of a run on the banks.

There was nothing like £20 million of idle, exportable bullion in London, the *Economist* went on to assert; there could not be, because nobody was rich enough, or foolish enough, to forego the interest on £20 million by holding that magnificent sum in sterile metal. (Even at 3 percent, the lost income would come to £600,000 a year.) London was the world's principal source of gold; since the French suspension of gold convertibility in 1870, it had become the world's only dependable source, and to secure gold for export, you had to apply to the Bank of England. The Bank's reserve

> is the ultimate reserve; our means of meeting a foreign payment
> depend on the magnitude of that final fund. The country must
> not go without a reserve while the London bankers and the
> Bank of England are squabbling who shall keep it. The import-
> ant question is not—does the Bank of England keep more cash
> in proportion than other bankers keep (which unquestionably it
> does), but does it keep enough to keep itself safe and all of us
> safe against the demands put upon us?[5]

If Bagehot wrote with special fluency on the question of the gold reserve, it was thanks to his years of practice with both sides of the argument. On the one hand, he would say, a system in which each bank keeps its own reserve was the best system. On the other, he would say that the system in which the Bank of England keeps a single reserve for all banks is the system in place and one too deeply engrained to change. He never attempted to show why change was out of the question, though he did, in one revealing passage, admit why, for bankers like him, change would be inexpedient:

> the main source of the profitableness of established banking is the smallness of the requisite capital. Being only wanted as a "moral influence," it need not be more than is necessary to secure that influence. Although, therefore, a banker deals only with the most sure securities, and with those which yield the least interest, he can nevertheless gain and divide a very large profit upon his own capital, because the money in his hands is so much larger than that capital.[6]

Which is to say that the Bank and its stockholders should bear the cost of the reserve because the private banks and their stockholders preferred not to.

Such contentions chased one another through the pages of the *Economist*. They likewise darted through the chapters of Bagehot's monetary masterpiece, *Lombard Street*.

It was a "little book," as Bagehot said, scarcely 73,000 words, and when it finally appeared, in the spring of 1873, the author apologized for it. He had been writing it at intervals since 1870—at Eliza's and his new home in Wimbledon, not far from what is today that tennis mecca's center court—but "pressing occupations" and "imperfect health" had interrupted him. He had needed a friend's help to correct the proofs.

What reception awaited *Lombard Street*, the author could not say. The book dealt, in a critical way, with financial institutions and the people inside them: the Bank of England, private London banks, publicly owned (joint-stock) banks, bill brokers. It recommended monetary policy suitable for times of "apprehension" (the Bank should husband its reserves against the possibility of a run) and "panic" (lend freely at a high rate of interest against good banking collateral). It prescribed how much gold the Bank should hold (£15 million was best but no less than £10 million). It described the cycles of the credit market. It warned against the piling on of credit obligations on an inadequate reserve of gold. And it warned, too—recalling the failure of Overend Gurney— against complacency. "Money will not manage itself," Bagehot famously cautioned, "and Lombard Street has a great deal of money to manage."

The author did allow his book one redeeming quality. He had entitled it *Lombard Street*, the City's fabled thoroughfare, and not "The Money Market" or any other such abstract name, "because I wish to deal, and to show that I mean to deal, with concrete realities." On this promise, Bagehot richly delivered. *Lombard Street* is a grand tour of living finance under the classical gold standard.

In 1873, Hankey brought out a second printing of his *Principles of Banking*, featuring a new preface aimed directly at "the able editor of the Economist."[7] Worthy and perhaps, in some ways, more farsighted than *Lombard Street*, Hankey's second edition was no more scintillating than the first.

Lombard Street scintillates. Not surprisingly, it begins with a paradox. "The briefest and truest way of describing Lombard Street," says Bagehot, "is to say that it is by far the greatest combination of economical power and economic delicacy that the world has ever seen." Money is power, and Britain had more money than any other country: the London banks held £120 million of deposits, three times more than the New York banks and nine times more than the Parisian ones. The collection of this vast floating pool in the City of London marked an epoch in financial history. For the first time no worthwhile enterprise, and no "civilized" government, need fail for a want of capital.[8] At the right rate of interest and against the correct collateral, or even on the strength of a sufficiently compelling story about future profits, a borrower would likely find accommodation.

It did not escape this critic of the 1867 Reform Act that the new structure of English commerce was democratic. Gone were the great merchant princes, "pushed out, so to say, by the dirty crowd of little men." Gone, too, were the good old standards of commercial probity. The "new men" flashed more credit than money in their hurry to get rich. Cutting corners, they produced shoddy wares. "They rely on cheapness, and rely successfully."*

On the other side of the ledger of that ostensible drawback was an undoubted advantage: no country was ever so keen as England to seize an opportunity. "The rough and vulgar structure of English commerce is the secret of its life," wrote Bagehot, still under Darwin's influence, "for it contains 'the propensity to variation,' which, in the social as in the animal kingdom, is the principle of progress."[9]

Part and parcel of up-tempo English trade was heavy English borrowing. Like Norman, Hankey, and Overstone, Bagehot worried that too little cash undergirded too much debt:

> There never was so much borrowed money collected in the world as is now collected in London. Of the many millions in Lombard street, infinitely the greater proportion is held by bankers or others on short notice or on demand; that is to say, the owners could ask for it all any day they please: in a panic some of them do ask for some of it. If any large fraction of that money really was demanded, our banking system and our industrial system too would be in great danger.[10]

But the collapse of the house of Overend Gurney—"one would think a child who had lent money in the City of London would have

---

* Bagehot seems not to have mentioned that the gold standard itself was a democratic institution. To all was accorded the equal right of converting notes into cash and cash into notes, and to each at the same universal rate.

lent it better"[11]—was a blow against lazy confidence. The time had come to see English high finance for the precarious structure it was.

Stuckey's was not unusual in showing next to no gold on its balance sheet.* No bank but one, Bagehot asserted, held more than trace amounts of legal tender (gold and notes of the Bank of England being the two forms of legally sanctioned final payment)—and that single exception was the Old Lady herself. On the year-end 1869 statement date, the Bank showed £11.3 million of such reserves against £27.2 million of liabilities.[12]

So all were leveraged to the Bank: it held not only its own reserve, but also the cash deposits of the rest of the London banking community. Nor was the Bank itself overendowed with real money. In each of the crisis years 1847, 1857, and 1866, as Bagehot pointed out, the Bank of England's cash reserve had dwindled to £3 million or less. On each occasion, Peel's Act had been suspended to allow for the emergency issuance of bank notes, and only then did the danger pass.

Not that these near misses were the products of a single bad law; they were, rather, the consequence of the "immense development of our credit system—in plain English, [of] the immense amount of our debts payable on demand and on the smallness of the sum of actual money which we keep to pay them if demanded." Cash was the Old Maid of English finance: no eager, profit-seeking banker or broker wished to be stuck with it.[13]

Not a few of the liabilities about which Bagehot worried were foreign; the Franco-Prussian War had put a scare into monied people. Searching for safe harbor, they had fixed on London, but they could just as easily pack up for another place. Foreign deposits were fickle.

---

* On the June 30, 1873, statement date, there is a line item for "Cash" in the sum of £235,505. The word almost certainly signified bank deposits and notes of the Bank of England more than gold coin. From Vincent Stuckey to Walter Bagehot, the management of Stuckey's had expressed a preference for paper money over sovereigns.

After the panic of 1866, especially after the suspension of Peel's Act (which many foreigners confound with a suspension of cash payments), a large amount of foreign money was withdrawn from London. And we may reasonably presume that in proportion as we augment the deposits of cash by foreigners in London, we augment both the chances and the disasters of a "run" upon England.[14]

A run on England meant a run on England's gold, and to Bagehot, if not to Hankey, that meant the Bank's gold. Most of these debts were contracted by private parties, yet the gold with which to settle them was locked in quasi-sovereign vaults. "[A]ll our credit system depends on the Bank of England for its security," Bagehot warned. "On the wisdom of the directors of that one Joint Stock Company, it depends whether England shall be *solvent* or *insolvent*."

It was therefore more than gratifying that the quality of the management of the Bank of England was on the upswing; the directors' intervention in the Panic of 1866 was their best response to any crisis since 1825.[15] Yet actions were not enough—"though the practice is mended the theory is not." The directors never made public how much gold they intended to keep or named the principle by which they arrived at their decision. "The result," said Bagehot, summing up the case against a system he insisted was unchangeable,*

is that we have placed the exclusive custody of our entire banking reserve in the hands of a single board of directors not particularly trained for the duty—who might be called "amateurs"—who have no particular interest above other people

---

* Later in the book, as was his wont, Bagehot made the case for a changed system of banking in which each bank looks after its own reserve. Self-interest would ensure adequate and informed provisioning. Yet, "the law and circumstances" have created a very different system, and England was stuck with it. Bagehot, *Lombard Street*, 104.

in keeping it undiminished—who acknowledge no obligation to keep it undiminished—who have never been told by any great statesman or public authority that they are so to keep it or that they have anything to do with it—who are named by and are agents for a proprietary which would have a greater income if it was diminished—who do not fear, and who need not fear, ruin, even if it were all gone and wasted.[16]

The more gold on the balance sheet, the less interest income on the profit-and-loss statement. What supposedly rendered the directors fearless was the Bank's status as a limited-liability company.

In one of the most famous passages in *Lombard Street*, Bagehot prescribes—for the benefit of the numerous, dim Thomson Hankeys on the Court of Directors of the Bank—how to treat a panic. Our twenty-first-century central bankers have taken it as their motto:

> A panic, in a word, is a species of neuralgia, and according to the rules of science you must not starve it. The holders of the cash reserve must be ready not only to keep it for their own liabilities, but to advance it most freely for the liabilities of others. They must lend to merchants, to minor bankers, to "this man and that man," whenever the security is good. In wild periods of alarm, one failure makes many, and the best way to prevent the derivative failures is to arrest the primary failure which causes them.[17]

In an earlier essay on the occasion of the centennial of *The Wealth of Nations*, Bagehot wrote that Adam Smith "evidently hurries over the abstract part of it, because he thinks his readers will not attend to it"; so does Bagehot scurry by the abstractions of central banking in *Lombard Street*. He wrote to change minds, not to expound theories, though the Bagehotian description of boom and bust suggests many fine theoretical possibilities. Thus, for example,

The good times too of high prices almost always engender much fraud. All people are most credulous when they are most happy; and when much money has just been made, when some people are really making it, when most people think they are making it, there is a happy opportunity for ingenious mendacity. Almost everything will be believed for a little while, and long before discovery the worst and most adroit deceivers are geographically or legally beyond the reach of punishment. But the harm they have done diffuses harm, for it weakens credit still further.[18]

Perhaps Bagehot was the one to nudge John Kenneth Galbraith, who coined the concept of the "bezzle" in 1955, to contemplate the pregnant interval between the commission of an embezzlement and the victim's discovery of his loss. Money could be two places at once, or at least in two minds at once, before anyone noticed it was missing.

IN 1915, THE THIRTY-TWO-YEAR-OLD John Maynard Keynes reviewed the works of Walter Bagehot in a new volume edited by Bagehot's biographer—and Eliza Bagehot's youngest sister—Emilie Barrington. Turning to *Lombard Street*, Keynes described it "in form and intention" as a "piece of pamphleteering," designed to knock some sense into the titans of the Bank and City. Keynes gave the book two cheers only. In it, he observed, Bagehot was dealing with the psychology of finance, not the theory of finance. The writing was luminous, but it had not held up well over time; much of the narrative dwelled on "obsolete facts" and "obsolete controversies."

The Great War would mark the end of the classical gold standard, though no one could predict that historical fact. So in one sense, Keynes was more correct than he knew. Gold convertibility, suspended in 1914, was only partly restored in 1925; it stopped for good in 1931, much to the dismay of the governor of the Bank of England, Montagu

Norman (grandson of our George W. Norman). Thus, the controversy
over the cost of holding the British gold reserve might seem dusty. As
for Bagehot's other injunction, that the Bank should lend in a crisis—
unreservedly, against good collateral and at a high rate of interest—that
counsel has become almost proverbial, though the part concerning the
high rate of interest is, these days, honored more in the breach than the
observance.[19] "The best way to avoid a panic is to meet the situation
like lions," Walter Cunliffe, governor of the Bank in 1914, announced to
a Treasury colleague on the first day of the fighting.*

By the second half of the twentieth century, bank runs seemed to
belong to the unlamented past. In Britain, there had been no run of
consequence since the collapse of the City of Glasgow Bank in 1878,
the year after Bagehot's death, so the long-drawn-out Victorian debate
over the role of a central bank in a crisis had itself come to appear irrelevant. But the developments of 2007–09 showed how misconceived
that assumption was. A century after Keynes passed judgment, *Lombard Street* is fresh again. So, too, is *The Principles of Banking*, by Thomson Hankey.

BAGEHOT AND HANKEY, WHO agreed on so little, did achieve a meeting
of the minds with respect to the business of commercial banking. It was
not so very difficult to manage, they independently decided. It was in

---

* Bagehot urged the Bank to employ senior permanent staff, knowledgeable in banking, to augment the twenty-six directors, of whom not one was a London banker by
trade. At this writing, the senior professional staff of the Bank of England numbers
170, at the head of which sits a permanent governor, an office that Bagehot hoped
would never be created: "Everybody in business would bow down to him and try to
stand well with him, for he might in a panic be able to save almost anyone he liked,
and to ruin almost anyone he liked." This proved a prescient warning. Bagehot,
Lombard Street, 98, 213.

fact as easy, claimed Hankey, as understanding the difference between a bill of exchange, against which one could safely lend, and a mortgage.

"Banking is a watchful, but not a laborious trade," Bagehot concurred, perhaps thinking of how relatively little time he devoted to Stuckey's, yet how plump was the Stuckey's P & L.

> A banker, even in large business, can feel pretty sure that all his transactions are sound, and yet have much spare mind. A certain part of his time, and a considerable part of his thoughts, he can readily devote to other pursuits. And a London banker can have the most intellectual society in the world if he chooses it. There has probably very rarely ever been so happy a position as that of a London private banker, and never perhaps a happier.[20]

If the business was a simple one, and if it required little capital—as Bagehot observed—to what did a rich London banker owe his wealth and spare mind? In some measure, he was beholden to the lender of last resort. As long as the government's bank bore the cost of holding the gold, and as long as that golden hegemon acknowledged a duty to lend in times of stringency, a bank could deploy the Stuckey's business model of heavy leverage: many safe and low-yielding assets piled on a small base of capital. His affairs so structured, the banker could pursue an avocation in authorship, like Bagehot, or in archeology, like Sir John Lubbock.

Bagehot saw nothing unwarranted in this state of things, and in none of his writings that I have seen did he address Hankey's contention that the mere existence of the doctrine of the lender of last resort was an incitement to financial recklessness.

The second printing of *The Principles of Banking* appeared almost simultaneously with the publication of *Lombard Street*. In it, Hankey objected to any law that would allow the Bank to slip the constraints of the Act of 1844. "I cannot conceive anything more likely to encourage rash and imprudent speculation," he began.

> All commercial and financial panics are caused by an excessive use of a system of credit, so valuable to commerce when carefully and prudently used; and any statutory enactment which encourages a belief that, under any circumstances, credit is equal to capital, is, in my opinion, a retrograde step, and most injurious to the best interests and prosperity of the whole community.[21]

Bagehot could hardly object to Hankey's description of the danger of over-borrowing—he shared it. What he rejected was Hankey's idea of how to run a central bank. There must be a lender of last resort, and that lender must be the Bank of England.

BAGEHOT, IN LIFE, stood for conservative banking and the gold standard. No more than Hankey would he have approved of the practices and institutions that crystallized the Great Recession. In 1909, long after Bagehot's death, Stuckey's sold out to Parr's Bank, thereby coming to form part of the corporate family tree of the National Westminister Bank.* In 2000, NatWest was acquired by the immense, fast-growing, thoroughly modern Royal Bank of Scotland Group. In 2008, RBS Group—overextended, mismanaged, illiquid, and caught up in what its management admitted was "a bull market culture"—spectacularly failed. It did not, however, go out of business, but continued to operate as a high-cost ward of the United Kingdom. The ultimate charge to British taxpayers has been reckoned at £45.5 billion.

The RBS balance sheet of 2008 bore no closer resemblance to the Stuckey's balance sheet of Bagehot's day than the twenty-first-century

---

* As did, in an earlier consolidation, Jones, Loyd & Co., Lord Overstone's bank.

paper pound does to the pre-1914 gold pound. Neither Bagehot nor Hankey could have foreseen such seismic change. Still, it was Hankey, and not Bagehot, who grasped the risk of the unintended consequences of a collective gold reserve and of a dependable, openhanded lender of last resort—along with the modern corollary that very large financial institutions should be treated as quasi-public property. A century and a half after Bagehot and Hankey stopped quarreling, it is the great author's obscure, rhetorically overmatched adversary whose foresight shines brighter.

IN 1873, BAGEHOT'S NEW BOOK found its way into the hands of at least one Bank director. William Lidderdale, who had joined the Court in 1870 at the relatively advanced age of thirty-eight and whose formative financial experience was watching his father lose his money in a Scottish bank failure,[22] set down his impressions of the Bagehot–Hankey controversy in a letter to a Liverpool business partner. We can all agree, said Lidderdale, that the English monetary and banking system is complex and interconnected, thus introducing what has come to be called systemic risks. The practice of taking

> enormous sums on deposit at call or short notice, on which interest has to be paid & which there is almost a necessity to employ if serious losses are to be avoided, is one which carries risk on its face. Mr. Bagehot says things *are* so & that it is useless trying to change the system & then throws upon the Bank of England the onus of providing a reserve adequate to the needs of all its competitors as well as regular customers.[23]

There is no better short-form summary of Bagehot's position. The gold question would not go away—*Lombard Street* failed to convince anyone to lay in more cash, as the *Economist*'s own figures would shortly prove. In 1879, the liabilities of eleven big banks, excluding the Bank of England, totaled £126 million; against these notes and deposits, the eleven showed £16.2 million in cash on hand or on deposit at the Bank of England. In 1889, liabilities had jumped to £170 million, against which cash and deposits at the Bank had increased by only £1.3 million.[24] Far from adding to their rainy-day cash positions in proportion to the growth of their liabilities, the leading banks made do with less.

In 1906, George Goschen, by now Viscount Goschen, made an after-dinner speech in the City of London. He put it to his friendly audience: Someone must hold the reserve, and a larger reserve, too, than the worryingly inadequate one on hand. Should that someone be you, the banks; the Bank of England; or the government? The *Financial News* reported the results:

> It was significant that there was dead silence, in an audience largely composed of bankers, when he spoke of the possible duty of the joint-stock banks in this connection, loud applause when he suggested the Bank of England as an alternative sufferer; and vehement cheers when the Government was mentioned as a last resort.[25]

It would take another century, and another system of monetary organization, but the government—many governments, along with their reluctant taxpayers—did finally bear the cost.

CHAPTER 17

"I WONDER WHAT MY EMINENCE IS?"

Bagehot saved his money; his friends smiled at his reluctance to spend it. He seemed not to speculate, and his only known investment was Stuckey's Banking Company. The branch of financial journalism that least engaged him was the securities-selection branch, which he identified with venality. He said—not in a boastful way, but as a matter of fact—that the *Economist* was the only financial periodical that didn't take bribes.

In the summer of 1873, with *Lombard Street* now on the bookstalls, Bagehot briefed the Wilson sisterhood on their financial position. James Wilson had left the *Economist* in trust to his family and named Bagehot a trustee under his will, and his favorite son-in-law was, likewise, as Bagehot modestly described his role, "Manager, Editor and principal-writer on business subjects" of that publication. He was, in fact, its voice, guiding spirit, and the principal writer on all subjects, though assisted in his present state of reduced health by Robert Giffen.

Wilson, who had died in 1860, left an estate worth £24,576, exclusive of the *Economist*. By year-end 1872, the value of the financial assets over which Bagehot and his co-trustees kept watch had climbed to £43,679. The portfolio was evenly divided between fixed-income securities—

Indian railway bonds, among others—and Stuckey's common stock. It was the Stuckey's shares that produced most of the £19,000 in mark-to-market appreciation.

In income generation, too, the Wilson estate was flourishing, though here the source of growth was the journalistic asset. Of the £3,486 in distributions in 1862 and £5,142 in 1872, the family newspaper contributed 43 percent and 54 percent, respectively. The Wilson sisters loved Bagehot dearly, and they loved him no less for producing the figures that he did.

Banking was inherently precarious, Bagehot reminded them. As for Stuckey's, its owners—"the proprietary"—formed a kind of club. For now, the sisters were members of that club, admitted as beneficiaries of the Wilson estate. It was Bagehot who must have secured the permission of the directors to allow the estate to hold the shares; if something were to happen to him, the directors might or might not allow the estate to continue to invest.*

Turning now to the *Economist*, Bagehot observed that its profits were unpredictable and sometimes nonexistent. The paper had earned little or nothing in the four consecutive years following the Overend Gurney failure; "[p]rogressively unprosperous" was how the editor described that dry spell.

Seeking a reason, Bagehot had first blamed rising competition, then thought again. The competition was not, in fact, rising, at least not in quality, and it had made no inroads on the *Economist*. The Wilsons' paper languished because the money market was dead. And when the financial currents quickened with the Prussian boom of the early 1870s, so did the *Economist*'s profits. In 1872, the stars came into alignment: a

---

* Just why the trustees had chosen to concentrate so much of the money they managed in the equity of a single bank, and a bank in which one of the trustees was so deeply interested, did not figure in Bagehot's presentation.

full-bodied 7 percent Bank Rate coincided with a record-high *Economist* circulation.

Of course, the *Economist*'s competitors did not employ Bagehot, who was banker and essayist rolled up into one. "Being in a Bank which always has large sums in London," the editor allowed, "I have better means of knowing than a mere writer what is happening and what is likely to happen; and it is a great deal in consequence of these opportunities that the *Economist* has been able to deal with the changes in the money market better than other papers." Competing journals had neither his talent (not that Bagehot put it that way), nor his probity (he did say that).

People read the *Economist* for its financial coverage, he advised the heiresses. The battle for free trade was over—the victory had been decisive—and there was no commercial legislation of consequence on the horizon. Political articles served their purpose only if they told "the men of business" the practical things they needed to know.

Bagehot was not averse to building the paper. For instance, he had created a supplementary investment publication, *Investors Monthly Manual* (no tips, just facts), which produced a "small profit." What he would not do was drum up advertising. "No attention must be paid to advertisements as an isolated source of income," he advised his wife and her sisters; if the *Economist* stayed true to itself, the ads would walk in the door. (In the councils of for-profit publishing, such a remark is rarely heard, but the editor of the *Economist* did say it.)

Just as Overstone had observed, Bagehot had his notions. To the sisters he laid it down that no hireling could faithfully succeed him in the editor's chair, because an employee, as distinct from an owner, could be bribed to puff shares. "The property is a delicate one and might easily be ruined by a person who had no interest in it before the parties interested were aroused to prevent it."

Yet Bagehot himself was not an owner of the paper. It would be most irregular if he were, explained the one-time law student, as "I am one of the Trustees of Mr. Wilson's will and of this very property and no permanent interest in it could possibly be given to me: trustees cannot convey to themselves."

Bagehot and his co-trustees had decided to convey to the editor a salary of £400 a year, space rates for his articles, and half the profits above £2,000 a year. On average since 1862, that profit participation had yielded him £780. He had recently been paying a portion of Giffen's salary out of his own pocket, "as I have not since my illness been able to do all which I used to do formerly."*

"I hope therefore," Bagehot closed his briefing, "that those concerned will not rely too much on their present prosperity, but that they will carefully bear in mind the nature of their principal source of income, and not regard that income as one which can be reckoned on in the same manner as one from funded property or land."[1]

In 1875, Bagehot was voted vice chairman of Stuckey's Banking Company, the high office that his father had filled. In 1876, the banker turned fifty. Outside the Stuckey's offices, he was a short- to middle-distance writer who excelled at explaining things. His strengths were versatility, erudition, vividness of perception, critical judgment, and brilliance of style. His books, with the exception of *Lombard Street*, were built from the articles he had published in the monthly or quarterly press. He had produced no serious theoretical work; it was not clear that he had the stamina. His contributions to the literature of political economy, besides *Lombard Street*, consisted of hundreds of thousands of words in the *Economist*, which he necessarily wrote against the clock.

Now he resolved to spread his wings, to make a substantial contri-

---

* In 1873, the circulation of the *Economist* stood at 3,690. Thirty years later, it averaged just 3,541. Today, it tops 1.1 million worldwide. Ruth Dudley Edwards, *The Pursuit of Reason: The Economist, 1843–1993* (Boston: Harvard Business School Press, 1993), 951.

bution to economic theory. He would clarify Ricardian doctrine and push the science of political economy past the seemingly immovable figure of J. S. Mill. There would be three volumes: a treatise on method, a survey of classical theory, and biographical sketches of the leading economists.

"The Postulates of English Political Economy," the first essay of the planned great work, made its appearance in the January and February 1876 issues of the *Fortnightly Review*.[2] And there the project stopped. To John Morley, the *Fortnightly*'s editor, Bagehot confided his fear that he would never finish the job "except in pieces"; Bagehot was correct. He was not a theorist, but a user of theories and a critic of theorists. Sifting through Bagehot's papers after he died, Giffen and Hutton found pages and chapters of the incomplete work. They pieced them together to form *Economic Studies*, a volume for which Alfred Marshall, Keynes's teacher and the ruling English economist of his day, was persuaded to write a preface. (Eliza Bagehot proved a devoted, persistent, and most persuasive widow.) Marshall's essay was dutiful, but privately, in 1889, the economist characterized the Bagehot fragments as "mostly brilliant, but very hasty and in reading him I alternately agree and admire much and differ and admire a little."[3] Bagehot's first drafts were not for the ages.

In lieu of a second essay such as "The Postulates of English Political Economy," Bagehot presented Morley with an upgrade: his commemorative profile of "Adam Smith as a Person" on the occasion of the hundredth anniversary of the publication of *The Wealth of Nations*. Bagehot was back to playing to his strengths: the reader comes first to feel as if he knows Adam Smith and, second, as if he would like to take the absent-minded Scottish scholar, European grand-tour guide, tutor, author, customs commissioner, and reasoner on free trade into his family. "Through life," Bagehot relates, "there was about Adam Smith a sort of lumbering bonhomie which amused and endeared him to those around him."[4] As usual, Bagehot left clues about himself as he wrote about others. Smith, he observed, like the historian Thomas Babington Macaulay, could "describe practical matters in such a way as to fasten them on the imagination, and not only get what they say read, but get it remembered and make it part of the substance of the reader's mind ever afterwards." It was Bagehot's gift, too.[5]

Bagehot deployed this talent to dazzling effect with another long essay that year. "Lord Althorp and the Reform Act of 1832" was history, biography, and Bagehot self-revelation built on the story of a fox-hunting nobleman who gave up the sport he loved in self-abnegating grief upon the death of his wife. Althorp was a bluff, rich, handsome Whig who would have no part of class-appropriate Conservative politics but championed radical reform in the ministry of Lord Grey. Bagehot describes the reactionary—the "savage"—spirit of the post-Napoleonic age and the turn against that ultraconservatism. He shows why the House of Commons voted to reform itself, even to the point of some members voting to extinguish their own constituencies.

The great Reform Act of 1832 did much, Bagehot allows, but perhaps undid more. The infamous pocket boroughs had sheltered a class of elevated statesmen who were spared the ordeal of having to face the voters, as the aristocrat in whose pocket the borough resided could command the requisite votes. "The reformers of 1832 destroyed intellectual constituencies in great numbers without saying, indeed without thinking, that it was desirable to create any," Bagehot writes.

> They thus by conspicuous action, which is the most influential mode of political instruction, taught mankind that an increase in the power of numbers was the change most to be desired in England. And of course the mass of mankind are only too ready to think so. They are always prone to believe their own knowledge to be "for all practical purposes" sufficient, and to be emancipated from the authority of the higher culture.[6]

Althorp, then, was of a type—the heedless type who has no conception of the unintended consequences of well-intended acts.

> Being without culture, they do not know how these institutions grew; being without insight, they only see one half of their effect; being without foresight, they do not know what will happen if they are enlarged; being without originality, they cannot devise anything new to supply, if necessary, the place of the old.[7]

Bagehot was always a tough critic, but perhaps the repeatedly frustrated seeker of parliamentary office wrote with special vehemence against the irreversible tide of the popular, and now twice reformed and enlarged, electorate.

Early in 1877, R. E. Welby, principal clerk of the finance division of the Treasury, paid a call at the *Economist*'s office in the Strand. Finding Bagehot at his post, Welby sat down to talk. The *Economist* had broached an idea that piqued the interest of the chancellor, Sir Stafford Northcote: to let the British government raise short-term debt by issuing a new kind of security. Treasury bills, as they came to be called, would run for three months, rather than, as with exchequer bills, twelve months. The chancellor could issue them whenever the need arose— not that the purpose of creating the new security was to enlarge the public debt. Treasury bills would look like London commercial bills, or the French government's *bons de Tresor*. Exchequer bills had been the Treasury's standby since the days of William and Mary, but they were antiquated, inflexible, and, because sparsely owned and thinly traded, illiquid. They came to market only in March and June and bore interest rates higher than those paid by prime commercial borrowers. It was a telltale fact that Her Majesty's Government paid higher money-market rates than the house of Barings did. Welby recalled Bagehot saying something like this:

The Treasury has the finest security in the world, but has not known how to use it. The market where you borrow deals in bills of exchange and is accustomed to that form of security. The security which you offer should resemble as nearly as possible a bill of exchange both in form and method of negotiation.[8]

Bagehot continued to press the idea in the pages of the *Economist*, though Sir Stafford needed no persuading. On March 7, 1877, Parliament enacted his legislation to allow the first issuance of Treasury bills. Neither the chancellor nor the *Economist* breathed a word about who had had the bright idea.

IN MARCH 1877, the equinoctial wind penetrated the undressed windows of the Bagehots' new London house at 8 Queen's Gate Place. William Morris had the commission for the curtains, wallpaper, and furniture, and the artist was not to be rushed. The eminent designer and poet was, said Bagehot, "composing the drawing-room as he would an ode."[9]

In that chilly March, Bagehot caught cold. No matter—he was often unwell. Eliza and he would still take the train to Langport to spend Easter with his widowed father. By the time the couple reached Herd's Hill, Bagehot was presenting the symptoms of his chronic bronchitis. A physician visited on March 24, morning and afternoon; he judged the prognosis favorable. After the second visit, Eliza took up station in the bedroom on a sofa behind a curtain, so as not to disturb her husband's rest. Bagehot complained of extreme weakness. At about 4 p.m., he struggled to sit up. He waved Eliza off when she leaned over to help— "Let me have my own fidgets." A moment later he called to her, then fell asleep "across the bed, breathing loud and hard." At 5:25, she knelt to take his pulse. "While I counted a little purple came on his lips and he became still and white; I called his aunt—then poured brandy down his throat. She said—it is of no use & I knew that he was gone."[10]

In London, they thought the reports of Bagehot's death were garbled. Surely, the deceased was the editor's father? *The Times* got the facts right but failed to grasp their significance. Its paragraph-length obituary resembled "the measure of the tribute that would be paid in the regular way to a deceased rear-Admiral or Colonial Bishop," said the Irish radical journalist E. D. J. Wilson. In the pages of *The Examiner*, Wilson did Bagehot justice:

> His friends used to say of him, and there was little exaggeration in the saying, that for a dozen years at least he was an unofficial member of every Cabinet, Conservatives as well as Liberal, which has governed these kingdoms. Successive Chancellors of the Exchequer and Secretaries of the Treasury called him into their counsels as a matter of course . . . And the most illustrious of the statesmen who thus consulted a journalist without a place in Parliament or any strength of party connection, would be the first to acknowledge how much they owed to the "white light" of his pure and clear intelligence.[11]

Gladstone was ready enough to credit Bagehot with some of the best advice he ever received in the chancellor's office, and he wrote Eliza to say so. Many years later, Welby, the Treasury official who in retirement had been created Lord Welby, told Emilie Barrington how much Bagehot had contributed to the government's finances: "The *machinery* of our financial administration is complicated, and Mr. Bagehot is the only outsider who had thoroughly mastered it. Indeed he understood the *machine* almost as completely as we who had to work it. This knowledge added to the soundness of his economical judgment, gave a special value to his opinion and advice."[12]

In the weeks, months, and years that followed his death, Bagehot's friends gave tribute. They marked the gift of his conversation (Lord Bryce to Hutton: "Is it going too far to say that he was the most interesting man in London to talk to?"),[13] the power of his thought, the glory of his prose. His posthumous fame spread to America. In 1889 Woodrow Wilson, then a professor at Wesleyan University, extolled Bagehot's writing in public lectures, saying that "you receive stimulation from him and a certain feeling of elation."[14]

In the same year, the Travelers Insurance Company of Hartford, Connecticut, published Bagehot's collected works in an edited, indexed, and annotated five-volume set, priced at $5. The scholarly president of Travelers, James Goodwin Batterson, assured policyholders that the company disowned any intention of proselytizing for Bagehot's favorite institutions—the gold standard, cabinet government, free trade. Its motive was simply to spread the fruits of "one of the foremost minds of any century." If it was a labor of love for Batterson, it was something very different for Forrest Morgan, the editor of the project, who devoted the first eight pages of his preface to raging against the long-deceased author for errors of commission and omission. Morgan wanted the readers to know—he really wanted them to know, as he had spent years of toil—that within the front ranks of English authors, Bagehot was the all-time, hands-down worst speller, fact-checker (he did not actually check facts), quotation-verifier (he made them up), and proofreader (he didn't even bother).*

WHEN HE HAD BEEN elected to membership in the Athenaeum in 1875, Bagehot had playfully wondered why: "By the rules they can only elect nine persons a year," he wrote to Eliza, "and those 'who have attained

---

* "No one," Morgan averred, "who does not—as probably no one save a future editor ever will—compare this edition, word by word, with any former ones, can form any adequate conception of the shocking state of Bagehot's text as heretofore given to the world; there is nothing even remotely approaching it in the case of any other English writer of high mark since Shakespeare's time." Forrest Morgan, ed., *The Works of Walter Bagehot*, vol. 1 (Hartford: The Travelers Insurance Company, 1889), ii.

eminence in Science, Literature, the Arts or public services.' I wonder what my eminence is?"[15]

His eminence was the near-literature of high journalism. Financial journalism is not so high, nor success, when achieved, so lofty. In that quotidian branch of the writing business, Bagehot was a superior commentator, though a middling seer—for every financial writer must squint into the future. His attitude was perhaps too cautionary in the short term, and much too complacent for the long term. He worried too much about the single gold reserve, and not enough about the distant adverse consequences of government control in banking and credit.

Bagehot lived and wrote in an era of monetary controversy and banking turmoil. For Britain, the wrenching failure of the City of Glasgow Bank in 1878 marked the close of the age of runs and panics. (Lidderdale, by then governor of the Bank of England, led a successful intervention to smother the effects of the Barings collapse in 1890.) Bagehot foresaw neither the calm that was to settle over the City during the rest of the nineteenth century, nor the upheaval that was to frighten the world half out of its mind in the twenty-first century.

Because Bagehot's words are so easily quoted, they are often misquoted. His prescription that, in a panic, a central bank should lend freely at a high rate of interest against good collateral has virtually become, following 2007, "Lend freely at low rates of interest while materializing immense sums of fiat money with which to raise the prices of financial assets in order to stimulate spending by the people who own the assets."

Can a man, even a genius, be fairly charged with failure to predict the distant evil consequences of the things he said, or didn't quite say, or said in a setting so foreign to that of his posterity that he was bound to be misinterpreted? Bagehot wrote in the context of the gold standard: of fixed foreign exchange rates, balanced budgets, convertible currencies, and the personal responsibility—either limited or unlimited—of bank shareholders for the solvency of the institutions in which they were invested. His world was one of institutionalized discipline. Today's world—one of paper currencies, floating exchange rates, enormous budget deficits, and governmental policies to protect both investors and depositors against the consequences of a bank's mismanagement—is largely one of institutionalized indiscipline.

In his indictment of the reformers of 1832, Bagehot said, "Probably they will do some present palpable good, but they will do so at a heavy cost; years after they have passed away, the bad effects of that which they did, and of the precedents which they set, will be hard to bear and difficult to change."[16] So, arguably, with Bagehot's ideas on central banking. If he did not invent the doctrine of the lender of last resort, he did canonize it. His epigrams did not lead today's central bankers to take actions that they would not have otherwise taken, but those words put the gloss of conservative authority on unprecedented monetary experiments.

Viscount Blakenham, former chairman of Pearson and chairman of the *Financial Times* from 1983 to 1997, was an environmentalist and a lover of the English countryside. Some time ago, on a visit to the *FT*'s offices, the then president of Italy told the chairman how much he admired Walter Bagehot, the great Victorian editor of the *Economist*. Not quite getting the name, Blakenham exclaimed, "Oh, I love badgers, too."

His name was impossible. His words live.

ACKNOWLEDGMENTS

The generosity of my creditors is exceeded only by their number. I am in debt, first, to Harrison Waddill, my enterprising and unflappable research assistant, who investigated (and discovered) Bagehot-related source material on both sides of the Atlantic. In the U.K., he and I incurred an especially heavy obligation to the staff of the Royal Bank of Scotland Archive, Edinburgh, in which are domiciled the records of Stuckey's Banking Company. Sally Cholewa and Lyn Crawford, along with Sophie Volker, Ruth Reed and Philip Winterbottom, went above and beyond the call of duty to welcome their visiting American patrons.

The papers of George Warde Norman contain a remarkable contemporary document describing Bagehot's views of money and banking. It was thanks to the help of Lucy Bonner, archivist on the Bromley Historical Collections at the Bromley Central Library, that Harrison was able to lay hands on it.

Barry and Janet Winetrobe, residents of Bagehot's hometown of Langport, contributed their time, encouragement, hospitality, and historical knowledge to this project. Their dedicated work at the Bagehot Fund is helping to perpetuate the great man's legacy in his birthplace and beyond.

Thanks, too, to Chris Thorn, who sacrificed his vacation days at Eton College to track down archival material.

Edward Chancellor, an English journalist and historian in the Bagehot mold, to whom this volume is dedicated, read my first draft, attempting, as he said, to rid the text of "Yankee solecisms." Adam Rowe, a rising young historian at the University of Chicago, made expert suggestions. And I thank my daughter, Alice Grant, for her perceptive reading. For any and all remaining errors, I claim full credit.

Whatever this book might be, it would be much less without the myriad editorial improvements effected by the all-seeing John A. Glusman, editor-in-chief of W. W. Norton & Co., Helen Thomaides, John's assistant, and Allegra Huston, who is not so much a copy editor—though she certainly is all of that—as the author's guardian angel. And thanks, too, for the intelligent and perceptive proofreading of Dassi Zeidel and John Gould.

NOTES

AUTHOR'S NOTE

1 Walter Bagehot, *The Works of Walter Bagehot with Memoirs by R. H. Hutton*, ed. Forest Morgan, 5 vols. (Hartford, CT: Travelers Insurance Company, 1891), 3:320.
2 Report from the Committee of Secrecy on the Bank of England Charter, 1832, 145–55.

PROLOGUE: "WITH DEVOURING FURY"

1 Edwin Canaan, ed., *The Paper Pound of 1797–1821: The Bullion Report 8th June 1810*, 2nd ed. (New York: Augustus M. Kelley, 1909), viii.
2 Philip T. Saunders, *Stuckey's Bank* (Taunton, UK: Barnicott and Pearce, 1928), 11.
3 Report from the Committee of Secrecy, 11.
4 Report from the Committee of Secrecy, 12.
5 Bray Hammond, *Banks and Politics in America from the Revolution to the Civil War* (Princeton, NJ: Princeton University Press, 1957), 35–36.
6 "With respect to the crisis which now agitates in the city . . . ," *The Times*, December 13, 1825.
7 Frank Whitson Fetter, *Development of British Monetary Orthodoxy: 1797–1875*, (Cambridge, MA: Harvard University Press, 1965), 94.
8 David Ricardo, MP, 40 Parl. Deb. (1st ser.) (1819) col. 746.
9 Report from the Committee of Secrecy, 69.
10 Frank Griffith Dawson, *The First Latin American Debt Crisis: The City of London and the 1822-25 Loan Bubble* (New Haven: Yale University Press, 1990), 246.

11 Edward Chancellor, *Devil Take the Hindmost: A History of Financial Speculation* (New York: Farrar, Straus and Giroux, 1999), 107.

12 John D. Turner, *Banking in Crisis: The Rise and Fall of British Banking Stability, 1800 to Present* (Cambridge: Cambridge University Press, 2014), 70.

13 Chancellor, *Devil Take the Hindmost*, 107.

14 Report from the Committee of Secrecy, 47.

15 Report from the Committee of Secrecy, 90.

16 Report from the Committee of Secrecy, 47.

17 13 Parl. Deb. (2d ser.) (1825) cols. 1272–4.

18 Report from the Committee of Secrecy, 400.

19 "The Money-Market," *The Times*, December 15, 1825.

20 Report from the Committee of Secrecy, 45.

21 Report from the Committee of Secrecy, 48.

22 Report from the Committee of Secrecy, 47.

CHAPTER 1: "LARGE, WILD, FIERY, BLACK"

1 Walter Bagehot, *The Collected Works of Walter Bagehot*, ed. Norman St John-Stevas, 15 vols. (London: the Economist, 1986), 15:308.

2 Philip T. Saunders, *Stuckey's Bank* (Taunton: Barnicott and Pearce, 1928), 24.

3 Russell Barrington, *Life of Walter Bagehot* (London: Longmans, Green and Co., 1914), 78.

4 Bagehot, *Collected Works*, 15:378.

5 Barrington, *Life of Walter Bagehot*, 64.

6 Bagehot, *Collected Works*, 15:6.

7 *Hampshire Chronicle*, April 27, 1801.

8 "Anne Beale, Governess and Writer: Extracts from her Diary," *Girls' Own Paper* (1901), 599.

9 Alastair Buchan, *The Spare Chancellor: The Life of Walter Bagehot* (London: Chatto and Windus, 1959), 25.

10 Barrington, *Life of Walter Bagehot*, 80–81.

11 Buchan, *The Spare Chancellor*, 21.

12 Buchan, *The Spare Chancellor*, 25.

13 David Melville Ross, *Langport and its Church* (Langport, UK: Herald Press, 1911), 347–48.

14 Ross, *Langport*, 344.

15 Ross, *Langport*, 345.

16 Buchan, *The Spare Chancellor*, 24.

17 Ross, *Langport*, 357.

18 William Irvine, *Walter Bagehot* (London: Longmans, Green and Co., 1939), 12.

19 Buchan, *The Spare Chancellor*, 28.

20 Buchan, *The Spare Chancellor*, 28.

21 Buchan, *The Spare Chancellor*, 98.

22 Irvine, *Walter Bagehot*, 13.

23 Barrington, *Life of Walter Bagehot*, 86.

24 Barrington, *Life of Walter Bagehot*, 91.

25 Barrington, *Life of Walter Bagehot*, 87–99.

26 Barrington, *Life of Walter Bagehot*, 75.

27 Irvine, *Walter Bagehot*, 17.

28 Barrington, *Life of Walter Bagehot*, 92.

29 Barrington, *Life of Walter Bagehot*, 72.

30 Bagehot, *Collected Works*, 15:378.

CHAPTER 2: "IN MIRTH AND REFUTATION— IN RIDICULE AND LAUGHTER"

1 Lee Jackson, *Dirty Old London: The Victorian Fight Against Filth* (New Haven: Yale University Press, 2014), 27.

2 Barrington, *Life of Walter Bagehot*, 101.

3 Irvine, *Walter Bagehot*, 27.

4 Barrington, *Life of Walter Bagehot*, 118.

5 Wikipedia contributors, "Augustus De Morgan," *Wikipedia, The Free Encyclopedia*, http://en.wikipedia.org/w/index.php?title=Augustus_De_Morgan&oldid=819004288 (accessed February 8, 2018).

6 George Macaulay Trevelyan, *The Life of John Bright* (London: Constable, 1913), 70.

7 Trevelyan, *The Life of John Bright*, 69.

8 Scott Gordon, "The London Economist and the High Tide of Laissez Faire," *Journal of Political Economy* 63, no. 6 (December 1955): 467.

9 Gordon, "The London Economist," 468.

10 Ruth Dudley Edwards, *The Pursuit of Reason: The Economist, 1843–1993* (Boston: Harvard Business School Press, 1993), 2.

11 Edwards, *Pursuit of Reason*, 16–17.

12 Edwards, *Pursuit of Reason*, 12.

13 Barrington, *Life of Walter Bagehot*, 123.

14 Irvine, *Walter Bagehot*, 26.

15 Barrington, *Life of Walter Bagehot*, 135–36.

16 Barrington, *Life of Walter Bagehot*, 146.

17 Buchan, *The Spare Chancellor*, 42-43.

18 R. W. Kostal, *Law and English Railway Capitalism 1825–1875* (Oxford: Clarendon Press, 1994), 25.

19 W. T. C. King, *History of the London Discount Market* (London: Frank Cass, 1972), 134.

20 King, *History of*, 134.

21 Kostal, *Law and English Railway Capitalism*, 28.

22 Kostal, *Law and English Railway Capitalism*, 28–29.

23 "Railway Speculation," the *Economist*, April 5, 1845, 310.

24 Chancellor, *Devil Take the Hindmost*, 137.

25 Chancellor, *Devil Take the Hindmost*, 139.

26 Chancellor, *Devil Take the Hindmost*, 142.

27 Chancellor, *Devil Take the Hindmost*, 143.

28 Stuckey's Banking Co., Ltd., Directors' Minutes, Royal Bank of Scotland Archives STU2.1, 277a.

29 Chancellor, *Devil Take the Hindmost*, 143.

30 Kostal, *Law and English Railway Capitalism*, 35.

31 Edwards, *Pursuit of Reason*, 77.

32 Gordon, "The London Economist," 484.

CHAPTER 3: "VIVE LA GUILLOTINE"

1 Report of Her Majesty's Commissioners appointed to inquire into The State, Discipline, Studies, And Revenues of the University and Colleges of Oxford, 1852, 76.

2 Barrington, *Life of Walter Bagehot*, 180–81.

3 Bagehot, *Collected Works*, 7:250.

4 Barrington, *Life of Walter Bagehot*, 167.

5 Barrington, *Life of Walter Bagehot*, 184.

6 G. M. Young, *Victorian England: Portrait of an Age* (London: Oxford University Press, 1936), 77–78.

7 Barrington, *Life of Walter Bagehot*, 190.

8 Roger Price, *The French Second Empire: An Anatomy of Political Power* (Cambridge, UK: Cambridge University Press, 2001), 15.

9 David Harvey, *Paris, Capital of Modernity* (New York: Routledge, 2006), 97.

10 Price, *The French Second Empire*, 17.

11 Price, *The French Second Empire*, 25.

12 *The Political and Historical Works of Louis Napoleon Bonaparte with an original memoir of his life* (London: Savill and Edwards, 1852), 1:141.

13 Alexis de Tocqueville, *Memoir, Letters, and Remains of Alexis de Tocqueville* (Cambridge, U.K.: Macmillan, 1861), 191.

14 Barrington, *Life of Walter Bagehot*, 195.

15 Russell Barrington, ed., *The Works and Life of Walter Bagehot*, 10 vols. (New York: Longmans Green, and Co., 1915), 1:313.

16 Barrington, *The Works and Life*, 1:318.

17 Barrington, *The Works and Life*, 1:314.

18 Barrington, *The Works and Life*, 1:315.

19 Barrington, *The Works and Life*, 1:312.

20 Barrington, *The Works and Life*, 1:316.

21 Barrington, *The Works and Life*, 1:339.

22 Barrington, *The Works and Life*, 1:320.

23 Barrington, *The Works and Life*, 1:337.

24 Barrington, *The Works and Life* 1:234, 1:239.

25 Buchan, *The Spare Chancellor*, 68.

CHAPTER 4: THE LITERARY BANKER

1 Stuckey's Banking Co., Ltd., Directors' Minutes, STU3.2, 207.

2 Barrington, *Life of Walter Bagehot*, 213.

3 Barrington, *Life of Walter Bagehot*, 211, 213.

4 Ben Wilson, *Heyday: The 1850s and the Dawn of the Global Age* (New York: Basic Books, 2016), 55.

5 Thomas Tooke and William Newmarch, *A History of Prices*, vol. 5, 1848–1856 (London: Longman, Brown, Green, Longmans, & Roberts, 1857), 271.

6 Tooke and Newmarch, *Prices*, 295–96.

7 "Business In 1852," the *Economist*, January 8, 1853, 33.

8 Stuckey's Banking Co., Ltd., Directors' Minutes, STU3.2, 124.

9 Daniel Hardcastle, Jun., *Banks and Bankers*, 2nd ed. (London: Whittaker and Co., 1843), 401.

10 Hardcastle, *Banks and Bankers*, 406.

11 Saunders, *Stuckey's Bank*, 43.

12 Saunders, *Stuckey's Bank*, 43.

13 Stuckey's Banking Co., Ltd., Directors' Minutes, STU3.2, 367.

14 Stuckey's Banking Co., Ltd., Directors' Minutes, STU3.2, 437.

15 Stuckey's Banking Co., Ltd., Directors' Minutes, STU3.3, 9.

16 Wilson, *Heyday*, 313.

17 Bagehot, *Collected Works*, 1:141.

18 Bagehot, *Works* (ed. Morgan), 1:269.

19 Bagehot, *Works* (ed. Morgan), 1:279.

20 Bagehot, *Works* (ed. Morgan), 1:280.

21 Bagehot, *Works* (ed. Morgan), 1:265.

22 Bagehot, *Works* (ed. Morgan), 1:283.

23 Bagehot, *Works* (ed. Morgan), 1:297.

24 Bagehot, *Works* (ed. Morgan), 1:1.

25 Bagehot, *Works* (ed. Morgan), 1:5.

26 Bagehot, *Works* (ed. Morgan), 1:14.

27 Bagehot, *Works* (ed. Morgan), 1:14.

28 Bagehot, *Works* (ed. Morgan), 1:22.

29 Bagehot, *Works* (ed. Morgan), 1:34.

30 Bagehot, *Works* (ed. Morgan), 1:43.

31 Bagehot, *Works* (ed. Morgan), 1:41.

32 Stuckey's Banking Co., Ltd., Directors' Minutes, STU3.3, 38.

CHAPTER 5: "THE RUIN INFLICTED ON INNOCENT CREDITORS"

1 Barrington, *Life of Walter Bagehot*, 230.

2 Barrington, *Life of Walter Bagehot*, 230.

3 Bagehot, *Collected Works*, 9:324.

4 D.P. O' Brien, ed., *The Correspondence of Lord Overstone*, 3 vols. (London: Cambridge University Press, 1970), 2:279.

5 "The Money Market," the *Economist*, October 17, 1857, 1145.

6 Lord Overstone, *Tracts and Other Publications on Metallic and Paper Currency* (1857; repr. Clifton, UK: Augustus M. Kelley, 1972), 65.

7 Overstone, *Tracts*, 356.

8 "The Bank And The Prospects Of The Money Market," the *Economist*, October 10, 1857, 1117.

9 The Bank And The Prospects Of The Money Market," the *Economist*, October 10, 1857, 1117.

10 "The Money Market," *Economist*, October 17, 1857, 1145.

11 David Kynaston, *The City of London: A World of its Own, 1815–1890* (London: Pimlico, 1995), 86.

12 D. P. O'Brien, *The Development of Monetary Economics: A Modern Perspective on Monetary Controversies* (Cheltenham: Edward Elgar, 2007), 94.

13 T. E. Gregory, *Westminster Bank through a Century*, vol. 2 (London: Oxford University Press, 1936), 173.

14 T.E. Gregory, *Westminster Bank*, vol. 2, 173.

15 Bagehot, *Collected Works*, 9:356.

16 Bagehot, *Collected Works*, 5:70.

17 Sir John Clapham, *The Bank of England: A History, Vol. 2 (1797-1914)* (London: Cambridge University Press, 1970), 226.

18 D. Morier Evans, *The History of the Commercial Crisis 1857–1858 and the Stock Exchange Panic of 1859* (1859; repr. New York: Augustus M. Kelley, 1969), 75.

19 *Western Bank of Scotland*, RBS Heritage Hub, http://www.rbs.com/heritage.html

20 King, *History of the London Discount Market*, 198.

21 "Money-Market and City Intelligence," *The Times*, November 7, 1857.

22 O'Brien, *The Correspondence of Lord Overstone*, 2:764.

23 "Money-Market and City Intelligence," *The Times*, November 10, 1857.

24 Evans, *The History of the Commercial Crisis*, 91.

25 Evans, *The History of the Commercial Crisis*, 73.

26 O'Brien, *The Correspondence of Lord Overstone*, 2:794.

27 *The Correspondence of Lord Overstone*, 2, 802.

28 148 Parl. Deb. (3d ser.) (1857), cols. 214–15.

29 Bagehot, *Collected Works*, 10:55.

30 Bagehot, *Collected Works*, 10:57.

31 Bagehot, *Collected Works*, 10:53–54.

32 Bagehot, *Collected Works*, 10:75.

33 Russell Barrington, ed., *The Love Letters of Walter Bagehot and Eliza Wilson: Written from 10 November 1857 to 23 April 1858* (London: Faber and Faber, 1933), 125.

34 Bagehot, *Collected Works*, 10:63.

35 O'Brien, *The Correspondence of Lord Overstone*, 2:823.

36 O'Brien, *The Correspondence of Lord Overstone*, 2:808.

37 O'Brien, *The Correspondence of Lord Overstone*, 2:822–23.

CHAPTER 6: "THE YOUNG GENTLEMAN
OUT OF MISS AUSTEN'S NOVELS"

1 Stuckey's Banking Co., Ltd., Directors' Minutes, STU3.3, 152.

2 Stuckey's Banking Co., Ltd., Directors' Minutes, STU3.3, 171.

3 Barrington, *The Love Letters*, 33.

4 Barrington, *The Love Letters*, 130.

5 Buchan, *The Spare Chancellor*, 104.

6 Buchan, *The Spare Chancellor*, 105.

7 Barrington, *Life of Walter Bagehot*, 168.

8 Barrington, *The Love Letters*, 18.

9 Martha Westwater, *The Wilson Sisters: A Biographical Study of Upper Middle-Class Victorian Life* (Athens, OH: Ohio University Press, 1984), 32–33.

10 Westwater, *The Wilson Sisters*, 43.

11 Westwater, *The Wilson Sisters*, 24.

12 Westwater, *The Wilson Sisters*, 45.

13 Barrington, *The Love Letters*, 59.

14 Westwater, *The Wilson Sisters*, 13.

15 Barrington, *The Love Letters*, 27-67.

16 Barrington, *The Love Letters*, 31.

17 Barrington, *The Love Letters*, 33–35.

18 Barrington, *The Love Letters*, 39.

19 Barrington, *The Love Letters*, 55.

20 Barrington, *The Love Letters*, 45.

21 Barrington, *The Love Letters*, 55.

22 Barrington, *The Love Letters*, 57.

23 Barrington, *The Love Letters*, 117.

24 Barrington, *The Love Letters*, 66.

25 Barrington, *The Love Letters*, 71.

26 "The Literary Examiner," *The Examiner: A Weekly Paper, on politics, literature, and the fine arts*, February 6, 1858, 84.

27 Barrington, *The Love Letters*, 83.
28 Barrington, *The Love Letters*, 53.
29 Barrington, *The Love Letters*, 97.
30 Barrington, *The Love Letters*, 98.
31 Barrington, *The Love Letters*, 60.
32 Westwater, *The Wilson Sisters*, 24.
33 Barrington, *The Love Letters*, 60.
34 Barrington, *The Love Letters*, 91.
35 Westwater, *The Wilson Sisters*, 44.
36 Barrington, *The Love Letters*, 153.
37 Barrington, *The Love Letters*, 111.
38 Barrington, *The Love Letters*, 52.
39 Barrington, *The Love Letters*, 197.
40 Barrington, *Life of Walter Bagehot*, 253.
41 Barrington, *Life of Walter Bagehot*, 255–56.
42 Barrington, *The Love Letters*, 177.

CHAPTER 7: A DEATH IN INDIA

1 Emilie I. Barrington, *The Servant of All*, 2 vols. (London: Longmans, Green and Co., 1927), 2:154.
2 Walter Bagehot, *Parliamentary Reform: An Essay* (London: Chapman and Hall, 1859), 4.
3 Bagehot, *Parliamentary Reform*, 13.
4 Bagehot, *Parliamentary Reform*, 10.
5 Bagehot, *Collected Works*, 13:547.
6 Barrington, *Servant of All*, 2:133–34.
7 Barrington, *Servant of All*, 2:137.
8 Eliza Bagehot, *Journal and Letters, Diaries of Eliza Bagehot, 1850–1921* (London: Oxford Microform Publications, 1977), 32.
9 Bagehot, *Collected Works*, 13:549.
10 Edwards, *The Pursuit of Reason*, 261.
11 Bagehot, *Collected Works*, 2:111.
12 Bagehot, *Collected Works*, 2:133.
13 Bagehot, *Collected Works*, 2:119.
14 Bagehot, *Collected Works*, 2:136.
15 Bagehot, *Collected Works*, 2:142.
16 Bagehot, *Collected Works*, 2:148.
17 Buchan, *The Spare Chancellor*, 114.
18 Eliza Bagehot, *Journal*, 28.
19 Bagehot, *Collected Works*, 13:552.
20 Bagehot, *Collected Works*, 13:549.

21 Barrington, *Servant of All*, 2:167.

22 Barrington, *Servant of All*, 2:167.

23 Barrington, *Servant of All*, 2:171.

24 Bagehot, *Collected Works*, 13:553.

25 Bagehot, *Collected Works*, 13:563.

26 Barrington, *Servant of All*, 2:217.

27 Barrington, *Servant of All*, 2:213.

28 Barrington, *Servant of All*, 2:232.

29 Barrington, *Servant of All*, 2:252.

30 Bagehot, *Collected Works*, 13:564–65.

31 Bagehot, *Collected Works*, 13:564.

32 Bagehot, *Collected Works*, 13:566.

33 Barrington, *Life of Walter Bagehot*, 337.

CHAPTER 8: THE "PROBLEM" OF W. E. GLADSTONE

1 Barrington, *Life of Walter Bagehot*, 327.

2 Barrington, *Life of Walter Bagehot*, 357.

3 Roy Jenkins, *Gladstone: A Biography* (New York: Random House, 1997), 223.

4 Jenkins, *Gladstone*, 222.

5 Jenkins, *Gladstone*, 224.

6 156 Parl. Deb. (3d ser.) (1860) col. 848.

7 156 Parl. Deb. (3d ser.) (1860) col. 850.

8 Walter Bagehot, *Biographical Studies*, ed. Richard Holt Hutton (London: Longmans, Green, and Co., 1907), 97.

9 Wikipedia contributors, "The Fortnightly Review," *Wikipedia, The Free Encyclopedia*, https://en.wikipedia.org/w/index.php?title=The_Fortnightly_Review&oldid=800433439 (accessed February 8, 2018).

10 Bagehot, *Biographical Studies*, 95.

11 Bagehot, *Biographical Studies*, 96.

12 Bagehot, *Biographical Studies*, 103.

13 Bagehot, *Biographical Studies*, 113.

14 Bagehot, *Biographical Studies*, 105.

15 H. C. G. Matthew, "Gladstone, William Ewart (1809–1898), prime minster and author," *Oxford Dictionary of National Biography*.

16 Jenkins, *Gladstone*, 48, 54.

17 Jenkins, *Gladstone*, 141–42.

18 Jenkins, *Gladstone*, 14.

19 D. A. Smith, "Lewis, Sir George Cornewall, second baronet (1806–1863), politician and author," *Oxford Dictionary of National Biography*.

20 Jenkins, *Gladstone*, 15.

21 Bagehot, *Collected Works*, 13:587–90.

22 Bagehot, *Collected Works*, 13:594–95.

23 Bagehot, *Collected Works*, 13:593.

24 Bagehot, *Collected Works*, 13:592.

25 "The Bank Notes Issue Bill," the *Economist*, May 27, 1865, 621.

26 "The Chancellor of the Exchequer has acted," *The Times*, June 3, 1865.

27 Hugh Brogan, "America and Walter Bagehot," *Journal of American Studies*, vol. 11, no. 3 (December 1977): 339.

28 Edwards, *The Pursuit of Reason*, 306.

29 Edwards, *The Pursuit of Reason*, 311.

30 Edwards, *The Pursuit of Reason*, 311.

31 Brogan, "America and Walter Bagehot," 339.

32 Edwards, *The Pursuit of Reason*, 308.

33 Jenkins, *Gladstone*, 237.

34 John Morley, *The Life of William Ewart Gladstone*, 3 vols. (London: Macmillan, 1903), 2:81–82.

35 Allan Nevins, *The War for the Union: War Becomes a Revolution, 1862-1863* (New York, Charles Scribner's Sons, 1960), 269.

36 "Recognition Or Mediation?," the *Economist*, October 18, 1862, 1149.

37 Adam Lynd Rowe, Teaching Fellow in the Social Sciences at The University of Chicago

38 "The Emancipation Proclamation," the *Economist*, October 25, 1862, 1177.

39 Brogan, "America and Walter Bagehot," 341.

40 Bryan Taylor, "The Confederate Cotton Zombie Bonds," *Global Financial Data*, March 19, 2014, https://www.globalfinancialdata.com/GFD/Blog/the-confederate -cotton-zombie-bonds.

41 Brogan, "America and Walter Bagehot," 341.

42 "Rumours Of Peace," the *Economist*, February 4, 1865, 126.

43 "The Fall Of Richmond And Its Effect Upon English Commerce," the *Economist*, April 22, 1865, 461.

44 "The Assassination Of Mr. Lincoln," the *Economist*, April 29, 1865, 495.

45 Allan Nevins, *The War For the Union: The Organized War, 1863-1864* (New York: Charles Scribner's Sons, 1971), 512.

CHAPTER 9: "THEREFORE, WE ENTIRELY APPROVE"

1 Bagehot, *Collected Works*, 9:389.

2 Bagehot, *Collected Works*, 9:397.

3 Viscount Goschen, *Essays and Addresses on Economic Questions 1865–1893: With Introductory Notes 1905* (London: Edward Arnold, 1905), 26.

4 Thomas J. Spinner, "Goschen, George Joachim, first Viscount Goschen (1831–1907), politician and financier," *Oxford Dictionary of National Biography*.

5 Goschen, *Essays and Addresses*, 17.

6 Goschen, *Essays and Addresses*, 37.

7 Goschen, *Essays and Addresses*, 19.

8 Goschen, *Essays and Addresses*, 24, 27.

9 O'Brien, *The Correspondence of Lord Overstone*, 3:1067.

10 O'Brien, *The Correspondence of Lord Overstone*, 3:1112.

11 O'Brien, *The Correspondence of Lord Overstone*, 3:1017.

12 King, *History of the London Discount Market*, 231.

13 Report of the case of The Queen v. Gurney and Others, 1870, 32.

14 The Queen v. Gurney and Others, 1870, 33.

15 The Queen v. Gurney and Others, 1870, 34.

16 Kevin Dowd and Martin Hutchinson, *Alchemists of Loss: How Modern Finance and Government Intervention Crashed the Financial System* (West Sussex: John Wiley & sons, 2010), 49.

17 The Queen v. Gurney and Others, 1870, 68.

18 King, *History of the London Discount Market, 249*.

19 The Queen v. Gurney and Others, 1870, 81.

20 The Queen v. Gurney and Others, 1870, 82.

21 The Queen v. Gurney and Others, 1870, 86.

22 David Kynaston, *Till Time's Last Sand: A History of the Bank of England 1694–2013* (London: Bloomsbury, 2017), 236.

23 The Queen v. Gurney and Others, 1870, 85.

24 King, *History of the London Discount Market*, 251.

25 The Queen v. Gurney and Others, 1870, 47.

26 "One of latest inventions of modern ingenuity . . . ," *The Times*, February 2, 1866.

27 "The Money Market," the *Economist*, February 3, 1866, 121.

28 "Money-Market and City Intelligence," *The Times*, March 19, 1866.

29 "The State Of The Money Market," the *Economist*, April 14, 1866, 437.

30 "The Panic of 1866," *The Bankers' Magazine and Journal of the Money Market*, June 1866, 639.

31 Bagehot, *Collected Works*, 13:608.

32 Bagehot, *Collected Works*, 10:85.

33 Bagehot, *Collected Works*, 10:86.

34 Bagehot, *Collected Works*, 10:92.

CHAPTER 10: "THE MUDDY SLIME OF BAGEHOT'S CROTCHETS AND HERESIES"

1 O'Brien, *The Correspondence of Lord Overstone*, 3:1114.

2 184 Parl. Deb. (3d ser.) (1866) cols. 1706–27.

3 184 Parl. Deb. (3d ser.) (1866) cols. 1746–54.

4 John H. Wood, "Bagehot's Lender of Last Resort: A Hollow Hallowed Tradition," *Independent Review* 7, no. 3 (Winter 2003): 344.

5 Frank Whitson Fetter, *Development of British Monetary Orthodoxy: 1797–1875* (Cambridge, MA: Harvard University Press, 1965), 238.

6 Fetter, *Development*, 263.

7 Fetter, *Development*, 260–61.

8 O'Brien, *The Correspondence of Lord Overstone*, 3:823.

9 Kynaston, *Till Time's Last Sand*, 201.

10 O'Brien, *The Correspondence of Lord Overstone*, 3:1112, 1113, 1115.

11 O'Brien, *The Correspondence of Lord Overstone*, 3:1115.

12 Bagehot, *Collected Works*, 11:21.

13 Bagehot, *Collected Works*, 11:15.

14 Thompson Hankey, *The Principles of Banking: Its Utility and Economy with Remarks on the Working and Management of the Bank of England*, 2nd ed. (London: Effingham, Royal Exchange, 1873), 29–30.

15 Hankey, *The Principles of Banking*, 34.

16 Hankey, *The Principles of Banking*, 26.

17 Hankey, *The Principles of Banking*, 29.

18 O'Brien, *The Correspondence of Lord Overstone*, 3:1119.

CHAPTER 11: THE GREAT SCRUM OF REFORM

1 Young, *Victorian England*, 201.

2 Trevelyan, *Life of John Bright*, 325.

3 Joseph Park, *The English Reform Bill of 1867* (New York: Longmans, Green & Co., 1920), 15–16.

4 A. N. Wilson, *The Victorians* (New York: W.W. Norton, 2003), 108.

5 Jose Harris, "Mill, John Stuart (1806-1873)," Oxford Dictionary of Biography.

6 "Election Intelligence," *Telegraph*, July 10, 1865.

7 *Telegraph*, July 10, 1865.

8 "Garibaldi," the *Economist*, April 9, 1864, 447.

9 Park, *The English Reform Bill*, 37.

10 Bagehot, *Collected Works*, 15:24.

11 Wilson, *The Victorians*, 109.

12 Helen Andrews, "Romance and Socialism in J.S. Mills," *American Affairs*, vol.1, no. 2 (Summer 2017), 199-208.

13 Bagehot, *Collected Works*, 5:210.

14 Bagehot, *Collected Works*, 5:211.

15 Bagehot, *Collected Works*, 5:230.

16 Bagehot, *Collected Works*, 5:243.

17 Bagehot, *Collected Works*, 5:275.

18 Bagehot, *Collected Works*, 5:279.

19 Bagehot, *Collected Works*, 5:262.

20 Bagehot, *Collected Works*, 5:208.

21 Bagehot, *Collected Works*, 5:208.

22 Bagehot, *Collected Works*, 13:610.

23 John Stuart Mill, *Considerations on Representative Government* (London: Longmans, Green, and Co., 1876), 70.

24 Mill, *Considerations on Representative Government*, 74.

25 A. V. Dicey, *An Introduction to the Study of the Law of the Constitution*, 4th ed. (London: Macmillan, 1889), 19.

26 Liza Picard, *Victorian London: The Life of a City 1840–1870* (New York: St. Martin's Press, 2005), 86, 97.

27 182 Parl. Deb. (3rd. ser.) (1866) cols. 18–115.

28 James Winter, *Robert Lowe* (Toronto: University of Toronto Press, 1976), 2.

29 Winter, *Robert Lowe*, 150.

30 Winter, *Robert Lowe*, 157.

31 Winter, *Robert Lowe*, 100.

32 Winter, *Robert Lowe*, 142.

33 Georgina Battiscombe, *Shaftesbury: The Great Reformer 1801–1885* (Boston: Houghton Mifflin, 1975), 205.

34 Arthur Patchett Martin, *Life and Letters of the Right Honourable Robert Lowe*, 2 vols. (London: Longmans, Green, and Co., 1893), 2:259.

35 "The Need Of Many Facts For A Good Reform Bill," the *Economist*, March 17, 1866, 313.

36 183 Parl. Deb. (3d ser.) (1866) cols. 75–113.

37 183 Parl. Deb. (3d ser.) (1866) col. 124.

38 Jenkins, *Gladstone*, 262.

39 183 Parl. Deb. (3rd ser.) (1866) cols. 151–52.

40 "After a debate prolonged through nine nights . . . ," *The Times*, April 28, 1866.

41 Martin, *Life and Letters of Robert Lowe*, 2:292.

42 "The Duty Of All Parties On The Reform Question," the *Economist*, May 5, 1866, 527.

CHAPTER 12: A LOSER BY SEVEN BOUGHT VOTES

1 "Representation Of Manchester: Meeting Of Liberals," *Manchester Guardian*, July 4, 1865, 6.

2 *Manchester Guardian*, July 4, 1865, 6.

3 H. J. Hanham, *Elections and Party Management: Politics in the Time of Disraeli and Gladstone* (London: Longmans, Green and Co., 1959), 303.

4 *Manchester Guardian*, July 4, 1865

5 *Manchester Guardian*, July 4, 1865.

6 Report of The Commissioners Appointed to Inquire Into the Existence of Cor-

rupt Practices at the Last Election and at Previous Elections of Members to Sit in Parliament, 1870, 444.

7 Report of the Commissioners, 308.

8 Hanham, *Elections and Party Management*, 263.

9 Report of the Commissioners, 444.

10 183 Parl. Deb. (3d ser.) (1866) cols. 1441–45.

11 "The Way To Reduce Electoral Corruption," the *Economist*, June 2, 1866, 642.

12 Hanham, *Elections and Party Management*, 266.

13 Report of the Commissioners, 566.

14 Report of the Commissioners, 1047.

15 Report of the Commissioners, 289.

16 Report of the Commissioners, 648.

17 Report of the Commissioners, 509.

18 Report of the Commissioners, xxviii.

19 Report of the Commissioners, 1029-30.

20 *Essex Standard*, October. 1, 1869.

21 Report of the Commissioners, 942.

22 Report of the Commissioners, xxxvii.

CHAPTER 13: BY "INFLUENCE AND CORRUPTION"

1 Robert Blake, *Disraeli* (London: Prion, 1998), 263.

2 Blake, *Disraeli*, 26.

3 Jonathan Parry, "Disraeli, Benjamin, earl of Beaconsfield (1804–1881), prime minister and novelist," *Oxford Dictionary of National Biography*.

4 Parry, "Disraeli."

5 Blake, *Disraeli*, 55.

6 Parry, "Disraeli."

7 "Mr. Disraeli," the *Economist*, July 2, 1859, 725.

8 Blake, *Disraeli*, 159.

9 "Why Mr. Disraeli Has Succeeded," the *Economist*, September 7, 1867, 1009.

10 "Merchant Taylors' Company," *The Times*, June 18, 1868.

11 Arthur Anthony Baumann, *The Last Victorians* (Philadelphia: J. B. Lippincott, 1927), 45.

12 Blake, *Disraeli*, 472–73.

13 Bagehot, *Collected Works*, 13:623.

14 Bagehot, *Collected Works*, 7:414.

15 Bagehot, *Collected Works*, 13:616.

16 Bagehot, *Collected Works*, 13:617.

17 Bagehot, *Collected Works*, 13:619.

18 Bagehot, *Collected Works*, 14:47.

CHAPTER 14: "IN THE FIRST RANK"

1 Bagehot, *Collected Works*, 13:632.

2 A. C. Howe, "Villiers, Charles Pelham (1802–1898), politician," *Oxford Dictionary of National Biography*.

3 Bagehot, *Collected Works*, 13:575.

4 Buchan, *The Spare Chancellor*, 257.

5 Bagehot, *Collected Works*, 13:586–87.

6 Barrington, *Life of Walter Bagehot*, 404.

7 Barrington, *Life of Walter Bagehot*, 377.

8 Bagehot, *Collected Works*, 13:599–600.

9 Bagehot, *Collected Works*, 13:609.

10 Bagehot, *Collected Works*, 13:638.

11 Bagehot, *Collected Works*, 13:638.

12 A. C. Howe, "Giffen, Sir Robert (1837–1910), economist and statistician," *Oxford Dictionary of National Biography*.

13 Barrington, *The Love Letters*, 45.

14 Bagehot, *Collected Works*, 7:43.

15 Walter Bagehot, *Physics and Politics* (New York: D. Appleton, 1893), 55.

16 Bagehot, *Collected Works*, 7:43.

17 Bagehot, *Physics and Politics*, 64.

18 Bagehot, *Physics and Politics*, 73.

19 Bagehot, *Collected Works*, 7:60-61.

20 Bagehot, *Collected Works*, 7:75.

21 Bagehot, *Collected Works*, 7:84.

22 Bagehot, *Collected Works*, 7:109.

23 Bagehot, *Collected Works*, 7:110.

24 Bagehot, *Collected Works*, 7:125.

25 Bagehot, *Collected Works*, 7:127.

26 Bagehot, *Collected Works*, 7:128.

27 Bagehot, *Collected Works*, 7:128.

28 Bagehot, *Collected Works*, 7:130.

29 Joseph Schumpeter, *History of Economic Analysis* (New York: Oxford University Press, 1954), 445.

CHAPTER 15: NEVER A BULLISH WORD

1 Report from the Select Committee on Loans to Foreign States, July 29, 1875, xiv.

2 Bagehot, *Collected Works*, 9:273.

3 "The Danger Of Lending To Semi-Civilised Countries," the *Economist*, November 23, 1867, 1320.

4 J. Carlile McCoan, *Egypt Under Ismail: A Romance of History* (London: Chapman and Hall, 1889), 65.

5 "The Danger of Lending To Semi-Civilised Countries," 1321.

6 Sidney Homer and Richard Sylla, *A History of Interest Rates*, 3rd ed. (New Brunswick, NJ: Rutgers University Press, 1991), 204.

7 "The Serious Danger Of Rash Foreign Loans," the *Economist*, April 30, 1870, 1392.

8 Searched for purposes of comparison were the *Scotsman* and the *Glasgow Herald*, and in London *The Times* and the *Daily Telegraph*, in each case between January 1, 1869, and February 28, 1877; and the *Money Market Review*, January 2, 1869, to June 26, 1875, on which date the relevant digital archival record ends.

9 Catalina Vizcarra, "Guano, Credible Commitments, and Sovereign Debt Repayments in Nineteenth-Century Peru," *Journal of Economic History* 69, no. 2 (2009): 7, doi:10.1017/S0022050709000813.

10 Vizcarra, "Guano, Credible Commitments," 17.

11 "The Peruvian Loan," the *Economist*, June 11, 1870, 723.

12 "The Foreign Loans Of The Week," the *Economist*, March 23, 1872, 352.

13 "The Peruvian Loan," the *Economist*, March 23, 1872, 352.

14 Vizcarra, "Guano," 41.

15 "The Present Position Of The New South American And Central American Loans—A Warning To Investors In Foreign Government Securities," the *Economist*, October 19, 1872, 1279.

16 "The Present Position," the *Economist*, October 19, 1872, 1279.

17 "The Egyptian Debt," the *Economist*, July 5, 1873, 809.

18 "The Causes And Effects Of The Recent Fall In Government Securities," the *Economist*, July 26, 1873, 900.

19 "The Turkish Repudiation," the *Economist*, October 9, 1875, 1190.

20 "The Duty Of The English Government With Reference To The Bankruptcy Of Turkey," the *Economist*, October 23, 1875, 1250.

21 "The Report Of The Delegation Of Turkish Bondholders," the *Economist*, June 17, 1876, 706.

22 Hamilton L. Jenks, *The Migration of British Capital to 1875* (New York and London: Alfred A. Knopf, 1927), 321.

CHAPTER 16: GOVERNMENT BEARS THE COST

1 Diaries, Letters, and Papers of George Warde Norman, 1754–1876, 9 vols., London Borough of Bromley Archives.

2 Kynaston, *Till Time's Last Sand*, 230.

3 Bagehot, *Collected Works*, 11:30.

4 Thomson Hankey, letter to the editor, *The Times*, November 12, 1872.

5 "The Dangerous Opinions Of A Bank Director," the *Economist*, November 16, 1872, 1397.

6 Walter Bagehot, *Lombard Street: A Description of the Money Market* (New York: E. P. Dutton, 1920), 232.

7 Hankey, *The Principles of Banking*, vii.

8 Bagehot, *Lombard Street*, 3–4.

9 Bagehot, *Lombard Street*, 10.

10 Bagehot, *Lombard Street*, 16.

11 Bagehot, *Lombard Street*, 18.

12 Bagehot, *Lombard Street*, 27.

13 Bagehot, *Lombard Street*, 32.

14 Bagehot, *Lombard Street*, 35.

15 Bagehot, *Lombard Street*, 37.

16 Bagehot, *Lombard Street*, 43.

17 Bagehot, *Lombard Street*, 51-52.

18 Bagehot, *Lombard Street*, 151.

19 Kynaston, *Till Time's Last Sand*, 280.

20 Bagehot, *Lombard Street*, 254.

21 Hankey, *The Principles of Banking*, xiii–xiv.

22 Richard Davenport-Hines, "Lidderdale, William (1832–1902), merchant and banking official," *Oxford Dictionary of National Biography*.

23 Kynaston, *Till Time's Last Sand*, 207.

24 Goschen, *Essays and Addresses*, 112.

25 Kynaston, *Till Time's Last Sand*, 261.

CHAPTER 17: "I WONDER WHAT MY EMINENCE IS?"

1 Bagehot, *Collected Works*, 14:422–26.

2 Barrington, *Life of Walter Bagehot*, 445.

3 Bagehot, *Collected Works*, 9:40.

4 Bagehot, *Biographical Studies*, 262.

5 Bagehot, *Biographical Studies*, 278.

6 Bagehot, *Biographical Studies*, 317.

7 Bagehot, *Biographical Studies*, 318.

8 Bagehot, *Collected Works*, 11:407.

9 Barrington, *Life of Walter Bagehot*, 442.

10 Edwards, *The Pursuit of Reason*, 318.

11 Bagehot, *Collected Works*, 15:41.

12 Bagehot, *Collected Works*, 15:58.
13 Bagehot, *Collected Works*, 15:70.
14 Bagehot, *Collected Works*, 15:166.
15 Barrington, *Life of Walter Bagehot*, 443.
16 Barrington, *Life of Walter Bagehot*, 318.

BIBLIOGRAPHY

List of notable cited works by Walter Bagehot.

"Bad Lawyers or Good?," *The Fortnightly Review*, January-June 1876.

"The First Edinburgh Reviewers," *The National Review*, October 1855.

"William Cowper," *The National Review*, July 1855.

"Business In 1852," the *Economist*, January 8, 1853.

"Festus," *The Prospective Review*, November 1847.

"The Money Market," the *Economist*, October 17, 1857.

"The Bank And The Prospects Of The Money Market," the *Economist*, October 10, 1857.

"The Money Market," the *Economist*, October 17, 1857.

"The General Aspect Of The Banking Question," the *Economist*, February 1857.

"The Act Of 1844 And The Convertibility Of The Note," the *Economist*, May 16, 1857.

"The Monetary Crisis of 1857," *The National Review*, January 1858.

Walter Bagehot, *Parliamentary Reform: An Essay* (London: Chapman and Hall, 1859).

"John Milton," *The National Review*, July 1859.

Walter Bagehot, *Biographical Studies*, ed. Richard Holt Hutton (London: Longmans, Green, and Co., 1907).

"The Bank Notes Issue Bill," the *Economist*, May 27, 1865.

"Recognition Or Mediation?," the *Economist*, October 18, 1862.

"The Emancipation Proclamation," the *Economist*, October 25, 1862.

"Rumours Of Peace," the *Economist*, February 4, 1865.

"The Fall Of Richmond And Its Effect Upon English Commerce," the *Economist*, April 22, 1865.

"The Assassination Of Mr. Lincoln," the *Economist*, April 29, 1865.

"The Money Market," the *Economist*, February 3, 1866.

"The State Of The Money Market," the *Economist*, April 14, 1866.

"The Prosperity Of The London Joint Stock Banks: Its Cause And Its Effect," the *Economist*, August 17, 1861.

"Limited Liability In Banking," the *Economist*, May 17, 1862.

"The State Of The City," the *Economist*, May 1866.

"What A Panic Is And How It Might Be Mitigated," the *Economist*, May 1866.

"Is It Better That The Banking Reserve Of A Country Should Be Kept In A Single Bank Or Be Distributed Between Several Banks," the *Economist*, March 1866.

"One Banking Reserve Or Many?," the *Economist*, September 1866.

"Garibaldi," the *Economist*, April 9, 1864.

"The Need Of Many Facts For A Good Reform Bill," the *Economist*, March 17, 1866.

"The Duty Of All Parties On The Reform Question," the *Economist*, May 5, 1866.

"The English Constitution," *The Fortnightly Review*, no. 1-9, May 15, 1865-January 1, 1867.

"The Way To Reduce Electoral Corruption," the *Economist*, June 2, 1866.

"Mr. Disraeli," the *Economist*, July 2, 1859.

"Why Mr. Disraeli Has Succeeded," the *Economist*, September 7, 1867.

"The Women's Degrees," the *Economist*, May 23, 1874.

Walter Bagehot, *Physics and Politics* (New York: D. Appleton, 1893), 55.

"The Danger Of Lending To Semi-Civilised Countries," the *Economist*, November 23, 1867.

"The Serious Danger Of Rash Foreign Loans," the *Economist*, April 30, 1870.

"The Peruvian Loan," the *Economist*, June 11, 1870.

"The Foreign Loans Of The Week," the *Economist*, March 23, 1872.

"The Present Position Of The New South American And Central American Loans—A Warning To Investors In Foreign Government Securities," the *Economist*, October 19, 1872.

"The Egyptian Debt," the *Economist*, July 5, 1873.

"The Causes And Effects Of The Recent Fall In Government Securities," the *Economist*, July 26, 1873.

"The Turkish Repudiation," the *Economist*, October 9, 1875.

"The Duty Of The English Government With Reference To The Bankruptcy Of Turkey," the *Economist*, October 23, 1875.

"The Report Of The Delegation Of Turkish Bondholders," the *Economist*, June 17, 1876.

"Investments," *The Inquirer*, July 31, 1852.

"The Dangerous Opinions Of A Bank Director," the *Economist*, November 16, 1872.

Walter Bagehot, *Lombard Street: A Description of the Money Market* (New York: E. P. Dutton, 1920).

"Will The Money Market Take Care Of Itself?," the *Economist*, April 1869.

"Why Not Issue Exchequer Bills At Short Dates?," the *Economist*, September 1876.

INDEX

Page numbers followed by *n* refer to footnotes.

Economist:

Bagehot as editor of, xiv, 107, 109, 113–14, 120, 122, 124–25, 132, 205, 230, 266, 283, 285, 286

Bagehot's writings in, xv-xvi, 66, 79, 88, 89, 90, 113, 170–72, 177, 179–80, 204, 208, 228–29, 234, 286

books published by, 31–33

circulation of, 286*n*

competition of, 284, 285

on Disraeli, 223–25, 232

on education for women, 228

on election bribery, 210–11, 213, 219

expansion of, 99–101, 284, 285

financial condition of, 284–86

on foreign investment, 248–59, 261–62

founding of, 22

on free trade, 49

on French politics, 45

and Gladstone, 116–18, 122

on government's roles, 33

on Great Exhibition (1851), 38

Hutton as editor of, 100, 101, 107, 114, 124, 132

incorruptibility of, xvi, 249*n*, 283

on international economies, 68

and *Investors Monthly Manual*, 285

left in trust to Wilson family, 283

on limited liability, 139

on neutrality, 238

Norman's contributions to, 263–66

and Overend Gurney, 153–62

and Panic of 1857, 69, 75, 76*n*

Peel's Act opposed by, 31, 32, 122, 142–43, 162, 170

on railroad speculators, 29, 31*n*

supporting statistics pioneered by, 101, 281–82

and U.S. Civil War, 124, 128, 130, 131–34, 135

Wilson as founder of, 22, 29

Edinburgh Review, 61, 63, 70, 90, 120, 142

Edwards, Edward Watkin, 146–51

Edwards, Ruth Dudley, 127

Egypt:

European control of finances of, 261–62

investments in, 248–49, 254–57, 258

Suez Canal Company, 259–62

Egyptian Trading Company, 142

Egypt Under Ismail (McCoan), 257, 258–59

Eldon, Lord, 61

elections, *see* voting franchise

Eliot, George, 184, 185*n*, 236, 237

Elizabeth I, queen of England, 1

Elizabeth, Princess Palatine of Bavaria, 202

Emancipation Proclamation, U.S., 129–32

Emerson, Ralph Waldo, 117*n*

Emile Erlanger & Co., 132

Encyclopedia Britannica, 89

Engels, Friedrich, 222*n*

English and Foreign Credit Company, 142

English Constitution, The (Bagehot), 185, 186–94, 230, 234

Estimates of Some Englishmen and Scotchmen (Bagehot), 90–91

Estlin, John Bishop, 4

Estlin, John Prior, 4

Estlin, Stuckey, 13

Examiner, 21, 90, 291

Federal Reserve Bank, roles of, xiv

Financial News, 282

Financial Times, 294

Finlason, W. F., 145

Fortesque, Albany, 21

Fortnightly; *Fortnightly Review*, 116, 184, 185, 186, 234, 240, 287

Fowler, William, *The Crisis of 1866*, 173

France:

bimetallism in, 86

bons de Tresor in, 289

coup d'état in, 40–45

Crédit Foncier and Crédit Mobilier, 89, 143, 157, 261

financial speculation in, 67

monetary innovations in, xxvii

revolution (1848), 39, 62, 199

and Suez Canal Company, 261

suspension of gold convertibility (1870), 270

Terror of 1793, 39

wars with Britain, xvii, xix, xx, 47

war with Austria, 100

interest rates:
  and Bank of England, xxi, xxviii, 28,
    29, 48, 69, 76, 139, 266
  cycles in, 47, 49, 68, 142, 153, 154,
    159, 176, 177
  discount rate, xxv, xxix, 29, 74, 149,
    248
  and foreign exchange, xxviii, 142, 254
  and gold standard, xxi
  Goschen on, xv, 139–42, 154
  and limited liability, 140, 142
  vs. risks, 247
  and speculation, 243
  Treasury bonds, xxvi
  and U.S. Civil War, 132–34
  and usury law, xx
International Financial Company, 142
International Land Credit Company, 142
investments:
  bubbles, xxvii, 26–31, 125*n*, 221, 248,
    253, 265
  bull and bear markets, 27*n*, 247, 262
  "finance" companies, 142, 143–53,
    157, 159, 166
  international, 30, 75, 140, 141–42,
    246–62
  margin of security in, 247, 271
  mortgage vs. bill of exchange, 172–73
  railroad shares, 27–28
  speculative, 26–31, 69, 81, 138, 143–
    44, 145–46, 243–44, 273
Investors Monthly Manual, 285
Irish potato famine (1845–1846), 31, 74
Irish Protestant Church, 231
Ismail, Khedive of Egypt, 248, 249, 256,
  257, 259–60, 261–62

Januarius, Saint, 220
Jefferson, Thomas, 15
Jeffrey, Francis, 61
Jenkins, Roy, 118
Jevons, William Stanley, 98*n*, 230, 237
Johnson, Samuel, 103
Joint Stock Companies Act (1844), 26, 122
Joint Stock Companies Act (1856;
  amended 1857, 1858), 195
Joint Stock Discount Company, 157–59
Jones, Frederick, xxviii, xix, xxx
Jones, Loyd & Co., 72, 280*n*

Joubert, M., 261
J. S. Morgan & Co., 250

Keightley, Thomas, 102, 103
Keynes, John Maynard, 277–78, 287
King, Henry S., 240
King, W. T. C., 144, 146
Kinnaird, Lady, 86
Kynaston, David, 164*n*

laissez-faire, 32, 87, 113, 139
Lancashire, textile industry in, 48, 153,
  181, 202
Landsdowne, Lord, 229
Langport, Somerset, 1–2
  eighteenth-century folkways in, 8
  religions in, 7–8
  as transportation hub, 8
Leeds Banking Company, 157*n*
lender of last resort:
  Bank of England as, xiv, 167–70, 171,
    174–75, 186, 266, 267, 268, 278,
    279, 280
  idea of, xiv, 281, 294
Lesseps, Ferdinand de, 254
Leveson-Gower, George, 235
Levy-Lawson, Edward, 238–39
Lewes, George Henry, 184*n*, 186
Lewis, Sir George Cornewall, 97, 102,
  107, 108, 201, 237
  on Bagehot's writing, 80
  as chancellor of the exchequer, 70,
    76, 128
  death of, 120
  and Peel's Act, 71, 77, 162
Lewis, Mary Anne, 222*n*
Lidderdale, William, 281
Liebling, A. J., xv
Lieven, Princess, xxvi
limited liability, 138–43, 195, 267, 276
Limited Liability Act, 143
Lincoln, Abraham, 124, 125, 126, 129–
  32, 135–36, 184
Liverpool, Lord, xxix
Liverpool and Manchester Railway,
  xxvi-xxvii
Lombard Street (Bagehot), xiv, 178, 188,
  271–77, 279, 283, 286
  and gold standard, 272, 273*n*, 277, 281